Stop Street Harassment

Stop Street Harassment

Making Public Places Safe and Welcoming for Women

HOLLY KEARL

 PRAEGER

AN IMPRINT OF ABC-CLIO, LLC
Santa Barbara, California • Denver, Colorado • Oxford, England

Library of Congress Cataloging-in-Publication Data

Kearl, Holly.
    Stop street harassment : making public places safe and welcoming for
women / Holly Kearl.
        p. cm.
    Includes bibliographical references and index.
    ISBN 978 -0-615-63461-6(hbk. : alk. paper)
    1. Sexual harassment of women—Prevention. 2. Public safety. 3. Public spaces—
Social aspects. I. Title.
HV6556.K43   2010
362.83—dc22   2010011872

ISBN: 978 -0-615-63461-6

14   13   12   11   10   1   2   3   4   5

This book is also available on the World Wide Web as an eBook.
Visit www.abc-clio.com for details.

Praeger
An Imprint of ABC-CLIO, LLC

ABC-CLIO, LLC
130 Cremona Drive, P.O. Box 1911
Santa Barbara, California 93116-1911

Manufactured in the United States of America

To my parents Alan Kearl and Beckie Weinheimer,
my partner Mark Hutchens,
and my sisters Heidi and Mary Kearl

Contents

List of Tables

Foreword

Street harassment has existed since the advent of streets, but for centuries it has been an overlooked problem. Today, men and women compete for equal access to public space—an area of our culture traditionally dominated by men. With the same tactics of intimidation and fear used when women demanded the right to own property, vote, and enter every occupation, men have become more overt in oppressing women's right to access public spaces. Consequently, women have learned to fear the streets.

Street harassment is about power, not sexual attraction. When women come into contact with street harassers, they only know one thing: this man made an unsolicited sexual advance. What will he do next? For the millions of women who experience harassment every day, it is not surprising that street harassment can quickly manifest itself into the fear of being at risk for assault or rape. These fears seep into women's lives and corrode their sense of security. We have collected hundreds of stories of women who have changed their commutes or their clothes in hopes of escaping harassment. This mental, physical, and emotional strain should not be accepted as part of being a woman or living in a city.

With a vision of creating a safer, more equitable world for women and lesbian, gay, bisexual, transgender, queer, and gender-nonconforming (LGBTQGNC) individuals, we launched RightRides for Women's Safety in 2004 and HollabackNYC in 2005. Each organization began as grassroots efforts with volunteer staffs, no funding, and a desire to combat harassment and assault.

RightRides for Women's Safety provides free, safe, late-night rides home for women and LGBTQGNC individuals. As of this writing, RightRides has driven 2,500 people home safely, across forty-five neighborhoods in New York City, thanks to hundreds of volunteers and nine donated Zipcar vehicles. RightRides is working to create chapters across the country, and one day, the globe.

HollabackNYC uses technology to give women an empowered response to street harassment by taking their harassers' pictures and posting them to HollabackNYC.com to "hollaback" at them. The initiative hit a nerve, resulting in more than 1,000 posts, twenty affiliate Hollaback sites, and more than 10,000 readers monthly. HollabackNYC is currently launching a new initiative, Hollaback!, which will map street harassment using an iPhone application, SMS texting, and an interactive Web site.

RightRides and HollabackNYC joined forces in 2009 to create New Yorkers for Safe Transit, the sole New York City coalition dedicated to eradicating gender-based harassment and violence in mass transit. Our goals include raising public awareness, pursuing educational campaigns, and fostering policy change to ensure New Yorkers can travel safely and securely. Like street harassment, harassment experienced in mass transit has been invisible to policy makers, law enforcement, and the general public for far too long.

Street-harassment activism is at a tipping point. Over the past five years, we have watched as the issue has moved from obscurity to urgency. We have worked to ensure this issue gains greater public awareness and action. Thousands of survivors have come forward with stories of harassment and assault. These accounts share a common narrative: street harassment isn't just annoying, it's scary and traumatizing. Nonetheless, it has been accepted as an everyday reality. Most concerning, however, is that street harassment acts as a gateway crime, opening the door for perpetrators to move to more serious expressions of violence and aggression such as stalking, assault, and rape.

We believe that street harassment can and will end. Survivors' stories are vital to shaping public understanding, but we also need action to reach the tipping point. We need not look far for inspiration: Only a couple decades ago, courageous women refused to continue accepting sexual harassment in workplaces. They won legal cases, changed policies, and held harassers accountable. Today, businesses take this issue seriously. In the coming decade, street harassment is poised to follow the same trajectory as workplace harassment and become a cornerstone women's issue.

Holly's book is incredibly brave, timely, and important. It will raise awareness and legitimize street harassment as it is experienced around the world. However, reading this book is only the first step. We encourage you to share this book and its suggestions for activism and mobilize your communities. Only a groundswell campaign can ultimately end street harassment.

We had few resources when we began RightRides and Hollaback, but we had unique approaches that altered the framework of social change. The result has been incredible. We've helped thousands of people feel safer on the streets, subways, and buses. We've helped fill a long-standing need to empower people to take action—everyday people who are fed up with experiencing harassment and assault and who deserve lives free from violence.

Use your vision and dedication to identify and pursue creative responses that resonate most within your communities. Your actions will be revolutionary, encouraging others to lend their resources and magnifying this collective movement to end gender-based harassment and assault. Your work can make a difference in the lives of millions. In the words of German writer Johann Wolfgang von Goethe, "Whatever you can do, or dream you can do, begin it. Boldness has genius, power, and magic in it. Begin it now."

Here's to your bold actions and to a world free from harassment!

Oraia Reid
Cofounder and Executive Director, RightRides for Women's Safety
Cofounder of New Yorkers for Safe Transit

Emily May
Cofounder of HollabackNYC
Cofounder of New Yorkers for Safe Transit

rightrides.org
hollabacknyc.com
nyfst.org

Acknowledgments

From a young age, my parents and my sister Heidi showed me the importance of working to make the world a fairer and more just place and their examples motivated me to tackle the issue of street harassment. Thank you to my parents for believing in me, suggesting I write this book, and helping me through every step.

Thank you to several people for their tremendous help: My partner, Mark Hutchens, for supporting my endeavors and offering useful feedback on my surveys and chapters; Brittany Shoot, Elizabeth Bolton, and Mary Kearl for their great feedback on my entire manuscript; and Maria Accardi, Dienna Howard, and Michelle Kunz for their input and help with various aspects of the project.

Thank you to the hundreds of anonymous people who had the courage to share their stories through my informal surveys and blog—you made this book possible. Thank you to the amazing anti-street harassment activists I interviewed and talked to for their time and for sharing their ideas to create a more equitable world. In alphabetical order, these activists include: Emily Aaron and Toby, Erin Armstrong, Kimberly Fairchild, Alyssa Fine, Ilona Granet, Dienna Howard, Nadia Ilahi, Erin Johnson, Ashley Lewis, Shannon Lynberg, Kari Mansager, Emily May, Jenga Mwendo, Jasmeen Patheja, Oraia Reid, Lisa Rahman, Tracey Rose, Katie Seitz, Chai Shenoy, Brittany Shoot, Joanne Smith, Carla Stokes, Lauren Taylor, Veronica Tirado, and Laura Tolton.

I am lucky that my employer AAUW, an organization that supports women's equity, was accommodating as I worked on the book.

Thank you to my many coworkers who supported my work and offered encouragement.

Many professors at Santa Clara University and George Washington University taught me ways to critically think and write about women's issues. Thank you to each, particularly Dr. Nancy Unger, my undergraduate advisor and Dr. Cynthia Deitch and Dr. Ami Lynch who oversaw my master's thesis on street harassment.

Lastly, I am indebted to other street harassment writers who made my work possible by breaking new ground and to Praeger Publishers for allowing me to publish my own work on the topic.

A Note about Survey Respondents

As part of my research on street harassment, I conducted four informal, anonymous online surveys using the service Survey Monkey. The first survey I conducted in 2007 was for my master's thesis on street harassment and there were 225 respondents. I conducted the second survey in 2008 in preparation for writing this book and there were 916 respondents. The third and fourth surveys were conducted as follow-up to the one I conducted in 2008, and I targeted specific audiences for them. Ninety women took the third survey in early 2009 and 85 men took the fourth survey in late 2009. The questions for each survey and how they were conducted are detailed on www.stopstreetharassment.com/book/surveys.

Many quotations from the surveys are included throughout the book. These quotes do not have endnote citations. Instead, within the text I identify which survey they are from.

Introduction

One sunny, spring afternoon in San Jose, California, I ran through a middle-class neighborhood near my college campus during a six-mile workout. Lost in my thoughts, I was startled to hear, "I like how your tits bounce when you run," coming from a white guy in his 20s who was standing on a driveway with his friends. My initial shock at hearing such vulgar language was quickly followed by strong feelings of horror, humiliation, and anger. I slowed my pace and turned around to glare at them. They continued laughing. I resumed my run, blushing with fury and mortification. The words and laughter echoing in my mind ruined the rest of my day.

This story describes only one of the many times when men I do not know have harassed me in public because I am female, a behavior termed "street harassment." I have been the target of whistles, honks, kissing noises, and less sexually explicit "hey baby" comments. I've been harassed during my running workouts, on the subway and bus, at gas stations, on the street as I walk to work or to volunteer, and while sightseeing. These incidents have made me feel startled at best, frightened at worst and, more commonly, disrespected, annoyed, or angry, especially when they happen frequently within a short time period.

At the scary end of the spectrum, men have followed me three times. Twice men followed me while I was running: once in southern California by car when I was 14, and once in northern Virginia by foot when I was 21. The third man followed me when I was sightseeing alone in Bruges, Belgium, as a 21-year-old, and it escalated to him approaching me and putting his arm around me. During each of these incidents, I was absolutely terrified, and I remember feeling shaky for hours afterwards. When the man chased me in Northern Virginia, we were alone in a park at dusk. I out-sprinted him to a well-lit neighborhood and he stopped. Did he intend me any harm, or was he just messing with me? I don't know. I went home and cried.

My most upsetting incident occurred during college. One evening, I was waiting for a friend outside a house after a party. A man at least three times my size grabbed my crotch and laughed as he walked by with his friends. I was in shock and afraid, but after I decided I was not in danger, I was horrified, angry, and disgusted. Sadly, my experiences are in no way unique. Compared with too many women, I feel lucky that this is the worst physical harassment I have experienced and that, except for my college years, I am not harassed on a daily basis.

Growing up, I rarely talked about street harassment with anyone. I did not even know the term. Like many young women, I had been told by family members, friends, and society in general that this behavior was "a compliment." I did not see my experiences in the larger context of women's inequality in society or piece together how many of us can't go about our daily lives without men objectifying, insulting, or threatening us. I didn't realize that so many of us restrict our access to public spaces in an attempt to stay safe and free from harassment. When I read the scores of women's stories posted on the anti-street harassment Web sites HollaBackNYC and Street Harassment Project, I finally began to make those connections.

In 2007, I wrote my master's thesis at George Washington University on how women were using Web sites like HollaBack to combat male harassment in public places in lieu of adequate laws or social recognition that street harassment damages women's lives. Because I had results from a survey I conducted for my thesis online, various reporters found them and contacted me. I imagine few people have had their master's thesis cited in the *Toronto Globe and Mail* or on *CNN*, which made me realize how few people study or write about this problem.

When I turned in my thesis, I was burned out and decided I was done working on street harassment. In 2008, however, encouraged by my male partner, I launched a Web site with resources and information on street harassment and a companion blog to provide a place to post women's stories and discuss street harassment in the news. Around then, my parents began encouraging me to write a book.

It took me months to start; it was a daunting task, and I wondered, who am I to write about this topic? Reading and hearing story after story about street harassment and knowing virtually no books existed on the topic finally made me decide to do it, as did the hope that it could be my contribution toward creating a world in which being female does not automatically make one a target for harassment and assault.

While all harassment is deplorable, this book, then, is focused on the underacknowledged but pervasive problem of men harassing women in public places because of their gender. In it, I illustrate that street harassment is a widespread problem and offer suggestions to stop it. In chapter one, I define street harassment and show its prevalence. Chapters two through six explore various facets of the problem, including the contexts in which the harassment occurs, how factors such as race and sexual orientation add layers to the harassment incidents, street harassment as a global problem, the many ways women perceive male attention in public, and all the strategies women practice to try to avoid harassment and assault. The final four chapters of this book discuss the ways we can work to stop street harassment, including strategies such as: educating men and engaging male allies, empowering women to know how to deal with harassers, creating public awareness initiatives, and making street harassment an issue akin to sexual assault or workplace harassment, complete with anti-harassment laws.

Ultimately, we need a full-blown global anti-street harassment movement to truly end this epidemic, and I hope this book can inspire activism on all levels. We need academics conducting research, activists tackling the issue in their communities, educators discussing it in their classrooms, nonprofits including it in their work, legislators passing anti-harassment laws, and the average person sharing stories. Most of all, we need men to stop harassing women.

I hope people will write more books, especially individuals who can represent a different background and experience than me, a white, heterosexual, able-bodied, college-educated, middle-class American ciswoman (a woman who conforms to her birth gender, unlike transwomen) in her midtwenties.

No time is better than now for each of us to play a part—no matter what it is—in stopping street harassment and in making all places safe and welcoming for women.

Part One

Complexities of Street Harassment

Chapter 1

Raise Your Hand If You've Experienced Street Harassment

Starting at a young age, as many as 80 percent of women around the world face at least occasional unwanted, harassing attention in public places from men they do not know; some women face it daily.[1] The harassment ranges from physically harmless leers, whistles, honks, kissing noises, and nonsexually explicit evaluative comments, to more insulting and threatening behavior like vulgar gestures, sexually charged comments, flashing, and stalking, to illegal actions like public masturbation, sexual touching, assault, and rape. This type of unwanted attention is termed street harassment. The following stories from four women who took an informal survey I conducted in 2008 help illustrate some of the behaviors street harassment most often entails.

I used to pass by this one particular corner to get to the bus stop. There were young men who'd hang out on the corner and make all kinds of comments to women who passed by. I admit to changing bus stops in order to avoid them.

—30–39-year-old heterosexual African American woman in Minneapolis, Minnesota

Before I had a car, I was always angry and a little scared when I had to use public transit because men harassed me on an almost daily basis. I was angry because there was nothing I could do to stop it overall. There would always be another guy the next day. I was angry that these men felt they had the right to intrude in my personal space and ask me personal questions and that they felt that I owed them attention. I carried pepper spray in my hand whenever I walked home.[2]

—20–29-year-old heterosexual Latina in San Diego, California

An old man started masturbating through his pants on the train while looking at me and my partner, moving closer and closer to us. We changed cars and he even had the nerve to follow us to the other car! No one else even seemed to notice how filthy the man was behaving.

—20–29-year-old bisexual/queer white woman
in New York City

I had an incident where late at night when I was alone and walking to my car a guy yelled out to me that I was beautiful. Not knowing who he was I ignored him. He caught up with me and got in my face and started yelling and swearing at me, pretty much telling me he thought I was conceited. I stood there and simply stared him in the eye. I'm not sure what he was trying to do, but finally he got tired and just walked away. It was pretty scary, but I'm glad I held my own.

—30–39-year-old heterosexual Asian American
woman in Chicago, Illinois

On the extreme end, street harassment can escalate to sexual assault, and it occasionally even ends in murder. In Savannah, Georgia, in May 2009, a woman was walking alone at night and three men approached her, trying to talk to her. She ignored the men and, without warning, they pushed her to the ground. Two men held her down while the third man sexually assaulted her until a passerby scared them away and helped the woman home.[3] In March 2009, a 29-year-old pregnant woman was walking home from work in Manhattan with a coworker when a van drove onto the sidewalk and hit them. Witnesses say the men in the van were "catcalling" the women, who were trying to ignore the men. The pregnant woman was killed, and her coworker was hospitalized.[4] After a Bradenton, Florida, high school football game in the fall of 2009, a young man approached four young women who were in a car and propositioned them for sex. When they refused, he came back with a gun and fired at them. One young woman died from her wounds.[5] For each woman who is sexually assaulted or murdered, countless others feel greater fear that it could happen to them, too.

Street harassment and the underlying fear of it escalating into something worse makes most women feel unwelcome and unsafe in public at least sometimes, especially when they are alone. It causes women to restrict their time in public alone and to be on guard while there, limiting their access to resources and leadership opportunities. It also reminds them that they live in a society in which, because they are female, men are allowed to interrupt and bother them at any time in annoying, disrespectful, creepy, and threatening ways, virtually without any consequences.

While public harassment motivated by racism, homophobia, transphobia, or classism—types of deplorable harassment that men can be the target of and sometimes women perpetrate—is recognized as socially unacceptable behavior, men's harassment of women motivated by gender and sexism is not.[6] Instead it is portrayed as complimentary or "only" a trivial annoyance. In reality, like other forms of harassment, street harassment is bullying behavior motivated by power and disrespect, and its negative impact on women can be as extreme as causing them to move neighborhoods, change jobs because of harassers along the commute, and stay home more often than they would otherwise. No country to date has achieved gender equality, and until street harassment is recognized as a serious problem and people work to end it, no country ever will. The second half of this book is full of strategies people can use to reach that goal, and it highlights amazing activists who are working hard to achieve harassment-free communities.

Because few people recognize street harassment as a problem or understand it, before discussing strategies to end it, the opening half of the book explores various facets of the problem. To start, in this chapter, I examine its definition and illustrate how infuriatingly common street harassment is for women.

DEFINING STREET HARASSMENT

Problems without names tend to stay hidden and inadequately addressed. I use "street harassment" to describe gender-based harassment in public spaces because it is the one most commonly used by academics and activists, but there is no universally used name or term for it like there is for "sexual assault" or "sexual harassment" at work or school. If someone uses terms like sexual assault or sexual harassment, most people understand what they mean, and if they do not, they can look them up in a dictionary. When people have asked me what my book topic is about and I say street harassment, most of them give me a blank stare until I say, "You know, when men say 'hey baby' and whistle at women or grope them on the subway." Then they nod and know exactly what I mean. Street harassment is not a term commonly used, it cannot be found in a dictionary, and not even everyone who writes about it or works to end it defines it the same way.

In my research, the earliest definition of street harassment I came across is from 1981 by University of California at Berkeley anthropology professor Micaela di Leonardo. She wrote that: "Street harassment occurs when one or more strange men accost one or more women . . . in a public place which is not the woman's/women's worksite. Through looks, words, or gestures the man asserts his right to intrude on the woman's attention, defining her as a sexual object, and forcing her to interact with him."[7]

Another early definition is by Carol Brooks Gardner, a sociologist who studied street harassment in Indianapolis in the late 1980s and early 1990s. She says, "Public harassment is that group of abuses, harryings, and annoyances characteristic of public places and uniquely facilitated by communication in public. Public harassment includes pinching, slapping, hitting, shouted remarks, vulgarity, insults, sly innuendo, ogling, and stalking. Public harassment is on a continuum of possible events, beginning when customary civility among strangers is abrogated and ending with the transition to violent crime: assault, rape, or murder."[8]

Since there is no universally recognized definition of the problem, I decided to find out how ordinary women define it. In the fall of 2008, I spent four weeks informally surveying more than 900 people, including more than 800 women, about their experiences in public places (see www.stopstreetharassment.com/book/surveys for more information). One question I asked was how respondents define street harassment. Nearly 400 women answered and the words they commonly used included "unwanted," "sexual," "uncomfortable," "touch," and "threat." Here are a few of their definitions.

Any sexualized or aggressive activity meant to make someone feel unsafe being in public, or to point out the person's sexualized or second-class status.

I think it's the exercise of power and intimidation. The people who do it are deliberately looking for attention and seek to intrude on other people's physical or mental space. They're not complimenting people because of beauty; they're doing it to make their presence felt because they need to feel stronger or better about themselves. . . . It's more the way things are done, and the intent behind them, than the actual thing.

Street harassment is when you make loud obnoxious general comments like "Heeeyy sexy!" or "Gorgeous body!" or lean in and say "mmmm." That's not respectful at all. No one responds to that positively. I think it can only be because the guy wants to make a show, make you uncomfortable.

For me, it's a strange man treating me differently than he would if I were accompanied by a man/older person/etc., i.e., someone he would respect and not view in a sexual way.

For me, street harassment constitutes unwelcome words and actions by men in public places that invade the physical and emotional space of unknown women in a disrespectful, creepy, startling, scary, or insulting way. Because the expectation for interactions between strangers is different in clubs and bars compared to other public places, I generally exclude such locations from the definition. Regardless of the specifics of its definition, all studies on the topic show that it is an alarmingly common experience for women.

STREET HARASSMENT IS A PERVASIVE PROBLEM

In May 2008, columnist Cath Elliot wrote an online news article for the *Guardian,* a British newspaper, discussing aspects of street harassment. Many comments on the article implied that such behavior is not a problem.[9]

One day someone will amuse themselves researching not why men wolf whistle but which women get wolf whistled at and why . . . Lighten up. Or wear a burka. Or find something serious to agonise over.[10]

Gosh, you poor little feminists. Being wolf-whistled at by lecherous builders [construction workers] and then having your boobs stared at. Whatever next? Next there'll be some middle-aged chap opening a door for you and saying "after you young lady," or a horrid chauvinist bus conductor calling you "sweetheart" or "darling"! My heart bleeds for you, it really does. Not.[11]

Is there really that much wolf-whistling around these days? I haven't heard one in years.[12]

In response, blogger Laura Woodhouse wrote an entry on the blog The F Word: Contemporary UK Feminism asking readers to give a "quick hands up" if they've experienced street harassment, "just a nod to show how depressingly normal street harassment is . . . I'll start the ball rolling with a big hands up."[13] Within two days the blog had about 200 comments. The majority of the comments were written by women "raising their hands" and sharing their street harassment stories. Over the next four months, more than one hundred more entries went up on the site. A year later, women were still posting their comments and stories. Here are a few:

How depressing that my first thought on reading this was "Who hasn't?" . . . so that would be a yes.[14]

Of course. I can't go out without being honked at, and people have asked me to "suck their cock" when I was just walking down the street. I live in a quiet little town as well, it'd probably be worse in a city. Whenever I mention it to my friends, they confirm that it's not just me, they get it all the time too.[15]

Oh, all the time. Like you said it's "depressingly normal." So much so that at times it hardly registers as harassment if you know what I mean. Disgusting.[16]

I also wondered "who hasn't?" when I saw this. I'm fifteen . . . and it's a bit creepy getting stupid comments when I pass much older guys.[17]

Perhaps we should ask "has any woman not experienced male sexual harassment?"[18]

I agree emphatically with Laura Woodhouse: street harassment is depressingly normal, and every street harassment study—from academic research to regional or countrywide investigations—shows that it is a significant problem.

Street Harassment Studies

In one of the first street harassment studies ever conducted, Gardner, associate professor of sociology and women's studies at Indiana University, Indianapolis, interviewed 293 women in Indianapolis, Indiana, over several years in the late 1980s and early 1990s. The women were from every race, age, class, and sexual orientation category of the general population in Indiana and the United States. She oversampled women of color to better represent their experiences. Gardner found that every single woman (100 percent) could cite several examples of being harassed by unknown men in public and all but nine of the women classified those experiences as "troublesome."[19]

Using a national sample of 12,300 Canadian women ages 18 and older from 1994, sociology professors Ross MacMillan, Annette Nierobisz, and Sandy Welsh studied the impact of street harassment on women's perceived sense of safety in 2000. During their research, they found that over 80 percent of the women surveyed had experienced male stranger harassment in public and that those experiences had a large and detrimental impact on their perceived safety in public.[20]

Laura Beth Nielsen, professor of sociology and the law at Northwestern University conducted a study of 100 women's and men's experiences with offensive speech in the California San Francisco Bay Area in the early 2000s. She found that 100 percent of the 54 women she asked had been the target of offensive or sexually suggestive remarks at least occasionally: 19 percent said every day, 43 percent said often, and 28 percent said sometimes. Notably, they were the target of such speech significantly more often than they were of "polite" remarks about their appearance.[21]

A 2002 survey of 200 citizens in Beijing, China, showed that 70 percent had been subjected to a form of sexual harassment. Most people said it occurred on public transportation, including 58 percent who said it occurred on the bus.[22]

During the summer of 2003, members of the Rogers Park Young Women's Action Team in Chicago surveyed 168 neighborhood girls and young women (most of whom were African American or Latina) ages 10 to 19 about street harassment and interviewed 34 more in focus groups. They published their findings in a report titled "Hey Cutie, Can I Get Your Digits?" Of their respondents, 86 percent had been catcalled on the street, 36 percent said men harassed them daily, and 60 percent said they felt unsafe walking in their neighborhoods.[23]

Groping on trains, subways, and transit stations in Tokyo, Japan, is rampant. In a 2004 survey of 632 women who travel during rush hour in Tokyo, nearly 64 percent of the women in their twenties and thirties said they were groped while commuting.[24] In 2008 in Tokyo alone there were 2,000 reported groping cases (and it is an underreported crime).[25]

In 2007, the Manhattan Borough President's Office conducted an online questionnaire about sexual harassment on the New York City subway system with a total of 1,790 participants. Nearly two-thirds of the respondents identified as women. Of the respondents, 63 percent reported being sexually harassed, and one-tenth had been sexually assaulted on the subway or at a subway station. Due to collection methods used, the report "Hidden in Plain Sight: Sexual Harassment and Assault in the New York City Subway System" is not statistically significant, but it suggests that a large number of women experience problems on the subway system.[26]

The Egyptian Centre for Women's Rights surveyed 2,000 Egyptian men and women and 109 foreign women in four governorates in the country, including Cairo and Giza, about sexual harassment on Egyptian streets. They published their findings in 2008. Eighty-three percent of Egyptian women reported experiencing sexual harassment on the street at least once, and nearly half of the women said they experience it daily. Ninety-eight percent of the foreign women surveyed reported experiencing sexual harassment while in Egypt. Wearing a veil did not appear to lessen a woman's chances of being harassed. About 62 percent of Egyptian men admitted to perpetrating harassment.[27]

In Yemen, the *Yemen Times* conducted a survey on teasing and sexual harassment in Sana'a in 2009. Ninety percent of the 70 interviewees from Sana'a said they had been sexually harassed in public. Seventy-two percent of the women said they were called sexually charged names while walking on the streets, and 20 percent of this group said it happens on a regular basis. About 37 percent of the sample said they had experienced physical harassment. Like those in Egypt, these survey results implied that being veiled did not lessen the harassment, because wearing a veil in public is so common.[28]

Throughout 2009, the Centre for Equity and Inclusion surveyed 630 women of all ages and socioeconomic status in New Delhi and Old Delhi, India. Ninety-five percent of the women said their mobility was restricted because of fear of male harassment in public places. Another 82 percent said the bus is the most unsafe mode of public transportation for them because of male harassers.[29]

While each of these studies has its imperfections, they all found a high percentage of women had been harassed by men (and many only focused on harassment on the transit system). Much more research on this topic is necessary, but from the studies that exist, it seems male street harassment is a common female experience, especially in cities, where women tend to encounter more people and are more likely to use public transportation. In my own informal research, I too, have found street harassment to be pervasive.

Nearly every woman I have talked to about this issue has been harassed by men. Furthermore, every woman can cite strategies, such as avoiding going in public alone at night, which she uses to avoid harassment and assault. To learn more about women's harassment experiences I conducted two informal, anonymous online surveys about street harassment: one in 2007 for my master's thesis at George Washington University and one in 2008 as preliminary research for this book. Between both surveys, there were 1,141 respondents (see www.stopstreetharassment.com/book/surveys for the full survey questions and how the surveys were conducted). Similar to the other studies conducted on street harassment, nearly every female respondent had experienced street harassment at least once.

In my first online survey, conducted during the spring of 2007, I asked 225 respondents: "Have you ever been harassed (such as verbal comments, honking, whistling, kissing noises, leering/staring, groping, stalking, attempted or achieved assault, etc) while in a public place like the street, on public transportation, or in a store?" Ninety-nine percent of the respondents, which included some men, said they had been harassed at least a few times. Over 65 percent said they were harassed on at least a monthly basis.

Over 99 percent of the 811 female respondents of the second informal survey I conducted in 2008 said they had experienced some form of street harassment (only three women indicated they had not). While I did not ask for any demographical information in my first survey, I did for the second survey and found that the 916 respondents came from a range of backgrounds and geographic locations. Survey-takers selected age categories from "13–19" through "80 and older," they represented every major American racial group; they identified as bisexual, gay, heterosexual, lesbian, queer, and "other"; and they came from forty-five American states, twenty-three countries, and five continents. In one question they could indicate the types of interactions they have had with strangers in public, and in two open-ended questions they had the opportunity to share a story illustrating those experiences. The following sampling of the shocking, horrific, and infuriating responses to those questions from the 811 women shows the omnipresence of street harassment across the United States and suggests it is a global problem.

Leering

Ninety-five percent of female respondents were the target of leering or excessive staring at least once, and more than 68 percent reported being a target 26 times or more in their life.

Lots of leering on public transportation.
> —13–19-year-old heterosexual Asian American
> woman in New York City

[When I was visiting] Seattle: honking, leering men in cars, I couldn't even walk past a bus stop at night without being hit on by creepy old men.
> —20–29-year-old pansexual white woman in Canada

When I went running and I had my backpack tied around my upper waist, some dude came up to me leering, and said, "Girl, I like the way you tie your backpack" while staring at my breasts. I just kept running and was disgusted by it for the rest of the day. I still am.
> —20–29-year-old heterosexual Latina in New York City

Honking and Whistling

Nearly 95 percent of female respondents were honked at one or more times, and 40 percent said they are honked at as frequently as monthly. Nearly 94 percent of female respondents were the target of whistling at least once, and nearly 38 percent said it occurred at least monthly.

Nothing too awful has happened to me, thank goodness, but I do get a few random annoyances. Take for example when I walk down the street, I get the occasional honks. The usual. And yeah, it's really depressing that it can be considered a usual.
—13–19-year-old heterosexual Portuguese woman in San Jose, California

When I lived in Florida, as a teenager I would be harassed by honkers and whistlers from cars almost daily as I walked to and from my school bus stop. It was humiliating and scary.
—20–29-year-old heterosexual white woman in Jersey City, New Jersey

Earliest thing I remember is a bunch of guys honking and shouting at me and my friends when we were walking downtown. It was creepy because we were only like 13.
—20–29-year-old bisexual white woman in Canada

One day, a female friend and I were walking in a residential area, when the taxi drivers just kept slowing down, honking, shouting, and whistling. We tried to stay as far away from the street edges on the pavement and walked quickly. But you can't really outrun a taxi.
—13–19-year-old heterosexual Latina in Lima, Peru

Making Vulgar Gestures

Nearly 82 percent of female respondents were the target of a vulgar gesture at least once. About 20 percent said they had been a target at least fifty-one times.

Walking [down] the street in my neighborhood, some strange guy stuck his tongue out at me in a sexual way.
—20–29-year-old bisexual African American woman in San Diego, California

My most recent incident was when a stranger stuck his tongue out repeatedly in what was meant to be a sexual way in the car next to me. It was disgusting.
—20–29-year-old queer white woman in Charlotte, North Carolina

Saying Sexually Explicit Comments

Nearly 81 percent of female respondents were the target of sexually explicit comments from an unknown man at least once. More than 41 percent have been the target at least twenty-six times in their lives.

I was walking to my dorm on campus when a group of guys drove past and one called me a "whore." They drove past me, laughing. I'd never seen these individuals previously and stopped in shock because this had never happened to me before.

> —20–29-year-old bisexual African American
> woman in Indianapolis, Indiana

I live in a busy neighborhood and one afternoon I was out shopping when a man yelled "hey, girl in the grey coat" from a car window. I thought maybe I had dropped something, so I turned to look and the man yells "I heard you like it up the a$$!" I was horrified . . .

> —20–29-year-old heterosexual white woman in Chicago, Illinois

I was waiting for a streetcar at a crowded stop, when a car pulled up to the red light and the bunch of guys inside commented loudly, for the duration of the light, that I looked like I'd be fun to rape.

> —30–39-year-old heterosexual mixed heritage (Asian, black
> and white) woman in Toronto, Canada

Following

Seventy-five percent of female respondents have been followed by an unknown stranger in public. More than 27 percent have been followed at least six times.

I've been followed in America, in France, in Bosnia, and groped in Croatia . . . I've been followed in cars and on foot, by men of all shades and probably many diverse backgrounds.

> —20–29-year-old heterosexual white American
> woman in Copenhagen, Denmark

I was followed by a man for at least six blocks until I ran into a local supermarket.

> —20–29-year-old heterosexual African American
> woman in New York City

In Toronto, in daytime business hours, a man followed me, breathing down my neck - all the way into a shop where I reported to a clerk that I was being followed. I was scared but did not want to show fear so I did not acknowledge his presence or change my pace.

> —50–59-year-old heterosexual white Dutch woman in the Netherlands

While driving home from school one night I was followed about 10 miles by another car to my home. I honked my horn which woke my father. As the people in the car ran towards my car my father ran out of the house and scared them away.

> —50–59-year-old heterosexual white woman in Bountiful, Utah

Sexual Touching or Grabbing

Nearly 57 percent of women reported being touched or grabbed in a sexual way by a stranger in public. About 18 percent said they have been touched sexually at least six times.

When I was about 10 years old, a man came up behind me on the sidewalk and groped me.
    —30–39-year-old heterosexual white woman in Lakeland, Florida

I was on a crowded bus in LA (express line, commuter hour) when a man sat next to me on my right side . . . A few moments later I felt something on my leg. I looked up from my book and noticed that he was using the coat to disguise the fact that his hand was on my thigh—a few inches higher and it would have been in my crotch.
    —20–29-year-old bisexual Latina woman in Oakland, California

Perhaps the most terrifying was when I was swept into a crowded corridor of a place of worship and [was] touched, groped, pinched, scratched, and had a piece of my clothing ripped by nameless, faceless, ageless men.
    —20–29-year-old heterosexual woman in Chennai, India

I was waiting in a cab for my friend, while he was getting a few things at the store. The cab driver and I started making small talk. Without warning he grabbed my breasts and tried to kiss me. I pushed him off of me. I was in shock. I didn't know what to do. Luckily my friend came out of the store. I sat in silence the entire ride. The cab driver was joking around with my friend like nothing happened.
    —20–29-year-old heterosexual white woman in Kalamazoo, Michigan

Masturbating

More than 37 percent of female respondents have had a stranger masturbate at or in front of them at least once in public.

Once while I was walking to the gym, a man pulled up beside me in his car and honked. He shouted vulgar things, exposed himself and proceeded to masturbate. I felt so bad and even defiled. I ran away and hid in the bushes while I called my fiancé to come and help me. He found me there shaking and sobbing a short while later.
    —20–29-year-old heterosexual white woman in Baltimore, Maryland

When I was a teenager in NYC, I twice had strangers masturbate in front of me on the subway. I was terrified and had no idea how to react.
    —30–39-year-old heterosexual Latina in Lakeville, Connecticut

Once I was in a public, outdoor area on a park bench when a man started talking to me and masturbating. He made sexually explicit comments towards me and tried to make me touch him. I was 13 and very embarrassed and uncomfortable about the situation, so I walked away.

　　　　　—20–29-year-old heterosexual white woman in Toronto, Canada

I was at a library and was masturbated at—I freaked out and chased the guy out of the library.

　　　　　—30–39-year-old heterosexual woman of mixed heritage
　　　　　(Latina and white) in New York City

Assaulting

About 27 percent of women report being assaulted at least once in public by a stranger.

I was raped when I was a teenager by an unknown person who had followed me into the park.

　　　　　—30–39-year-old heterosexual white woman in San Jose, California

I was sexually assaulted once when I was walking my dog near my residence.

　　　　　—20–29-year-old heterosexual in Singapore

I was coming home from work at a bar one night, and I didn't notice that someone I'd served at work followed me out. He honked at me, going down the freeway, and when I tried to lose him, it wasn't working. I drove to a police station and honked my horn, hoping someone would come out to help me. Before they did, he got out of his car and attacked me. He bashed in the side of my car with a baseball bat, until help came. I still have a restraining order on him after all this time.

　　　　　—30–39-year-old heterosexual Native Hawaiian in Phoenix, Arizona

I have been sexually attacked on the street in an upscale, quiet neighborhood. My instincts and experience being harassed on the street enabled me to fight him off. Fortunately, I was able to fight as no one came to my rescue.

　　　　　—60–69-year-old heterosexual white woman in Somerville, Massachusetts

Other Common Experiences

Sexist comment: Over 87 percent of women said they were the target of a sexist comment, and about 45 percent said they've been a target of a sexist comment in public at least twenty-five times in their life.

Kissing noises: Just over 77 percent of women said they were the target of kissing noises from men, and 48 percent said they've been the target at least twenty-five times in their life.

Blocking path: About 62 percent of women say a man has purposely blocked their path at least once, and 23 percent said this has happened at least six times.

Harassment Begins Early

These numbers and stories, though they were collected informally and barely touch upon the range of women's experiences, are appalling. Before I examined my results, I expected the number of women who had been whistled or leered at by men to be high, but I did not expect some of the other percentages to be so high. I find it scary that 75 percent of women have been followed by an unknown man at least once. I find it disturbing that over half of the women respondents were less than 30 years old and already had experienced so much harassment.

In a later survey question, I asked how old respondents were when they were first harassed by male strangers in public. The results were shocking: 87 percent had been harassed by age 19, including 22 percent by the time they were 12 years old and 66 percent by the time they were 15. Many of my 2008 survey respondents shared stories illustrating the young age at which girls start being harassed by men:

I was followed and harassed so much during my teens and 20s that I was often frightened to go out. It started when I was as young as 8 or 9 and it seemed to happen almost every day. Either someone followed me making sexual comments, or tried to get me into their car, or flashed me or worse. I felt vulnerable and violated and it often made me cry. Now that I am almost 40, the base level of street harassment has gone down a lot and I feel like I can breathe again. (. . . The harassment seemed to be at its worse when I was 14–28 . . . I still get harassed and my 78 year old mother and I have been harassed together!), but it's not a constant.
                    —30–39-year-old bisexual woman (no race specified)
                                                    in New York City

The very first time I got honked at, I was so confused. I was around 11 or 12, walking down the street to my friend's house to play dolls. A car of men honked at me. I was confused because I wasn't in their way, I didn't understand why they were honking. Then as they drove past they smiled and waved at me and I understood. But still . . . I was a little girl, wearing unflattering clothes, huge glasses, and probably unwashed hair.
                    —20–29-year-old heterosexual white woman in Chicago, Illinois

Many boys and men harass girls on their way to and from school. Later in the book I discuss several examples on a global scale, including girls who were groped on the subway in Japan and assaulted walking to school in rural Zambia.[30] As another example, in Afghanistan, Taliban members have thrown acid at girls going to school. In 2008, several men sprayed acid at fifteen girls walking to school; three of the girls sustained severe burns and one girl permanently lost her sight.[31] Harassment happens to girls commuting to school in the United States, too. Here are two stories from my 2008 survey respondents on the topic.

When I was a freshman in high school, a girlfriend and I were followed home by a car of teenage boys who shouted remarks and the occasional lewd comment. We veered off our route and onto the campus of the elementary school where we went to a former teacher's classroom and asked her if we could stay for a while, until we felt sure those guys were gone.

—20–29-year-old bisexual white woman in Murfreesboro, Tennessee

One day in 8th grade (when I was 13), I was running late. The train was crowded, but I had to get on. As I shoved myself in, a fat man suddenly came out of nowhere and wedged himself in behind me. . . . He started rubbing his crotch against my leg and panting. I was so scared, I didn't know what to do or say. When the train reached the next stop and a lot of people got off, I tried to get away from him. He followed me and continued rubbing his crotch against my leg. . . . He didn't stop until more people got off and I finally found a seat.

—13–19-year-old heterosexual Asian American woman in New York City

What is equally shocking is how many girls are harassed by grown men who are old enough to be their fathers and grandfathers. Over and over, girls and women said they were disgusted when this happened. Also, in one of my survey questions, 62 percent of women selected a five, six, or seven on a scale from one to seven (with seven being the most threatening) for how they felt if the harasser was older than them.

Frequently Harassed

While many girls and women have only been harassed a handful of times in their lifetimes (still a handful too many), others are harassed multiple times a day. Men who harass women can be undiscerning in their targets,[32] but there are circumstantial factors that seem to contribute to the likelihood that one woman will be harassed more frequently than another. Some of these factors include relying on public transportation or walking, being in public alone, living in populated areas, being young, and living in an area with low evidence of gender equality. Also, overall, women of color may face more harassment than white women.[33] Thus, an older white woman who lives in the suburbs, drives to her destinations, and is rarely in public alone likely will experience less frequent (but not a complete absence of) harassment than a young woman of color who walks or takes the bus to her destination and is often in public alone.

The following comments from the 2008 survey speak to the sheer volume of street harassment many women endure.

Regularly when walking around at home (I live in a countryside area) I am hooted at or have men yell out of cars at me.
—13–19-year-old heterosexual white woman in the United Kingdom

In my old neighborhood, I would get street harassed EVERY time I left the apartment. It didn't matter what I was wearing. I do not remember a single time I did not get harassed. I did not feel unsafe, but I was in a constant state of irritation.
—20–29-year-old queer Asian American woman in New York City

It happens so often, that they all kind of blend into one large experiences of constant uncomfortable-ness and vigilance.
—20–29-year-old heterosexual white woman in Raleigh, North Carolina

I could write a full-length manuscript about it, like so many black girls and women.
—30–39-year-old heterosexual African American woman in Bronx, New York

In Chile, street harassment is a regular and quite accepted behavior.
—30–39-year-old heterosexual Latina in Chile

When women regularly face harassment, it tends to become a part of their existence and something they must learn to cope with if they want to be able to participate in public life. Too often their coping mechanisms also restrict their ability to go in public and to have peace of mind while there.

CONCLUSION

Street harassment is a pervasive problem. How can women ever hope to achieve equality with men when so many are routinely harassed simply for leaving their homes, especially if they are unaccompanied by a man? What does it mean that young women grow up in a world in which they likely will be the target of male harassment in public several times—probably before they reach their twenties? At the very least, it means that across the world, there is gender inequality.

NOTES

1. Carol Brooks Gardner, *Passing By: Gender and Public Harassment* (Berkeley, CA: University of California Press, 1995), 89–90; see also Ross

MacMillan, Annette Nierobisz, and Sandy Welsh, "Experiencing the Streets: Harassment and Perceptions of Safety among Women," *Journal of Research in Crime and Delinquency* 37, no. 3 (August 2000), 319; see also Laura Beth Nielsen, *License to Harass: Law, Hierarchy, and Offensive Public Speech* (Princeton, NJ: Princeton University Press, 2004), 43; see also Prime Minister's Office, "Violence Against Women—Just Because They're Women!" November 26, 2002, http://www.pmo.gov.il/PMOEng/Archive/Press+Releases/2002/11/Speeches6916.htm; see also "Harassment Rampant on Public Transportation," *Shanghai Star*, April 11, 2002, http://app1.chinadaily.com.cn/star/2002/0411/cn8-4.html; see also Amaya N. Roberson, "Anti-Street Harassment," *Off Our Backs,* May–June 2005, 48; see also *ABC News*, "Japan Tries Women-Only Train Cars to Stop Groping," June 10, 2005, http://abcnews.go.com/GMA/International/story?id=803965&CMP=OTC-RSSFeeds0312; see also Scott M. Stringer, "Hidden in Plain Sight: Sexual Harassment and Assault in the New York City Subway System," July 2007, http://mbpo.org/uploads/HIDDEN%20IN%20PLAIN%20SIGHT.pdf; see also Sewell Chan, "Subway Harassment Questionnaire Garners a Big Response," *New York Times*, July 26, 2008, http://cityroom.blogs.nytimes.com/2007/07/26/big-response-to-subway-harassment-question/; see also Cynthia Johnston, "Two-Thirds of Egyptian Men Harass Women?" *Reuters*, July 17, 2008, http://www.reuters.com/article/email/idUSL1732581120080717; see also Ali Saeed and Nadia Al-Sakkaf, "Sexual Harassment Deters Women from Outdoor Activities," *Yemen Times*, January 21, 2009, http://www.yementimes.com/article.shtml?i=1226&p=report&a=2; see also *Indian Express*, "82% Delhi Women Find Buses Most Unsafe: Study," November 14, 2009, http://www.indianexpress.com/news/82-delhi-women-find-buses-most-unsafe-study/541230.

2. M.C. (a 2008 survey respondent) e-mail message to author, August 20, 2009.

3. Sheila Parker, "Metro Police Investigate Sexual Assault," WSAV, May 25, 2009, http://www2.wsav.com/sav/news/local/article/metro_police_investigate_sexual_assault/12822.

4. Barry Paddock, Henry Karoliszyn, Jotham Sederstrom, Alison Gendar, and Wil Cruz, "Van Crashes in Midtown; Kills Pregnant Woman Driver Allegedly Attempted to Flirt With," *New York Daily News*, March 27, 2009, http://www.nydailynews.com/ny_local/2009/03/27/2009-03-27_van_crashes_in_midtown_kills_pregnant_wo.html.

5. Joey Johnston, "ESPN's Vitale to Help with Bradenton Teen's Funeral Expenses," Tampa Bay Online, September 8, 2009, http://www2.tbo.com/content/2009/sep/08/081251/counselors-attend-students-after-bradenton-cheerle/news-metro.

6. Martha Langelan, *Back Off! How to Confront and Stop Sexual Harassment and Harassers* (New York: Fireside Press, 1993), 51; see also Gardner, 14–16.

7. Micaela di Leonardo, "Political Economy of Street Harassment," *Aegis,* Summer 1981, 51–52; quoted in Cynthia Grant Bowman, "Street Harassment and the Informal Ghettoization of Women," *Harvard Law Review* 106, no. 3 (January 1993): 524.

8. Gardner, 4.

9. Cath Elliot, "So Angry I Could Strip!" *Guardian,* May 28, 2008, http://www.guardian.co.uk/commentisfree/2008/may/28/soangryicouldstrip.

10. Jeremy James, comment on "So Angry I Could Strip!" comment posted on May 28, 2008 (accessed July 30, 2008).

11. Bisonex, comment on "So Angry I Could Strip!" comment posted on May 28, 2008 (accessed July 30, 2008).

12. Staybryte, comment on "So Angry I Could Strip!" comment posted on May 28, 2008 (accessed July 30, 2008).

13. Laura Woodhouse, "Hands Up If You've Experienced Street Harassment," The F Word Contemporary UK Feminism Blog, May 28, 2008, http://www.thefword.org.uk/blog/2008/05/hands_up_if_you.

14. Graceless Atthis comment on "Hands Up If You've Experienced Street Harassment," comment posted on May 28, 2008 (accessed July 15, 2008).

15. Redheadinred comment on "Hands Up If You've Experienced Street Harassment," comment posted on May 28, 2008 (accessed July 15, 2008).

16. Deviousdiva comment on "Hands Up If You've Experienced Street Harassment," comment posted on May 28, 2008 (accessed July 15, 2008).

17. Marlow comment on "Hands Up If You've Experienced Street Harassment," comment posted on May 28, 2008 (accessed July 15, 2008).

18. Jenniferdrew comment on "Hands Up If You've Experienced Street Harassment," comment posted on May 28, 2008 (accessed July 15, 2008).

19. Gardner, 89–90.

20. MacMillan, Nierobisz, and Welsh, 318.

21. Nielsen, 43.

22. "Harassment Rampant on Public Transportation."

23. Roberson, 48.

24. ABC News, "Japan Tries Women-Only Train Cars to Stop Groping"; see also Erin Johnston, "Women Feel Tokyo Train Gropers," *Guardian,* November 24, 2004, http://www.guardian.co.uk/world/2004/nov/24/japan.

25. Takahiro Fukada, "In Anonymous Packed Train Lurk Gropers," *Japan Times,* August 18, 2009, http://search.japantimes.co.jp/cgi-bin/nn20090818i1.html.

26. Stringer, "Hidden in Plain Sight: Sexual Harassment and Assault in the New York City Subway System"; see also Chan, "Subway Harassment Questionnaire Garners a Big Response."

27. Johnston, "Two-thirds of Egyptian Men Harass Women?"; see also Magdi Abdelhadi, "Egypt's Sexual Harassment 'Cancer,'" *BBC News*, July 18, 2008, http://news.bbc.co.uk/2/hi/middle_east/7514567.stm.

28. Saeed and Al-Sakaaf.

29. All Headline News, "Survey Finds Majority of Delhi Women Fear Sexual Harassment in Public Places," November 17, 2009, http://www.all headlinenews.com/articles/7017019900; see also *Indian Express*, "82% Delhi Women Find Buses Most Unsafe: Study."

30. Fukada, "In Anonymous Packed Train Lurk Gropers"; see also Lewis Mwanagombe, "Education-Zambia: Bicycles Help Girls Go Further," IPS, September 7, 2009, http://ipsnews.net/news.asp?idnews=48349.

31. Farangis Najibullah, "Acid Attack on Afghan Schoolgirls Causes Fear, Anxiety among Parents," Afghanistan Online, November 15, 2008, http://www.afghan-web.com/woman/acidattacks.html.

32. Gardner, 110; see also Langelan, 51.

33. Nielsen, 41.

Chapter 2

Context in Which Street Harassment Occurs

Women "cat call" toward men as well. I have been yelled at by cars full of females passing by and I take no offense to it.[1]

As a man I could only wish women catcalled when they see me. "HEEEEY YOU BALDHEAD HANDSOME SON OF A GUN!"

MANY women do dress in an inviting manner! Low cut tops or their thong pulled up in effort to show it! I see it EVERYDAY! These types are looking for that attention! Am I wrong?[2]

These responses to a CNN article on catcalling[3] are the type of comments many men (and some women) make when they hear a woman talk about street harassment or read an article about it. The comments downplay and trivialize street harassment as a problem and portray it as a compliment or behavior that women universally want. The people making such comments have failed to consider the context in which street harassment occurs. Context helps explain why so many women do not like street harassment and why male harassment of women differs from other forms of harassment.

This chapter explores three important contexts of street harassment. First, street harassment occurs in a culture of worldwide gender inequality. When men harass women, it reminds women of this inequality—because it happens at all, because the point is often to evaluate women as sex objects, and because there are few legal remedies to pursue against harassers. Second, street harassment occurs in a context of rape culture, causing most women to have an underlying fear of being raped by men in public when they are alone and wary of any man who approaches them. Combined, these two contexts create a third one, a context of victim blaming where women are put at fault for the harassment instead of the men who perpetrate it. These contexts prevent direct comparisons between gender-based street harassment of women by men and other types of harassment that occur in public.

GENDER INEQUALITY

Street harassment is one of many manifestations of global gender inequality. People who believe male street harassment is complimentary or comparable to the occasions when women harass men fail to recognize the underlying power dynamics. Each year, the World Economic Forum measures gender equality with the Global Gender Gap report. They assess 134 countries on how well they divide their resources and opportunities among female and male populations by measuring categories such as labor force participation, income, literacy, school enrollment, political leadership, life expectancy, and the existence of legislation punishing acts of gender-based violence. As of 2009, no country had achieved gender parity in all areas. Iceland, Finland, Norway, and Sweden came closest; each country scored over 0.8 out of 1.0.[4] Consequently, around the world, including the United States, men have more opportunities and access to resources than women.

Ranked thirty-first in the report with a score of 0.7173, the United States is far from achieving gender equity.[5] While there is gender equity regarding literacy and opportunity for school enrollment and women have a longer life expectancy than men, the following statistics show how in areas like political leadership and the labor force—and additional areas not measured by the Global Gender Gap Report—men hold the most power, causing them to be more powerful overall than women.

- **Political leaders:** No woman has served as president or vice president of the United States. In 2009, a mere 12 percent of state governors were women.[6] Women have only held 17 percent of the seats in the U.S. House of Representatives and the U.S. Senate during a congressional session.[7]

- **Workplace leaders:** In 2009, only fifteen of the Fortune 500 companies, or 3 percent, had female CEOs, including only one black woman CEO.[8] A 2008 study of CEO pay at 3,242 North American companies showed women's salaries were 85 percent of men's salaries.[9]

- **Law enforcement:** In 2008, 14 percent of all police officers and 1 percent of all police chiefs were women.[10] Women comprise only 22 percent of the justices on the U.S. Supreme Court and 30 percent of judges in state courts.[11]

- **News makers:** In 2006, only 28 percent of all U.S. broadcast network evening newscast stories were reported by women.[12] An underwhelming 16 percent of guests on influential Sunday morning political talk shows are women, and only 15 percent of the authors of the nonfiction books on the *New York Times* best-selling list are women. Only 20 percent of op-eds in newspapers are written by women, and only 13 percent of the online Wikipedia entries have been authored by women.[13]

- **Media makers:** Of the top 250 domestic grossing films of 2008, only 9 percent had women directors, 12 percent had women writers, and 23 percent had women producers.[14] For the 2008–2009 television season, women comprised only 9 percent of directors, 29 percent of writers, and 35 percent of producers.[15] In 2009, overall, twice as many men as women worked in the television industry, with nearly three times as many men as women employed in the film industry.[16]

- **Workplace discrimination and economic disparity:** Compared with men, women at work are more likely to face sexual harassment[17] (especially if they are in a managerial position[18]), discrimination for performing caregiver duties,[19] and unequal pay.[20] Salary and industry analysis shows that women make less than men in both the ten lowest-paying and the ten highest-paying occupations for women.[21] Single women, particularly mothers, are much more likely than single men and single fathers to live in poverty.[22] One of the long-term impacts of workplace inequality is that poverty is twice as high among older women as among older men and three times as high among older African American women as among older white women.[23]

- **Household inequality:** One in every four women will experience domestic violence in her lifetime, and an estimated 1.3 million women are victims of physical assault by an intimate partner each year.[24] In the majority of households, including those in which women work full time outside the home and households in which there are unemployed men, women do more housework, cooking, and caregiving than do their male counterparts.[25]

Combined, these statistics reveal that women as a group hold less power than men in government, in the workplace, and in their own homes. They show that Americans are ruled by laws written and enforced primarily by (white) men and that American society is disproportionately shaped by (white) male viewpoints through the news we read and hear, the television shows and movies we watch, and the books and public opinions we read.

In the context of a male-shaped society, women learn from a young age that how attractive they are to men matters more than anything else. A 2007 report by the American Psychology Association (APA) Task Force on the Sexualization of Girls found that girls are socialized by the media, parents, and peers to believe that their worth is their sexuality and ability to please men.[26] Here are a few of the APA findings regarding the primarily male-run media's habit of sexualizing women's bodies:

- In 81 episodes of prime-time programming, 84 percent of the episodes contained at least one incident of sexual harassment, and most of it was focused on demeaning terms for women or the sexualization of their bodies (such as talking about their body parts or men ogling women).[27]
- An analysis of music videos showed that 57 percent of the videos featured women portrayed only as a decorative sexual object.[28]
- A study of nudity in movies showed that female nudity occurs at a 4 to 1 ratio to male nudity.[29]

Women's intellect, sense of humor, and athleticism is too often secondary to whether or not they are "hot." For example, during the 2008 presidential election, Republican vice presidential nominee Sarah Palin's sex appeal became her biggest asset or liability[30]—depending on the voter and the media spin—while Democratic presidential candidate Hillary Rodham Clinton was mocked for being past her sexual prime when her blouse revealed a bit of cleavage[31] and when the media commented on her "cankles."[32] Similarly, there are world-class female athletes who pose half or fully nude for magazines to show that they are feminine and "hot" as well as athletic.[33]

Underrepresented in positions of real power, from a young age women are taught that being beautiful and sexy is their way to achieve (temporary, fleeting) power over men and power in general. Toddlers and elementary-school-age girls see ads for and may own impossibly proportioned and beautiful Barbie dolls, "princess" paraphernalia, and age-inappropriate items like padded bras,[34] high heels,[35] thong underwear,[36] and stripper poles.[37] If women are deemed attractive enough by narrow societal standards, they can be paid more for their looks as models and for selling their bodies as prostitutes than for their intellect and nonsexual skills.[38] University of Michigan Law School professor and pioneer of the legal claim for sexual harassment, Catharine MacKinnon, studied salaries for occupations in the United States comprised almost entirely of women, such as secretaries, preschool teachers, bank tellers, and food service workers, and she found that the average street walker in Manhattan makes double to quadruple the salaries of women in the occupations she studied.[39] In part because of sex discrimination, there are women who become part-time or temporary sex workers to make extra money because the pay is so much better than jobs like waitressing or running a cash register and, in the short term, may be worth the increased risk of workplace violence.[40]

Street Harassment Reinforces Gender Inequality

Street harassment is just one more manifestation of gender inequality. Most men are free to walk around in public largely unharmed and unharassed. Women, however, are interrupted, touched, and followed by men just because they are women in public. Male harassment enforces spatial boundaries for women and causes what law professor Cynthia Grant Bowman calls the "informal ghettoization of women"; women are pushed to the "private sphere of hearth and home" to avoid harassment.[41]

In their article "Beauty Is the Beast: Psychological Effects of the Pursuit of the Perfect Female Body," Elayne A. Saltzberg and Joan C. Chrisler, wrote that "street harassers put women 'in their place' by commenting loudly on their beauty or lack of it. Beauty norms limit the opportunities of women who can't or won't meet them."[42] Street harassment can shock women into remembering that they exist "to be sexually enjoyed by men."[43] When men say "mmm-mmm" at women's butts or tell women they are fat cows, they remind women how some men and how society in general value them, and they are forced to see themselves as men see them.[44] Thus, a woman who is conventionally beautiful is reminded of her value when men harass her "positively." One of my 2008 online survey respondents said when answering 2009 follow-up questions, "Sometimes I wish I was fat or ugly so that I would not be sexualized by strangers. But then I remember that they would instead taunt me for being unattractive and not sexually pleasing to them."

She is right, many women who are not conventionally beautiful are reminded that they are "undesirable" despite their other qualities when men harass them with negative comments or when they see men harass "pretty" women but not them. A woman in Vancouver, Canada submitted the following to my blog:

I am fat and considered very unattractive. I am often told that I'm a dog/ugly/cow/pig/barked and oinked at by strange men in public. Two men recently followed behind me on the street for several blocks, loudly discussing what they would have to do in order to make me "f***able" (i.e., put a bag over my head, get me to go to a plastic surgeon, etc.) I try very hard not to take these experiences to heart but this recent one was very disturbing. I realized that I have been avoiding crowded public areas because of this. It also reinforces my feeling that despite my achievements and personality, in this world what really matters is my outward appearance.[45]

This is such a heartbreaking story, but it is the reality for this woman and for so many others.

Street harassment is not against the law, which means women have virtually no legal recourse against a harasser if he has not touched her or masturbated in front of her or directly threatened her.[46] Yet there are laws and city ordinances against pick pocketing, solicitation, panhandling, and not picking up dog waste, problems that have the potential to negatively impact men, which street harassment does not. Since men are the main legislators, laws tend to reflect issues that impact them.[47] Men also are the primary law-enforcers. So when a man has assaulted, threatened, or masturbated in front of a woman and she reports him and maybe ends up in court, chances are the police officer and judge will be (white) men. They may be men who do not completely understand why the woman is upset or who will dismiss her problem as trivial,[48] particularly if she is a woman of color or a transwoman.

Recognizing gender inequality helps explain why women do not like street harassment and why it is different from other forms of harassment (in which other forms of inequality may instead be at play), particularly when women harass men.

LIVING IN A RAPE CULTURE

An underlying fear of stranger rape that many women have when they are alone in public is another context for gender-based street harassment. Notably, since it is a fear that few men have, it creates a unique context for harassment perpetrated by men against women.

Historically, male harassment and the threat or reality of rape has restricted women's mobility in public places, particularly in patriarchal and patrilineal societies. According to feminist author and scholar Marilyn French, this is because men wanted to ensure paternity, especially of male heirs, by controlling the sexual activities and movements of their mate.[49] In particular, wealthy/upper-class men closely monitored their wives and daughters in an effort to ensure their property or power went to their legitimate offspring and that their daughters were "pure" when they began bearing off-spring for their husbands. Consequently, many upper class women were cloistered away or were always accompanied by a male member of the family or a male servant. Economic necessity meant lower-class women usually left their homes unaccompanied to work, so they had more freedom of movement than their upper-class counter-parts, but that meant that these women were vulnerable to harassment and sexual assault by men of all classes.[50]

Yet rape and sexually controlling behavior are not innate to humans: most men (and women) do not rape, and there were (and are) societies, particularly those that are matrilineal, in which it appears such crimes never or very rarely occurred. In the 1980s, anthropologist Peggy Reeves Sanday studied ninety-five tribal societies and the evidence of rape. She concluded that 47 percent of the tribal societies were rape-free, and 53 percent were rape-prone. She defined a "rape prone society" as "one in which the incidence of rape is reported by observers to be high, or rape is excused as a ceremonial expression of masculinity, or rape is an act by which men are allowed to punish or threaten women." Conversely, a "rape free society" is "one in which the act of rape is either infrequent or does not occur" and where "sexual aggression is socially disapproved and punished severely."[51]

Sanday found that the difference between the two types of cultures was, unsurprisingly, a respect for women. Rape-free societies have sexual equality and reflect the idea that the sexes are complementary and deserve the same rights and privileges.[52] She wrote:

Rape is not an integral part of male nature, but the means by which men programmed for violence express their sexual selves. Men who are conditioned to respect the female virtues of growth and the sacredness of life do not violate women. It is significant that in societies where nature is held sacred, rape occurs only rarely. The incidence of rape in our society will be reduced to the extent that boys grow to respect women and the qualities so often associated with femaleness in other societies.[53]

As part of her research, she spent twenty-four months with the Minangkabau, a rape-free Indonesian society, which was at that time the largest and most modern matrilineal society in the world. She found that sex was neither a commodity nor a "notch in the male belt" and that a man's sense of himself was not predicated by his sexual functioning. Aggression was not linked to sex. Minangkabau custom, law, and religion forbids rape and severely punishes rapists.[54] The existence of rape-free societies like the Minangkabau and the existence of men who live in rape-prone societies but do not rape women shows that rape and sexual assault are learned, not natural, behaviors.

Most countries today are rape-prone societies, and the United States is one of the worst. One out of every six American women has been the victim of rape or attempted rape in her lifetime.[55] The rape rate in the United States is 26 times that of Japan, 23 times that of Italy, 20 times that of Portugal, 15 times that of England, and 8 times that of France.[56] As a rape-prone society, it also is one with a rape culture. Milkweed Editions cofounder, editor, and publisher Emilie Buchwald defines "rape culture" in the anthology *Transforming a Rape Culture* as "a culture of intimidation. It keeps women afraid of being attacked and so it keeps women confined in the range of their behavior. That fear makes a woman censor her behavior—her speech, her way of dressing, her actions. It undermines her confidence in her ability to be independent."[57] Blogger Melissa McEwan wrote a fantastic "Rape Culture 101" post describing rape culture. It is a long post but well worth the read (http://shakespeares-sister.blogspot.com/2009/10/rape-culture-101.html). I will excerpt part of it here (note that she links to articles throughout her post).

Rape culture is encouraging male sexual aggression. Rape culture is regarding violence as sexy and sexuality as violent. . . . Rape culture is the media using euphemisms for sexual assault.[58] Rape culture is stories about rape being featured in the Odd News.[59] . . . Rape culture is boys under 10 years old knowing how to rape.[60] . . . Rape culture is blurred lines between persistence and coercion. Rape culture is treating diminished capacity to consent as the natural path to sexual activity. . . . Rape culture is rape being used as entertainment, in movies and television shows and books and in video games. . . . Rape culture is pretending that non-physical sexual assaults . . . [are] totally unrelated to brutal and physical sexual assaults, rather than viewing them on a continuum of sexual assault.[61]

When you read the post online, the citations are extensive and stunningly illustrate how pervasive the reality of rape is in our society. This reality of rape and a rape culture impacts how women experience street harassment.

Fearing Rape

Women, especially young women, consistently list rape as one of their top fears. In their book *The Female Fear: The Social Cost of Rape* published in 1991, Margaret T. Gordon and Stephanie Riger found that one-third of the women they studied reported worrying at least once a month about being raped. Many said they worried daily about that possibility. A third of the women said that their fear of rape is "part of the background" of their lives and "one of those things that's always there." Another third claimed they never worried about rape but still reported taking precautions, unconsciously or consciously, to try to avoid being raped.[62] Furthermore, they found that over 60 percent of women living in twenty-six of the largest U.S. cities reported feeling "very unsafe" or "somewhat unsafe" alone at night in public.[63]

In 1972, sociologist Mark Warr examined the fear of rape among urban women by surveying 339 people in Seattle, Washington. On a scale of 0 to 10, respondents rated how fearful they were of sixteen unpleasant or horrible incidents, such as "having your car stolen," "being beaten up by someone you know," "being murdered," "being sold contaminated food," and "being raped." Of the options, the number one fear for women ages 18 to 35 years of age was being raped. A follow-up question showed that, unlike many of the other options that women also feared, being raped was one they felt was both very serious and likely to occur, while they saw most other crimes as either very serious but unlikely to occur or not serious and likely to occur.[64]

I used the same sixteen incidents and fear scale in a question in early 2009, with ninety female respondents from my 2008 online survey who said I could contact them with follow-up questions (see www.stopstreetharassment.com/book/surveys). Eighty-nine women answered it. "Being raped" was selected by a majority of women as being a "10," causing them to be "very afraid." The second options women selected the most for being a "10" was the fear of "having someone break into your home while you're home." This was significantly higher than the fear of "having someone break into your home while you're away," suggesting an underlying fear of rape or assault by the burglar. Only two percent of women selected "0" or "not afraid at all" for "being raped."

This fear of rape can make street harassment—even the seemingly "innocent" forms—threatening and unnerving for women. A woman tends to be more afraid in certain circumstances, such as if she is alone or in an isolated area, it is dark out, the man is larger than her, there are several men, she has been assaulted or seriously harassed in the past by a male stranger in public, or she knows another woman has been harassed or raped in that area. One woman who took my 2008 online survey shared a story illustrating the latter:

I was going to school in Cleveland, Ohio. . . . I would get followed down the street [walking to campus] with strange men shouting sexually sugges- tive comments at me about my body. I would have cars slow down and honk at me, and the drivers ask me to get in and sit in their laps (which inci- dents were especially frightening because a girl in my school was abducted in broad daylight by a driver and taken to a warehouse and brutally raped).

Several scholars who conducted street harassment research found that women's fear of rape strongly correlated to how they felt about male harassment in public. In the conclusion of Carol Brooks Gardner's book *Passing By: Gender and Public Harassment*, she wrote that "it is impossible to state too strongly how constant the theme of fear was" among the nearly 300 women she interviewed in Indianapolis on male harassment; this was true for women from every social class, race, age, sexual preference, occupational group, and whether or not they were disabled.[65] In her book *Back Off! How to Confront and Stop Sexual Harassment and Harassers*, Martha Langelan wrote that for women, an underlying tension is always wondering how far the ha- rasser will go, if he will become violent.[66] Cynthia Grant Bowman, author of a legal article "Street Harassment and the Informal Ghettoiza- tion of Women," found that when women discussed their feelings about street harassment, they usually cited their fear of rape.[67] Lastly, a study of more than 12,000 Canadian women by Canadian sociologists Ross MacMillan, Annette Nierobisz, and Sandy Welsh showed that stranger harassment has a more consistent and significant impact on women's fears in public than non-stranger harassment.[68]

Rapists Don't Wear Signs

A main reason for the fear of rape in public is that any man could escalate his actions into a physical and/or sexual attack.[69] Former executive director of the D.C. Rape Crisis Center Martha Langelan and legal scholar Deborah Thompson have noted that some men use street harassment for "rape-testing." If a woman is passive when he harasses her, he may assume she also will be passive if he rapes her.[70] At the very least, the words and actions men use when they street harass women can make women feel similarly violated and remind women that they are susceptible to assault from men just by being female.

Rapists don't wear signs: women must assume that any man poses a potential threat. As French wrote, "Women are afraid in a world in which almost half the population bears the guise of the predator, in which no factor—age, dress, or color—distinguishes a man who will harm a woman for one who will not."[71] One woman who took my 2008 online survey said, "I always feel uncomfortable when I am out alone at night in my neighborhood. As every man walks past me, I silently evaluate how likely he is to rape me and what I would do if that happened. I always notice how many people are around, what their gender is, etc."

I love going running outdoors. When I am running alone on trails where I feel isolated, however, I always have an underlying fear of rape or attack and am wary of any men I encounter. Unfortunately, my fear and that of other women who like to go walking, running, or bicycling in parks or isolated areas is not unfounded, as several 2009 news stories show. A man in a Philadelphia park forced a woman into the bushes at gunpoint and raped her;[72] a man robbed and raped several women on at least four separate incidents over the summer in a park in Chicago;[73] a man slashed a woman with a knife as she ran in a park in New York City;[74] a man kidnapped a woman taking a routine evening walk in Georgia,[75] and a man murdered a woman running through a park in Vancouver, Canada.[76] Many women opt to exercise at a gym instead of outdoors because of the risk of harassment and assault they face outdoors.

While most male harassers do not intend to rape women, women do not know which ones have that intention and so are wary of all harassers. Journalist and feminist activist Susan Brownmiller eloquently said, "A world without rapists would be a world in which women moved freely without fear of men. That some men rape provides a sufficient threat to keep all women in a constant state of intimidation, forever conscious of the knowledge that the biological tool must be held in awe, for it may turn to weapon with sudden swiftness born of harmful intent."[77] Street harassment reminds women of this threat and prevents many of them from moving freely in public places. As men who are harassed rarely feel this threat when someone harasses them and as women who perpetrate harassment rarely pose this threat to their target, the threat of rape largely is a unique context for street harassment.

BLAMING WOMEN, TRIVIALIZING HARASSMENT

Usually victims of crimes like robbery or kidnapping by strangers in public places are not blamed for the crime, unless perhaps it took place in an area known to be unsafe. But, given the contexts of gender inequality and rape culture, women who are harassed and even raped tend to be blamed for those crimes.[78] The blame often is subtle: people draw attention to what the woman was wearing or what time of day the crime took place, as if it were her fault she was attacked, not the fault of the assailant. Through victim blaming, the male harassment of women is trivialized and its seriousness downplayed; these women brought it upon themselves.

Look at What You're Wearing

While crimes like rape and sexual harassment are motivated by power and control, not by uncontrollable sexual urges, there are people who believe that men "can't help" raping an attractive woman (or girl) and that women "bring it on themselves" by dressing "provocatively" and "teasing" men with their looks.[79] This also is true of street harassment, as these comments to online articles illustrate.

When men see a sexually attractive woman walking on the street, it's actually hard not to be tempted to do something to express approval, sorry, it's probably hardwired into the brain.[80]

I accept your point about the wolf whistling. It's something I would never do, and I consider it inappropriate behaviour. As for staring at breasts, well there are some men who take this too far by staring, but there's a reason men look at breasts, and that is that THEY ARE GREAT!!!! Blame Darwin. Trying to get men to stop looking at or thinking about breasts is like trying to stop human beings thinking about sex. It's never going to happen.[81]

It would be hard to convince me that women do not dress enticingly in order to be sexually appealing to men (or other women). That men respond verbally is in their genes and hormones, and the continuation of our species depends on this elaborate mating game.[82]

People who share these beliefs are not going to take women's complaints of street harassment seriously, because they consider street harassment to be a natural reaction to a woman's attractiveness. Of course, they conveniently exclude all the non-"complimentary" harassment so many women endure, such as being called fat or ugly or hearing racist slurs connected with their body parts. How many people actually end up dating and mating because of harassment on the street? Contrary to what these people say, most men do not regularly harass women and thus must not be "hardwired" to do so.

The victim blaming of women whom men harass is extremely common in the United States and in other rape-prone societies. Women engage in self-blame as well, although they seem to do it more in an effort to explain harassment and to figure out ways to not get harassed. For example, one woman who took my 2008 online survey wrote,

This past week I was walking back from class to my apartment, an 8-block walk. An older man made eye contact with me, then stopped walking as he passed me and said, "Do you want to get a drink with me, lady?" . . . I was furious that I don't have the right to walk down a public street without being treated like a sex object. I was also upset that my first reaction was to see if I'd done anything wrong. It was still light out, I wasn't wearing a tank top or shorts or a skirt. Yet none of that should matter!

I found that the victim blaming falls into two main categories. The most common form I have found is people blaming women for harassment because of what they were wearing, as the following quotes from men illustrate.

If they're walking around with revealing clothes, they're going to get comments made from gentleman. . . . It's as simple as that. If you don't want comments passed you should dress a little more conservative and you'll have no problem.[83]

Look at what you're wearing, look at what you're wearing, look at what you're wearing.[84]

Girls walking 'round here with those short dresses and stuff on . . . a man . . . they're gonna treat you like you acting . . . like the slut you is.[85]

Whenever a woman dresses in a skanky way . . . she will receive more attention whether she want it or not. Not saying they are a 'ho' . . . but they are wearing a 'ho's' uniform, so it shouldn't come as a surprise.[86]

If women stroll around half naked then obviously men are gonna have a look. That's just the way it is. Ladies, put some clothes on that ass if you respect yourself.[87]

Victim blaming is inappropriate, and in this context it is also completely false. Men in countries where women are completely veiled and otherwise wear "conservative" clothing harass those women too. Some do so daily.[88] The problem is not women's clothing; it is the ignorance, disrespect, and arrogance of harassing men.

Because of victim blaming, many women feel the need to explain their outfits, to convince the listener that they are not the ones at fault. For example, one of the women who took my 2008 online survey wrote,

"One day I went shopping at CVS for some things I needed, and a man followed me back to my dorm from CVS. I was wearing jeans and a jacket, nothing overtly sexy or even attractive, and at one point I actually broke out into a run because I was frightened." Another woman wrote, "I was wearing a conservative sweater and loose jeans at 4 P.M. in Chelsea when a stranger walked by me and at the last moment thrust his hand out and grabbed my vagina. It was awful. I'm still not over it."

There also are women who counter the victim blaming by saying they should be free to wear what they want and others who say it does not matter what they wear because men harass them in all kinds of clothing. One of my 2008 online survey respondents wrote, "In my old neighborhood, I would get street harassed EVERY time I left the apartment. It didn't matter what I was wearing. I do not remember a single time I did not get harassed."

The second category of victim blaming focuses on where and when women are in public. Women are more likely to be blamed for harassment or assault if they are in public at a time or in a place deemed inappropriate or dangerous, such as on an isolated trail or in a parking lot after dark. For example, in early 2009 I read an article on KOLD News 13 about the sexual assault of a woman in Phoenix, Arizona. She was at a convenience store looking for a ride home late at night. The man who offered her a ride allegedly sexually assaulted her in a parking lot. Among other victim-blaming remarks, the article, which was full of grammatical errors, states, "Police say this woman could've probably used better judgment, but that doesn't change the fact she was taken somewhere against her will and forced into a very bad situation."[89] Why does she not have a right to get a ride home without being sexually assaulted? Because she is a woman and it is late at night?

Just as numerous, women counter clothing-related victim blaming by explaining what they were wearing, many women counter the claim that women are only harassed and assaulted at night or in deserted areas by saying that it was daytime or that they were in a populated area when they share a harassment experience. The following two stories from women who took my 2008 online survey illustrate effect:

I was standing in front of my house saying goodbye to a friend when a man in a car pulled up and asked us how much we were (insinuating we were prostitutes). He had this disgusting smile on his face and obviously thought he was really funny. Mind you, it was a Saturday afternoon and we were not wearing anything revealing.

I was walking down the street, in daylight, and a man (who was with two friends) jumped in front of me and waved his arms and stuck his tongue out as he made an "arrghhhh" noise.

While these types of victim blaming occur after a woman is harassed or assaulted, some of the most pervasive victim blaming occurs before anything bad happens. From a young age, girls and women are told to be careful about what they wear and how they wear it as well as how and where and when they walk. They are told whether or not they should make eye contact, smile, scowl, or give out their real name or phone number to a stranger. They are told to always assess their surroundings, never let their guard down, plan an escape route, take self defense classes, carry mace and a cell phone. Women who study abroad or plan to travel alone are given more precautions than men.[90] Women on college campuses are at a higher risk of rape than any other category of women, and people and organizations tend to give them advice on "how not to get raped."[91]

Girls and women learn from this advice that they are not safe in public. They also learn that it is THEIR responsibility to be safe. If they are harassed or assaulted, it must be because they did not follow every single guideline. They must have let their guard down.[92] Instead of focusing on changing the habits of girls and women, we should be figuring out why perpetrators harass and assault people and how to make them stop.

CONCLUSION

Men who claim that they would love to have women harass them or individuals who try to compare male harassment of women to other forms of harassment tend to ignore the context in which street harassment occurs. Around the world, men are more powerful than women, and street harassment is one more manifestation of that power. In rape-prone societies, women fear rape and may be wary of any man who approaches them. Given the context of gender inequality and rape culture, people tend to blame women for causing street harassment instead of blaming the real perpetrators: men. These contexts make it clear how street harassment differs from other forms of harassment and why it is harmful and an unpleasant experience for most women.

NOTES

1. Kevinelle comment on "Catcalling: Creepy or a Compliment?" CNN, comment posted on May 14, 2008, http://www.cnn.com/2008/LIVING/personal/05/14/lw.catcalls/index.html (accessed May 14, 2008).

2. trey_trey comment on "Catcalling: Creepy or a Compliment?" comment posted on May 14, 2008 (accessed May 14, 2008).

3. Anna Jane Grossman, "Catcalling: Creepy or a Compliment?" CNN, May 14, 2008, http://www.cnn.com/2008/LIVING/personal/05/14/lw.catcalls/index.html.

4. Ricardo Hausmann, Laura D. Tyson, and Saadia Zahidi, "The Global Gender Gap Report," World Economic Forum, 2009, http://www.weforum.org/pdf/gendergap/report2009.pdf.

5. Ibid.

6. National Governors Association, "Current Governors," 2009, http://www.nga.org/portal/site/nga/menuitem.42b929b1a5b9e4eac3363d10501010a0/?vgnextoid=d54c8aaa2ebbff00VgnVCM1000001a01010aRCRD&vgnextfmt=curgov.

7. Mildred Amer, Jennifer E. Manning, and Colleen Shogan, "Women in the United States Congress: 1917–2009," Congressional Research Service, July 27, 2009, http://www.senate.gov/CRSReports/crs-publish.cfm?pid='0E%2C*PLS%3D%22%40%20%20%0A.

8. Nadira Hira, "Fortune 500 Women CEOs," *CNN*, April 21, 2009, http://money.cnn.com/galleries/2009/fortune/0904/gallery.fortune500_women_ceos.fortune/index.html; see also Daryl C. Hannah, "First Black-Woman Fortune 500 CEO," *DiversityInc*, May 22, 2009, http://www.diversityinc.com/public/5879.cfm.

9. Matt Krantz, "Women CEOs Slowly Gain on Corporate America," *USA Today*, January 2, 2009, http://www.usatoday.com/money/companies/management/2009-01-01-women-ceos-increase_N.htm.

10. Jacqueline Mroz, "Female Police Chiefs, a Novelty No More," *New York Times*, April 6, 2008, http://www.nytimes.com/2008/04/06/nyregion/nyregionspecial2/06Rpolice.html.

11. Sally J. Kenney, "Gap on Federal Bench? 8th Circuit Here We Come," *Women's E News*, April 17, 2009, http://www.womensenews.org/article.cfm?aid=3983.

12. Media Report to Women, "Industry Statistics," February 2009, http://www.mediareporttowomen.com/statistics.htm.

13. The OpEd Project, "More about the OpEd Project," n.d., http://www.theopedproject.org/cms/index.php?option=com_content&view=article&id=57&Itemid=63; see also Andrew LaVallee, "Only 13% of Wikipedia Contributors are Women, Study Says," *Wall Street Journal*, August 31, 2009, http://blogs.wsj.com/digits/2009/08/31/only-13-of-wikipedia-contributors-are-women-study-says.

14. Martha M. Lauzen, "The Celluloid Ceiling: Behind-the-Scenes Employment of Women on the Top 250 Films of 2008," Center for the Study of Women in Television & Film, 2009 http://womenintvfilm.sdsu.edu/files/2008_celluloid_ceiling.pdf; see also Jenny Peters, "Female directors on the hunt for work," *Variety*, June 11, 2009, http://www.variety. com/article/VR1118004830.html?categoryid=3284&cs=1&query=Few+Females.

15. Martha M. Lauzen, "Behind-the-Scenes Women in the 2008-09 Prime-time Television Season: Executive Summary," Center for the Study

of Women in Television & Film, 2009 http://womenintvfilm.sdsu.edu/files/ 2008-09_Boxed_in_Summary.pdf.

16. Writers Guild of America, West, "Rewriting an All-Too-Familiar Story? The 2009 Hollywood Writers Report," November 2009, http:// www.wga.org/uploadedFiles/who_we_are/hwr09execsum.pdf.

17. AAUW, "Sexual Harassment in the Workplace: Facts and Statistics," n.d., http://aauw.org/advocacy/laf/lafnetwork/library/workplaceharssmentfacts. cfm.

18. Zosia Bielski, "Female Managers Face More Harassment, Study Says," *Globe and Mail*, August 13, 2009, http://www.theglobeandmail. com/life/work/female-managers-face-more-harassment-study-says/article1247187.

19. CCH Aspen Publishers, "Employment Law: EEOC Examines 'Caregiver Discrimination,'" May 4, 2007, http://hr.cch.com/news/employ-ment/050407a.asp; see also Holly Kearl, "Women Still Face Pregnancy Discrimination," AAUW Legal Advocacy Fund Update Newsletter, Winter 2009, http://aauw.org/publications/updates/upload/LAF-Update-Winter-2009.pdf.

20. AAUW, "Pay Equity Statistics," n.d., http://aauw.org/advocacy/laf/ lafnetwork/library/payequity_stats.cfm.

21. Institute for Women's Policy Research, "The Gender Wage Gap by Occupation," April 2009, http://www.iwpr.org/pdf/C350a.pdf.

22. National Poverty Center, "Poverty in the United States, FAQ," n.d., http://www.npc.umich.edu/poverty/#4; see also Allison Stevens, "Moore: Women's Poverty Should Top Our Agenda," *Women's eNews,* January 14, 2009, http://www.womensenews.org/article.cfm/dyn/aid/3887; see also ERA: Women and Poverty, "Women and Poverty," n.d., http://www.equalrights.org/ professional/welfare/welfback.asp; see also Alexandra Cawthorne, "The Straight Facts on Women in Poverty," Center for American Progress, October 8, 2008, http://www.americanprogress.org/issues/2008/10/women_poverty.html.

23. Sunhwa Lee and Louis Shaw, "From Work to Retirement: Tracking Changes in Women's Poverty Status," AARP, February 2008, http:// www.aarp.org/research/ppi/econ-sec/low-income/articles/from_work_to_ retirement_tracking_changes_in_women_rsquo_s_poverty_status.html.

24. National Coalition against Domestic Violence, "Domestic Violence Facts," n.d., http://www.ncadv.org/files/DomesticViolenceFactSheet%28 National%29.pdf.

25. Cathy Arnst, "Will the Recession Change Gender Roles?" *Business Week*, February 6, 2009, http://www.businessweek.com/careers/working parents/blog/archives/2009/02/will_the_recess.html.

26. American Psychology Association, "Report of the APA Task Force on the Sexualization of Girls," 2007, http://www.apa.org/pi/women/programs/ girls/report.aspx?item=2.

27. Ibid., 5.

28. Ibid., 5.

29. Ibid., 7.

30. Campbell Brown, "Commentary: Sexist Treatment of Palin Must End," *CNN*, September 24, 2008, http://www.cnn.com/2008/POLITICS/09/24/campbell.brown.palin/; see also The Sarah Palin Sexism Watch Blog, http://palinsexismwatch.blogspot.com.

31. Robin Givhan, "Hillary Clinton's Tentative Dip into the New Neckline Territory," *Washington Post*, July 20, 2007, http://www.washingtonpost.com/wp-dyn/content/article/2007/07/19/AR2007071902668.html; see also Charlotte Allen, "Cleaving over Hillary's Cleavage," *Los Angeles Times*, August 5, 2007, http://www.latimes.com/news/opinion/sunday/commentary/la-op-allen5aug05,0,4948945.story; see also Jill Colvin, "Hillary's Cleavage Problem," *New York Press*, August 15, 2007, http://www.nypress.com/article-16988-hillarys-cleavage-problem.html.

32. Emily Miller, "Cankles Make Hillary Clinton One of the Girls," *Free Republic*, July 23, 2009, http://www.freerepublic.com/focus/chat/2301301/posts.

33. Laura Boswell, "Olympians Posing Nude, Poses Questions," *ESPN Magazine*, n.d., http://sports.espn.go.com/espn/page3/story?page=boswell/040823.

34. Jessica Valenti, "Padded Bras for Six Year-Olds," Feministing.com, September 11, 2006, http://feministing.com/archives/005685.html.

35. Jessica Valenti, "High Heels for Babies. Really," Feministing.com, June 13, 2008, http://www.feministing.com/archives/009385.html.

36. *CNN Money*, "Abercrombie's Sexy Undies 'Slip,'" May 28, 2002, http://money.cnn.com/2002/05/22/news/companies/abercrombie/; see also Gloria Blackwell, "Back to School for the Media: Tweens, Thongs, and 'Coffee Sluts,'" AAUW Blog, September 1, 2009, http://blog-aauw.org/2009/09/01/back-to-school-for-the-media-tweens-thongs-and-coffee-sluts.

37. Colin Fernandez, "Tesco Condemned for Selling Pole Dancing Toy," *Daily Mail*, October 24, 2006, http://www.dailymail.co.uk/news/article-412195/Tesco-condemned-selling-pole-dancing-toy.html; see also Gizmodo, "Pole Dancer Doll Doesn't Really Set the Perfect Role Model," August 30, 2009, http://gizmodo.com/5348675/pole-dancer-doll-doesnt-really-set-the-perfect-role-model.

38. Naomi Wolf, *The Beauty Myth* (New York: Anchor Books, 1992), 50.

39. Ibid., 50–51.

40. Feminist.com, "The Sex Industry," n.d., http://www.feminist.com/resources/ourbodies/viol_sexind.html; see also Neil McKeganey and Marina Barnard, *Sex Work on the Streets: Prostitutes and Their Clients* (Buckingham, UK: Open University Press: 1996), 26–27; see also Sudhir Venkatesh, "Skinflint: Did Eliot Spitzer Get Caught Because He Didn't Spend Enough on Prostitutes?" *Slate*, March 12, 2008, http://www.slate.com/id/2186491/; see also African Press International, "Few Available Jobs Pay as Well as Sex Work," November 18, 2009, http://africanpress.wordpress.com/2009/11/18/few-available-jobs-pay-as-well-as-sex-work/; see also Rosie Campbell Pitcher, Phil Hubbard, Maggie O'Neill, and Jane Scoular, *Living*

and Working in Areas of Street Sex Work: From Conflict to Coexistence (York, UK: Joseph Rowntree Foundation, 2006), 18–19.

41. Cynthia Grant Bowman, "Street Harassment and the Informal Ghettoization of Women," *Harvard Law Review* 106, no. 3 (January 1993), 517–580; see also Elizabeth Arveda Kissling, "Street Harassment: The Language of Sexual Terrorism," 1991 *Discourse & Society* 2 (4), 454.

42. Elayne A. Saltzberg and Joan C. Chrisler, "Beauty Is the Beast: Psychological Effects of the Pursuit of the Perfect Female Body," in *Women: A Feminist Perspective*, Fifth Edition, ed. Jo Freeman (Palo Alto, CA: Mayfield Publishing Company, 1995), 312.

43. Norma Anne Oshynko, "No Safe Place: The Legal Regulation of Street Harassment," Thesis for Masters of Law in Faculty of Law, University of British Columbia, 2002, 15.

44. Margaret T. Gordon and Stephanie Riger, *The Female Fear: The Social Cost of Rape* (Urbana: University of Illinois Press, 1991), 6; see also Oshynko, 15–16.

45. Stop Street Harassment Blog, "An Ugly Girl's Story," August 31, 2009, http://streetharassment.wordpress.com/2009/08/31/an-ugly-girls-story.

46. Bowman, 517–580.

47. Oshynko, 5–6.

48. Bowman, 517–580.

49. Marilyn French, *From Eve to Dawn: A History of Women in the World, Volume 1* (New York: The Feminist Press at CUNY, 2008).

50. French, *From Eve to Dawn*; see also Patricia Cline Cohen, "Safety and Danger: Women on American Public Transport, 1750–1850," in *Gendered Domains: Rethinking Public and Private in Women's History*, ed. Dorothy O. Helly and Susan M. Reverby (Ithaca, NY: Cornell University Press, 1992), 121; Joan Fayer, "Changes in Gender Use of Public Space in Puerto Rico," in *Voices in the Street: Explorations in Gender, Media, and Public Space*, eds. Susan J. Drucker and Gary Gumpert (Cresskill, NJ: Hampton Press, Inc, 1996), 213; see also Susan J. Drucker and Gary Grumpert, "Shopping Women, and Public Space," in *Voices in the Street: Explorations in Gender, Media, and Public Space*, eds. Susan J. Drucker and Gary Gumpert (Cresskill, NJ: Hampton Press, Inc, 1996), 120; see also Ray Oldenburg, "The Sexes and the Third Place," in *Voices in the Street: Explorations in Gender, Media, and Public Space*, eds. Susan J. Drucker and Gary Gumpert (Cresskill, NJ: Hampton Press, Inc, 1996): 16; see also Gordon and Riger, 48–50.

51. Peggy Reeves Sanday, "Rape-Prone Versus Rape-Free Campus Cultures," *Violence against Women* 2 (2) June 1996: 191–192, available online at http://www.sas.upenn.edu/~psanday/rapea.html.

52. Peggy Reeves Sanday, "The Socio-Cultural Context of Rape: A Cross-Cultural Study," in *Confronting Rape and Sexual Assault*, ed. Mary E. Odem and Jody Clay-Warner (Lanham, MD: The Rowman & Littlefield Publishing Group, Inc., 1998), 105.

53. Sanday, "The Socio-Cultural Context of Rape: A Cross-Cultural Study," 107.

54. Sanday, "Rape-Prone Versus Rape-Free Campus Cultures," 191–192.

55. RAINN, "Who Are the Victims?" n.d., http://rainn.org/get-information/statistics/sexual-assault-victims.

56. Esther Madriz, *Nothing Bad Happens to Good Girls: Fear of Crime in Women's Lives* (Berkeley, CA: University of California Press, 1997), 4.

57. Emilie Buchwald, "Raising Girls for the 21st Century," in *Transforming a Rape Culture*, eds. Emilie Buchwald, Pamela R. Fletcher, and Martha Roth (Minneapolis, MN: Milkwood Editions, 1993), 188.

58. Melissa McEwan, "CNN Still Doesn't Know How to Cover Sexual Assault," Shakesville, October 6, 2009, http://shakespearessister.blogspot.com/2009/10/cnn-still-doesnt-know-how-to-cover.html.

59. McEwan, "How Odd!" Shakesville, November 2, 2007, http://shakespearessister.blogspot.com/2007/11/how-odd.html.

60. McEwan, "Three Boys under 10 Charged with Rape," Shakesville, November 19, 2007, http://shakespearessister.blogspot.com/2007/11/three-boys-under-10-charged-with-rape.html.

61. McEwan, "Rape Culture 101," Shakesville, October 9, 2009, http://shakespearessister.blogspot.com/2009/10/rape-culture-101.html.

62. Gordon and Riger, 20–22.

63. Ibid., 9.

64. Mark Warr, "Fear of Rape among Urban Women," *Social Problems*, 32, no. 3 (Feb. 1985), 238–250.

65. Carol Brooks Gardner, *Passing By: Gender and Public Harassment* (Berkeley, CA: University of California Press, 1995), 240.

66. Langelan, 41.

67. Bowman, 535.

68. Ross MacMillan, Annette Nierobisz, and Sandy Welsh, "Harassment and Perceptions of Safety among Women," *Journal of Research and Crime Delinquency* (2000), 315.

69. Kissling, 455; see also Deborah Thompson, "'The Woman in the Street:' Reclaiming the Public Space from Sexual Harassment," 1994 *Yale Journal of Law and Feminism* 6 (1994), 320–321; see also Oshynko, 63; see also Lisa J. Curtis, "Street Fight: Arts Organization Creates an Exhibit in DUMBO Born Out of One Harrowing Night," *Brooklyn Paper*, July 29, 2002, http://www.brooklynpaper.com/stories/25/29/25_29catcalls.html.

70. Thompson, 321; see also Martha Langelan, *Back Off! How to Confront and Stop Sexual Harassment and Harassers* (New York: Fireside Press, 1993), 45.

71. Marilyn French, *The War Against Women* (New York: Ballantine Books, 1992), 197.

72. CBS News, "Female Jogger Reportedly Raped in Fairmount Park," August 13, 2009, http://cbs3.com/topstories/fairmount.park.philadelphia.2.1125141.html.

73. Rummana Hussain, "Suspect Held without Bail in Jackson Park," *Chicago Sun Times*, August 21, 2009, http://www.suntimes.com/news/24-7/1728510, jackson-park-rapes-suspect-bail-082109.article.

74. Michael Wilson, "Woman Slashed While Jogging in Park Behind Gracie Mansion," *New York Times*, January 4, 2009, http://www.nytimes.com/2009/01/05/nyregion/05jogger.html?_r=2&ref=nyregion.

75. Steve Osunsami, Chris Strathmann, and Joshua Gaynor, "Finding Kristi Cornwell: Missing Georgia Mother Snatched Off the Street," ABC News, August 17, 2009, http://abcnews.go.com/GMA/story?id=8341741&page=1.

76. CBC News, "Mounties Scour Vancouver Park for Clues in Jogger's Killing," April 6, 2009, http://www.cbc.ca/canada/british-columbia/story/2009/04/06/bc-jogger-slaying.html.

77. Susan Brownmiller, "Against Our Will: Men, Women, and Rape," in *Feminism in Our Time: The Essential Writings, World War II to the Present*, ed. Mariam Schneir (New York: Vintage Books, 1994), 282.

78. Jessica Valenti, *The Purity Myth* (Berkeley, CA: Seal Press, 2009), 158; see also Thompson, "'The Woman in the Street:' Reclaiming the Public Space from Sexual Harassment," 317; see also Carole J. Sheffield, "Sexual Terrorism," in *Women: A Feminist Perspective, Fifth Edition*, ed. Jo Freeman, (Palo Alto, CA: Mayfield Publishing Company, 1995), 14–15; see also Gordon and Riger, *The Female Fear: The Social Cost of Rape*, 2.

79. Canada.com, "Priest Blames Girls for Abuse He Caused," January 18, 2007, http://www.canada.com/nationalpost/news/story.html?id=a9b28207-58bd-4e0d-b8fe-57be11a56f73; see also McEwan, "Judge Blames 10-Year-Old Victim for Her Own Rape," Shakesville, June 28, 2007, http://shakespearessister.blogspot.com/2007/06/judge-blames-10-year-old-victim-for-her.html; see also Donovan Slack, "Fearless in the City: Some Women Still Party as if Invulnerable," *Boston Globe*, March 9, 2006, http://www.boston.com/news/nation/articles/2006/03/09/fearless_in_the_city/; see also Martha MacCallum, "Have Fun Girls," Fox News, March 8, 2006, http://www.foxnews.com/story/0,2933,187244,00.html; see also Dan Parkinson, "Should Women Be More Responsible?" *BBC*, November 16, 2006, http://news.bbc.co.uk/2/hi/uk_news/6153822.stm; see also McEwan, "Take My Cunt, Please," Shakesville, January 4, 2007, http://shakespearessister.blogspot.com/2007/01/take-my-cunt-please.html; see also Ann Friedman, "Girls Just Wanna Have Fun . . . Without Getting Raped," Feministing, March 28, 2006, http://feministing.com/archives/002955.html (accessed November 22, 2009); see also Thompson, 317; see also Mike, "Hemlines Don't Rape People, Rapists Do," Science Blogs, January 3, 2007, http://scienceblogs.com/mikethemadbiologist/2007/01/hemlines_dont_rape_people_rapi.php.

80. Tlwinslow, comment on "Why Do Men Catcall," Alternet.org, comment posted on October 21, 2009, http://www.alternet.org/sex/143383/why_do_men_catcall/?page=2 (accessed November 22, 2009).

81. Strangebrew, comment on "So Angry I Could Strip!" *Guardian*, comment posted on May 28, 2008, http://www.guardian.co.uk/commentisfree/2008/may/28/soangryicouldstrip (accessed July 30, 2008).

82. Peter, comment on "Taking Back the Streets," WNYC, comment posted on July 17, 2007, http://www.wnyc.org/shows/bl/episodes/2007/07/16/segments/82164 (accessed October 1, 2009).

83. Maggie Hadleigh-West, *War Zone*, Film Fatale, Inc., 1998.

84. Ibid.

85. Girls for Gender Equity's, 2007, 20-minute documentary *Hey . . . Shorty*.

86. Dave, comment on "Catcalling: Creepy or a Compliment?" CNN, comment posted on May 14, 2008, http://www.cnn.com/2008/LIVING/personal/05/14/lw.catcalls/index.html (accessed November 22, 2009).

87. Okani, comment on "So Angry I Could Strip!" *Guardian*, comment posted on May 28, 2008, http://www.guardian.co.uk/commentisfree/2008/may/28/soangryicouldstrip (accessed July 30, 2008).

88. Ali Saeed and Nadia Al-Sakaaf, "Sexual harassment deters women from outdoor activities," *Yemen Times*, January 21, 2009, http://www.yementimes.com/article.shtml?i=1226&p=report&a=2; see also Cynthia Johnston, "Two-thirds of Egyptian Men Harass Women?" *Reuters*, July 17, 2008, http://www.reuters.com/article/email/idUSL1732581120080717.

89. Som Lisaius, "Sexual Assault Suspect Caught on Surveillance Tape at Circle K," CBS KOLD News 13, April 28, 2008, http://www.kold.com/Global/story.asp?S=10267317&nav=menu86_3.

90. Sara Savage, "Study Abroad Safety Tips for Female Students," IIE-Passport, n.d., http://info.iiepassport.org/tipsforfemalestudents.html (accessed November 8, 2009); see also David S. Katz, "Personal Safety for Women Traveling Abroad on Business," WITI, 2004, http://www.witi.com/careers/2004/travelsafety.php (accessed November 8, 2009); see also University of Chicago, "Safety Tips for Students Studying Abroad," n.d., http://study-abroad.uchicago.edu/safety.html (accessed November 8, 2009); see also Authentic Ireland Travel, "A Woman's Guide to Safe Travel," n.d., http://www.authenticireland.com/womens+guide+to+safe+travel (accessed November 8, 2009).

91. eHow, "How to Avoid Being Raped at College," n.d., http://www.ehow.com/how_2126457_avoid-being-raped-college.html (accessed November 20, 2009); see also RAINN, "RAINN's 2009 Back-To-School Tips for Students," August 10, 2009, http://www.rainn.org/news-room/sexual-assault-news/2009-back-to-school-tips.

92. McEwan, "Rape Culture 101," Shakesville, October 9, 2009, http://shakespearessister.blogspot.com/2009/10/rape-culture-101.html.

_____ *Chapter 3* _____

Multilayered Harassment

In the United States, factors like race, sexual orientation and gender expression, age, socioeconomic class, weight, nationality, and disabilities can add multiple layers to women's street harassment experiences. Scholar Carol Brooks Gardner wrote in her book *Passing By: Gender and Public Harassment*, "individuals who are members of multiple situationally disadvantaged groups often balance and counterbalance the experiences that they associate with membership in each category."[1] In her book *License to Harass*, law professor Laura Beth Nielsen wrote, "Street harassment certainly is a form of gender domination, but it represents a more complicated process because multiple hierarchies are in play at the same time." Thus, a lower-class lesbian Latina who walks with a cane may face many more forms of street harassment or experience harassment differently than an upper-class white heterosexual able-bodied woman. Understanding how women from all backgrounds experience street harassment is an essential step toward working to end it. In this chapter, I explore some of the ways in which race, sexual orientation and gender expression, socioeconomic status, and disability create multiple layers in many women's street harassment experiences. Socioeconomic status and disability are not covered as thoroughly as the former two topics, and that in part is an unfortunate reflection on the lack of research on those topics. More research on all layers of street harassment is necessary to better understand the problem.

RACE

"If I was white . . . I wouldn't have this daily problem"

A Native American teenager who answered follow-up interview questions to my 2008 online survey told me that she was first harassed in eighth grade by a group of older boys outside her school. She said, "They whistled then proceeded to follow me, they tried to grope me and grab me, but I managed to get away, I remembered to scream, and run. . . . The next time it happened about the same place except this time they slapped me around . . . one of the reasons they noticed me was that I am Native American in a small white town, where racism still exists."[2]

Racism still exists throughout the United States, and it can intersect with sexism to create multiple layers of discrimination, starting with which women are targeted the most. I found that anecdotally, women of color believe men harass them more often than men harass white women. Since all forms of street harassment are about power and control—not about compliments and making women feel good about themselves and safe in public—it makes sense that men would more frequently target women they perceive to be the least powerful. Two of my 2008 survey respondents wrote in response to follow-up questions I asked in 2009 about race:

I do feel like girls of color get more street harassment than white girls.

Because I'm a dark skinned black female, black men feel I only deserve to be exploited for sex. Black men in general find no value in black women. If I was white and around white men, I wouldn't have this daily problem.

A few white women mentioned in their 2009 follow-up survey responses that they felt men bothered them less because of their race:

I'm white, and I suspect I'm not harassed nearly as often because of that.

Sometimes I think that because I'm white, I'm less likely to be attacked, because living on the South Side of Chicago, people know that if a white girl gets hurt the cops will be all over it.

The little research that exists on how race impacts the volume of harassment women experience also suggests that women of color are harassed more than white women. In Laura Beth Nielsen's street harassment study in the San Francisco Bay Area in the early 2000s, 68 percent of women of color said they experienced sexually suggestive speech "every day" or "often," compared with 55 percent of white women. Forty-six percent of persons of color experienced race-related speech "everyday" or "often" versus 5 percent of white people.[3] Crime statistics show that women of color face more overall sexual violence than white women.[4] One reason why women of color may be harassed more is a myth that they are sexually promiscuous.

Jezebel, Temptress, Whore: Sexually Available Women

For centuries, people have stereotyped women of color as overly sexual, promiscuous, and/or sexually available, particularly compared to white women.[5] These stereotypes persist today and shape how and why some men harass women of color. For example, Lori, an Asian American[6] woman interviewed by filmmaker Maggie Hadleigh-West for the 1998 anti-street harassment documentary *War Zone*, said many men make comments to her implying that she is just a sex toy and that she believes they do so because of her race.[7] One of the women who answered follow-up survey questions in 2009 wrote, "I definitely think because I am Latina I get [harassed] a lot more. I think there is a tendency to respect us less, or [to think] that we are more sexually available."

The stereotype of sexually available black women is particularly pervasive and has a long history in the United States. White male slave owners and/or other male members of the household sometimes forced sexual acts on their slave women. On the auctioning block, white people openly scrutinized black women's bodies for their reproductive capabilities.[8] In her 1992 book *Black Looks: Race and Representation*, bell hooks wrote in depth about the ways white people have dehumanized and animalized the black female body and how, in addition to other humiliations associated with slavery, some white men displayed black women in cages as physical oddities and charged a fee to white people to see them.[9] One of my survey respondents wrote that while African American men harass her the most, when white men harass her "they're usually more likely to ask me to 'dance for' them or 'shake it' for them or something. I usually feel more degraded and angry when white men do this—it's like an extra level of dehumanization like they 'own' me."[10]

Deirdre Davis explored this further in her article "The Harm that Has No Name: Street Harassment, Embodiment, and African American Women." She wrote that from the time of slavery through the present, creating and perpetuating a myth that African American women are promiscuous, sexual animals, and Jezebel temptresses has been a racist way to justify the sexual, economic, and social subjugation of African American women.[11] These myths seep into the ways some men treat and talk to African American women in public spaces. In her book *Black Feminist Thought: Knowledge, Consciousness, and the Politics of Empowerment*, Patricia Hill Collins discussed how some men view African American women as "sexually promiscuous and potential prostitutes who can be sexually consumed on the street through touch or other sexualized gestures."[12] I found this experience to be true among several of my African American survey respondents.

As a light skinned African American woman I am always street harassed by both men of color and non men of color on the street. But I feel that because I am African American that these men assume that I want their sexual advances and I don't!

Well most of the guys that harass me are black. I'm black. . . . I feel that my race + gender has impacted my life because they feel that I'm some easy chick they can get in the bed.

I went to a store just up the block from my home, to get some food. I was on the phone—though not really talking to anyone, just talking to ward people off. But still, a guy came up to me and was beyond vulgar and . . . propositioned [me] for sex!

Not only do some men on the street treat women of color as if they were sexually available, American laws—largely written by white men—have done so too. In examining case law on street harassment from the 20th century, legal scholar Cynthia Grant Bowman found evidence that many times in the courtroom judges and juries assumed that black women were more likely than white women to be prostitutes. She found court decisions that concluded a white man was honestly and innocently mistaken if he believed a black woman on the street was a prostitute and, therefore, the woman should not be offended or alarmed by his proposition. Meanwhile, the courts found that a white woman who was not a prostitute should take offense at being mistaken for one.[13] A woman in Santa Barbara, California, who will be featured in a forthcoming anti-street harassment documentary *BACK UP! Concrete Diaries* alludes to these legal realities and attitudes that continue today when she said:

Honestly [street harassment] has a lot to do with issues of how people in this society structure femininity and womanhood and types of womanhood that are worth being protected. And the unfortunate reality is that people think that black women should not be protected. We've never been protected by law. . . . All the privileges in terms of people thinking that our femininity, our womanhood is something that's worth protecting, we've never had that. White women get it but we don't.[14]

The way some law enforcement officers, the majority of whom are white men, treat and respond to harassment crimes reported by women of color also shows the tendency to disbelieve and trivialize their experiences.[15] Someone submitted a story to my blog about a man on the street who had harassed, threatened, and chased her. She escaped and called the police. The 911 dispatcher and the police officer who arrived on the scene were nonchalant and unhelpful. She noted in a follow-up comment to her post that "I hate to go there, but I feel if I were white, that officer would've acted in a heartbeat."[16]

"Bin Laden's Sister": Racist Speech

Sexual harassment expert Martha Langelan said in *Back Off! How to Confront and Stop Sexual Harassment* that women of color "often experience a combination of sexual and racial harassment, sometimes within a single incident."[17] Unsurprisingly, given the continued pervasiveness of racism in the United States I found that to be true in my research. Many women of color said men had harassed them with racist and sexist speech and slurs. Before examining this aspect of street harassment, I want to note that my informal survey showed that women of all races experienced sexist speech far more frequently than racist speech (see Table 3.1). I would guess this is because blatant racism is socially unacceptable (even though it still happens) while sexist speech is still socially acceptable.

Women who appear to be Muslim or from countries in the Middle East said they feel targeted by men in public places in the United States because of both their race and their sex, especially since the September 11, 2001, terrorist attacks. During a workshop I attended at a Street Harassment Summit in New York City on May 5, 2007, one attendee shared the following story:

Street harassment is a huge part of my day, and it makes me very angry. I think it's always tied in with my racial identity. The worst thing that

Table 3.1
Sexist and Racist Speech

	Sexist Speech (daily/weekly)	Racist Speech (daily/weekly)
African American	13 percent (of 85 women)	2 percent
Anglo American	14 percent (of 555 women)	2 percent
Asian American	11 percent (of 39 women)	3 percent
Latina	21 percent (of 60 women)	0 percent
Other	13 percent (of 114 women)	2 percent

happened to me lately was I was on my way to work at a new job and I was very happy, and this guy said something to me and I kept walking and he came up around me in my face and said, "You look just like Bin Laden's sister." My mouth was closed, and I was like, why aren't I responding? He continued to scream at me and I kept walking, and he said, "You should get home, women like you don't work. Don't your men keep you locked up? Oh that's right; your men aren't real men. I'll show you what a real man is." And he proceeded to tell me the actions that real men do to their women. People on the street were stopped and were staring at me but no one said anything.[18]

She was visibly upset and shaken when she relayed this horrifying incident. Given the hostility that some Americans feel toward people they perceive to be potential terrorists, these kinds of street harassment incidents can be very frightening because of the implied threat of violence. One woman who took my 2008 survey said, "As a Muslim woman who wears hijab (the headscarf and modest clothing), most of the feelings I have are due to religious discrimination and anti-immigrant sentiments. (Even though I am not an immigrant.) I am constantly worried about being attacked verbally or physically because it has happened to friends of mine."

Several Asian American women mentioned men making racist remarks to them. As one of my 2008 survey respondents said, "A man on the bus was making racist and sexist comments toward me, calling me a 'fucking FOB,' [fresh off the boat] 'job stealing Chinese,' 'illiterate bitch' and other such comments." A young Asian American woman interning at the Kirwan Institute for the Study of Race and Ethnicity at Ohio State University wrote in a blog post: ". . . Every day I walk to and from work, and just about every day I face some form of street harassment. Whether it be receiving ogling looks, lewd comments, or being ching-chonged, I've come to expect it. It has become an undeniable part of my experience as a woman of color."[19]

An African American woman who took my 2008 survey and answered follow-up questions in 2009 said the first time she was harassed was when she was seven or eight years old. Her family had recently moved to a predominantly white neighborhood. She wrote, "I was riding my bike when a neighbor kid called me the n-word."[20] Another woman said that most of her harassers are the same race as she is, but when white men harass her, the comment is almost always racialized. She wrote, "They either comment on my skin color ('Hey, chocolate/mocha/etc') or they grab or comment on my butt."[21] Men regularly include references to the skin tone of one of my friends, who is a light-skinned African American woman, in their harassment, calling her "light" or "redbone."

A few white women who took my survey noted being the recipient of racist speech too. Usually it entailed being called a "white bitch" after ignoring or refusing to comply with street harassers' demands, but not always. For example, one of my survey-takers wrote, "In certain neighborhoods there is more of a racist/sexual commenting combo. This is what makes me feel the worst, i.e. 'Hey snow white, you lookin' sexy.'"

Women who appear racially ambiguous may face racist comments about that or about specific physical features. One mixed-race Indian and white woman who took my 2008 survey and answered follow-up questions in 2009 said that her "ethnicity is at the heart of almost every instance of street harassment" and men often ask her what she is, "I'm walking down the street, so men need to know my pedigree."

Intra-racial Harassment and Racism

With the exception of Native Americans[22] and possibly Asian Americans,[23] men are more likely to harass and assault women of their own race than another race,[24] just as with other forms of gender-based violence in the United States. In part, this is due to proximity: people tend to live near, be friends with, and have family members of their same race. Thus, the people they interact with the most—positively or negatively—are of their same race. Cities and a growing number of suburbs with more racial diversity mean there is an increased chance that a man will harass a woman of a different race. This is an area in which more research is necessary, but it seems that much harassment is intra-racial. Anecdotally, the experiences of many women who took my survey showed this.

I have noticed black men are the leaders in public sexual aggression in New York City. They honestly think nothing is wrong with their behavior, and if you as black girl or woman don't give into their nasty advances, look out! I have been hit, spit on, glass bottles thrown at me, cursed out and physically threatened just because I wouldn't bow down to the Black Man.

Same race men seem to think themselves entitled to say something to me when they're so inclined.

I am white, and I have found that almost all of the street harassment I've experienced has been from white men.

Latinos, Mexican men in particular, will cat call, whistle at or approach me and it infuriates me. They do it . . . because they think they can get away with it, because they think that I "speak their language," because they don't fear that, like a white woman, I might call the cops or file for harassment.

This last comment speaks to an important point. The United States is a racist society in which there is police brutality against and swift and harsh sentencing of men of color. This reality makes many women of color unwilling to publicly call out or report men of their race who engage in acts of gender violence, including street harassment. They know it is likely that the men will be brutalized and treated unfairly. The authors of the book *Shifting: The Double Lives of Black Women in America* and the article "Making Sense of Our Difference: African American Women on Anita Hill" discussed how often African American women feel unable to speak out against sexism, particularly if the perpetrator is an African American man, because of the pressure to do everything possible to overcome racism and protect "their" men against anti-black prejudices.[25] Yet, many men of color benefit from the patriarchy of American society and when they engage in street harassment, they engage in what Bowman and University of Wisconsin–Madison political science professor Hawley Fogg-Davis describe as "raced patriarchy," because the men use their power to intimidate, shame, and humiliate women of color.[26] Fogg-Davis takes these points a step further and says that some African American men use street harassment "to monitor, intimidate, and control black women. . . . Intra-racial street harassment exemplifies . . . inclusionary control."[27]

While women of color may be more hesitant to identify the behavior of men of color as harassment or to report it because of racial solidarity, white women may be more inclined to identify men of color as harassers because of racism. Through my research and in conversations with people in general, I found that it is a common stereotype that men of color (or lower-class men and racism ensures that the two overlap a lot) harass women more than white men.[28] In particular I hear women say Hispanic men harass the most because it is socially acceptable in their culture.[29] This is such a strong stereotype that HollaBack anti-street harassment Web sites—geographically specific Web sites that publish women's street harassment stories and photos of their harassers—post an antiracism policy.[30]

Women who perpetuate the stereotype that men of certain racial or cultural backgrounds harass women more than other men may live in an area where there are few white men and so yes, in *their area* men of color harass more, or they may be interpreting harassment differently based on the race of the man. The stereotypes that men of color are more violent or sexually predatory than white men—a stereotype that has served as a racist social control mechanism in post-slavery America by which white people justified lynching and still justify locking up black men—may mean that women are more fearful when they see or are harassed by men of color than when harassed by white men. For example, one woman who answered follow-up questions to my 2008 online survey in 2009 said, "I am white, and I feel bad that I still feel more cautious and nervous around African American and Latino men. It's hard to stop those feelings." Another woman wrote, "Sadly, I feel more afraid when it is a man of color or one not dressed 'appropriately' as in a suit and tie. And I am especially afraid of a group of teenagers." So the same behavior by a man of color and a white man may feel different to her.

These women may experience differently the same behavior performed by a man of color and by a white man. If women have internalized racist hierarchies, they may feel flattered if a white man whistles at them or makes a sexual comment, especially if he appears to be middle or upper class. Conversely, women may feel insulted or afraid of the same actions done by a man of color, particularly if he appears to be lower class.[31] These stereotypes and this underlying racism also may cause harassment by men of color to stick out more in women's minds, making them believe men of color harass them more. One self-identified mixed-race Asian woman wrote the following in the comments section to a post about class, race, and street harassment on the blog Feministe:

I initially perceived all of my harassers to be men of color. As I learned more about the way racism and classism operate . . . the observed racial demographic of my harassers changed. I think that women—especially White women—are trained not to interpret much inappropriate behavior by middle and upper-class White men as harassment. . . . Once I started working on my classism and racism, I started noticing a HELL of a lot more harassment that I was experiencing from White men.[32]

Some people, including commenters on the blogs Feministe and Racialicious, have theorized, that upper-class (mainly white) men do not harass women on the streets as much as lower-class men.

They think it is because upper-class men harass women at clubs, bars, conferences, and in white-collar workplaces. But, they say, the streets are where many lower-class men work (as delivery men, construction workers, or gardeners, etc.) and where unemployed men hang out and harass women.[33] At the end of the day, there has not been a comprehensive study on race and male street harassers, but depending on the racial makeup of one's area, it is likely that a woman will experience most harassment from the men of her race.

SEXUAL ORIENTATION AND GENDER EXPRESSION

The United States is not only a country that still experiences racism, it also is a place where people often feel unwelcome if they are not heterosexual and if they do not express their gender in a way that matches their birth sex. Some men think that being a lesbian is an affront to their masculinity, and so to "punish" all women who ignore or otherwise rebuff their street harassment attention, they even may call their target a lesbian or a dyke. In the anti-street harassment documentaries *War Zone* and *Hey . . . Shorty*, several men said the women must be lesbians when the filmmakers asked them why they are ignored by the women they harass.[34]

Passing as Heterosexual

People cannot always assess someone's sexual orientation by sight. Men still proposition and sexually harass women who appear to be heterosexual, even if they are not. This is the epitome of heterosexual male privilege: assuming every woman he sees on the street is single, heterosexual or bisexual, and interested in his attention. This assumption wholly denies the sexual identity of lesbian women.[35] While many, even most, heterosexual women want nothing to do with the men who approach them on the street, women who have no sexual interest in men especially do not. Male harassers do not give women that choice. A white lesbian in her twenties in Vancouver wrote in response to my survey that despite being interested in women, "[Street harassment by men] happens a million times a day. . . . I don't like walking by a dude or a bunch of dudes together and then they make comments as I walk by, or greet me like I've just been waiting for them to come by and rescue me from the mundanity of my life."

Scholar Tiffanie Heben wrote in her article "A Radical Reshaping of the Law: Interpreting and Remedying Street Harassment" how street harassment by a man who interprets a woman to be hetero-sexual can function to deny the woman her sexual identity. His actions remind her that her true sexual identity is a "deviance" from the sexual orientation norm he is projecting onto her.[36] She may also be frightened because she fears that if he finds out her sexual orientation he will become violent. One of my 2008 online survey respondents, a teenager in Fayetteville, Arkansas, wrote about this fear, "The trouble is that I'm gay, but I really enjoy dressing up. Guys always notice how I'm dressed, but I can never quite get up the courage to tell them 'I'm not doing this for YOU!' . . . I know I can't say I'm gay, because he'd either leer even more, or take it as a challenge. Honestly, I never feel quite safe when I'm alone."

And unfortunately, that fear is justified. In 2003, 15-year-old Sakia Gunn was murdered while waiting with four friends for a bus in Newark, New Jersey. The teenagers were on their way home from Manhattan when two men got out of a car and sexually propositioned them. When the women said they were lesbian, one of the men fatally stabbed Gunn in the chest. He is now serving a twenty-year prison sentence. Gunn's story inspired Hawley Fogg-Davis's article "Theorizing Black Lesbians within Black Feminism: A Critique of Same-Race Street Harassment."[37] The threat of violence means that women have a vested interest in appearing straight in order to stay safe, but heterosexual women are attacked too, so nothing guarantee safety.

Gender Nonconforming

People who are openly homosexual or visibly do not conform to the gender they were born to can face homophobic and transphobic slurs and assault. Gary David Comstock, a professor of religion at Wesleyan University, studied violence against lesbian and gay people and found that 86 percent of the openly lesbian women he surveyed had been the victims of anti-lesbian verbal harassment as a result of their sexual orientation. More women of color than white women reported such harassment.[38] The frequency of targeted harassment and assault against lesbian, bisexual, queer, and transgender (LBQT) people means they may view all forms of street harassment as threatening or unwelcome.[39] (While gay men are harassed and attacked for their sexual orientation, I am not focusing on them in this chapter.)

Street harassing men who reference a woman's sexual orientation and/or gender expression often do so with hostility, making their aggression clear. They may use homophobic and hateful comments as a way to try humiliate and silence individuals they think do not conform to male patriarchy (or whom they believe are sinners within the context of their religion).[40] For example, a bisexual white woman in her twenties in Washington, D.C., wrote in a follow-up interview to my 2008 survey, "I've been called homophobic slurs by men who I've ignored or who have made assumptions about my sexuality based on my appearance." A mixed race (Korean and white) woman in her twenties in Brooklyn, New York, shared a specific incident in my 2008 survey about a time when a man targeted her because of her sexual orientation: "5th Avenue Park Slope, Brooklyn at 4 pm on a Sunday afternoon. I was so horrendously verbally attacked by a crazed man that I called the cops and ID'd him from mug shots at the station. He was eventually caught on drug charges but was also slapped with a hate crime because he repeatedly yelled 'fuckin dyke' and harassed me only because he could not tolerate my butch presence."

While heterosexual ciswomen (women who conform to their birth gender, unlike transwomen) may experience a reprieve from male street harassers when they are visibly with a male significant other, women whose significant other is female do not have that luxury. Indeed, the harassment may be even worse, especially if two women appear to be a couple. One woman I interviewed said that when she was in public with her ex-girlfriend, she was afraid to touch her in any way other than as a friend, because she was afraid it might provoke comments or harassment she did not want to deal with.[41] Maria, a college librarian in her thirties in Louisville, Kentucky, shared a story on my blog Stop Street Harassment in May 2009, about how a man cursed and spit at her and her girlfriend one evening when they were walking home from a poetry reading. She said:

As an openly gay woman, I've had to train myself to not notice people on the street. I've taught myself to not pay attention to other people's reactions when they see my girlfriend and me holding hands or acting affectionate in public. You know, the same way straight couples act in public, only they don't get spit at or cursed. This kind of deliberate tuning out of the world is the only way I'm able to enjoy being out and visible with my girlfriend.[42]

Conversely, some men will treat a female couple as if the women exist for their viewing pleasure. One of my 2008 survey takers, a white lesbian in her twenties in Fairfield, California, said, "Occasionally, being out with my girlfriend has provoked specifically lez-focused comments, like guys yelling 'Hey, make out for us!'" Another survey respondent, a teenage white woman in New York City said, "Male police officers have been as guilty of leering and staring at my girlfriend and I, as civilian men." Any way it is done, such behavior toward a female couple is unwanted and, as Maria pointed out, not something heterosexual couples deal with.

As women who conform the least to their birth gender, transwomen tend to face a huge volume of harassment in public places and some of the worst violence. In Queens, New York, in 2009, cismen attacked two transwomen in separate incidents within a month. First, two men assaulted Leslie Mora with a belt buckle in a targeted hate crime. Less than a month later, men shouted anti-gay slurs and threatened to slit the throat of Carmella Etienne. They also threw rocks and a beer bottle at her, and the resulting injuries put her in the hospital. The *New York Daily News* reported that "Etienne is now afraid to leave her home" and quoted her as saying, "'The law will hopefully bring them to justice. I love being myself.'"[43] It's unfair and not right that just being one's self can trigger so much hate and violence.

Not only do people harass and attack transwomen for being who they are: transwomen also face scrutiny from both ciswomen and cismen over "what" they are. On the Community Feministing blog, contributor Josh T. wrote about the specific harassment and difficulties transpeople face in public spaces.

I am trans bashed on the street constantly. People who present as cismen will start yelling, getting upset, moving to the other side of the street as if I am scary, a threat. Groups of teenagers will discuss me as I walk by; what "it" is. . . . I also experience this strange highbred [hybrid] of bashing and catcalling when someone simultaneously mocks my presentation and sarcastically expresses attraction. My experience is different from what ciswomen experience on the street. Ciswomen are followed and targeted by cat calling because of their proximity to fitting into the predefined role of men's inferior. Trans folk have these experiences because we *don't* fit. But both groups are targets of the everyday vocalizations that reassert male supremacy because we are the other. We are not men, so we are objects.[44]

From January to November, there were ninety-nine recorded murders of transgender persons in the United States in 2009.[45] Yet there are police officers who trivialize and dismiss the harassment and assault experiences of transwomen, as they do for many ciswomen. Officers also may unfairly judge a transwoman or question her identity, deterring transwomen from viewing law enforcement as an option for seeking justice and staying safe. Rebecca Ashling wrote a comment about this on the blog Bird of Paradox, "It would never occur to me to actually make any complaints about transphobic harassment to the police. I know instinctively that I don't belong to any of the categories of people they would take seriously."[46]

Thanks to the 2009 Matthew Shepard and James Byrd, Jr. Hate Crimes Prevention Act, however, crimes against transgender people are now recognized as hate crimes. This is the first time a federal law has included protections for transgender people. Mara Keisling, the executive director of the National Center for Transgender Equality, said about the occasion, "Every day transgender people live with the reality and the threat of personal violence, simply because of who they are. This must end and it must end now. The new law provides for some vital first steps in preventing these terrible crimes as well as addressing them when they occur."[47]

SOCIOECONOMIC STATUS

One of the common unifiers of women of all socioeconomic classes is their vulnerability to male harassment and assault. Women in lower classes are more susceptible to frequent male stranger harassment in public places, but upper-class women are certainly not immune. Martha Langelan found many lower-class men who said they street harassed women out of frustration over the class difference.[48] In her *Yale Journal of Law and Feminism* article "The Women in the Street: Reclaiming the Public Space from Sexual Harassment," legal scholar Deborah Thompson included a story from a summer law associate who was harassed by construction workers while she walked to lunch with a partner and an associate at the law firm. The woman wrote, "I instantly went from feeling professional and in control to feeling powerless and embarrassed."[49]

Access to resources and wealth can reduce street harassment. Wealthy women can afford a car or a taxi, which may shield them from many forms of street harassment. They may not have to work outside the home and thus be less likely to go in public alone. On the other hand, lower-class women are more likely to have a job (or jobs) outside the home to which they may travel alone and on public transportation, by bicycle or on foot. Significantly, they may have fewer resources or connections to help them cope with harassers or to take action against them. Young women of all socioeconomic statuses also face many of these problems.

Poverty can lead to crime, including more extreme forms of street harassment. Based on a study of seventy-five African American teenagers in an impoverished area of St. Louis, researcher Jody Miller found that gender-based violence is "particularly acute for adolescent girls in neighborhoods characterized by intense disadvantage."[50] Sexual violence was a common theme in the interviews she conducted, and the young women often spoke specifically about the dangers posed by the nighttime in their neighborhood, where there were gang and drug-related violence and predatory males. People in the neighborhood were fairly desensitized to violence and many girls cited times when people would stand by and sometimes even laugh when assaults occurred (between intimate partners and between strangers).[51]

Prostitutes who regularly work on the streets tend to be lower-class women and they are very vulnerable to harassment and assault, by passersby, the police, and clients.[52] One study in the United States found that eight out of ten prostitutes had been sexually assaulted before the age of 14.[53] In another study in England, where prostitution is legal, women who worked on the streets saw violence as an everyday risk and most had personal experiences with violence.[54] This is not surprising considering how so many people talk about prostitutes and treat them. For example, in the Grand Theft Auto video game series players can have sex with a prostitute and kill her to retrieve their money. In real life, many serial killers, including the Yorkshire Ripper, the Brooklyn Strangler, Jack the Ripper, Kendall Francois, Maury Travis, and Robert Hansen, have targeted prostitutes.[55] There are even men who justify treating women who are not prostitutes with violence and disrespect if the men feel the women are "dressed" like prostitutes. The men will ask the women "how much" or call them a ho or a slut.

Because low-income and homeless women are more likely to be sex workers than wealthy women, there is significant overlap in crimes against homeless women and sex workers. As such, homeless women are also extremely vulnerable to harassment and assault and often have little refuge from the street. Scholar Stephanie Golden wrote about the difference between the historical male and female tramps in her article "Lady Versus Low Creature: Old Roots of Current Attitudes Toward Homeless Women":

The image of the male tramp or hobo commonly involved forceful action and power . . . a form of noble conquest, with his personal erratic mobility blended into the nation's manifest destiny. The female tramp, in contrast, was immediately and completely defined by her sexuality. . . . while a male tramp had a certain place in relation to society, a woman had no place as a tramp unless she could be defined as a prostitute—that is, degraded and marginalized.[56]

Today, homeless women are still treated as sexually available. Golden wrote in her article how in 1998, the director of a twenty-four-hour center for women in Manhattan said that male guards in the city shelters and men on the streets commonly assumed "'homeless women are fair game.' Men who harass homeless women feel the women belong to them because they're on the streets."[57]

PERSONS WITH DISABILITIES

Historically, persons with disabilities have been kept isolated by being locked away in almshouses, institutions, or attics, abandoned or legislated out of sight. Until 1973, Chicago prohibited persons who were "deformed" and "unsightly" from exposing themselves to public view.[58] Mark Weber, author of *Disability Harassment* writes, "Isolation dehumanizes, and those who are not considered human are apt targets for mistreatment."[59] Today there are able-bodied people who still try to keep all persons with disabilities isolated and who treat them as inferior, including on the streets.

Gardner discussed the intersectionality of gender-based street harassment and the harassment of persons with disabilities in her book *Passing By*. Many of the women with disabilities she interviewed reported being told by able-bodied persons to go home or that they should be locked up.[60] She wrote, "It is not simply a matter of exclusionary practices that affect women (and men) with disabilities, it is also different evaluative practices. A first difference is that a woman with a disability that is regarded as disfiguring can regularly be faulted on her appearance by men evaluators."[61] So, like overweight women, women with disabilities who do not look like the "ideal" woman can face male harassment for that specific reason. Gardner also found that some of the women liked mild gender-based harassment by men because it meant they were being treated like a woman instead of like a woman with a disability.[62]

Several women with disabilities I heard from in my research felt that if they were harassed it was because they were a woman or because of their disability, but not necessarily because of a combination of the two. For example, blogger Never That Easy wrote a comment to a blog post I wrote about street harassment and disabilities:

Unfortunately, I do think that people with disabilities are quite vulnerable to this kind of harassment. Luckily, I have not experienced any sexualized harassment since needing to use my wheelchair, but I do get the people who just move you, who think nothing of pushing your chair out of their way, as if you weren't a real person for them to have to even acknowledge – the fact that it's your body they are moving means nothing to them.[63]

Another example is blogger Andrea Shettle who commented on the same blog post.

I'm a deaf woman. I've had a few incidents with sexual harassment, though I'm not sure that my being deaf necessarily played a role in any of these incidents. (In fact, in one of those incidents, the perpetrator was deaf.) I can believe, though, that sometimes disability may play a role in who is targeted. Research about violence against people with disabilities does often find that some abusers target people with disabilities because they see them as more vulnerable, less able to fight back, less able to speak up (especially if a speech-related disability or intellectual disability), less able to identify them (if blind), less able to escape, less likely to be believed (esp. if intellectual disability or psychosocial disability) etc. I would guess that a similar dynamic comes into play with street harassment or bullying.[64]

Persons with visible disabilities also may be treated similarly regardless of gender because of the stereotype that they are asexual. Of all the factors that can impact street harassment, disability is the one about which there is the least research and that shortcoming needs to be rectified.

CONCLUSION

Racism, homophobia and transphobia, classism, and ableism give additional meanings and layers to gender-based street harassment. The discussions in this chapter touched on how varied women's experiences are, yet the unifying factor is that they are being targeted in part because they are female. This perpetuates a less-safe environment for women and makes them less welcome in public than men. Further research on each area covered here can provide more needed insight into all women's harassment experiences.

NOTES

1. Carol Brooks Gardner, *Passing By: Gender and Public Harassment* (Los Angeles, CA: University of California Press, 1995), 229.

2. M. H. (a 2008 survey respondent) e-mail message to author, August 19, 2009.

3. Laura Beth Nielsen, *License to Harass: Law, Hierarchy, and Offensive Public Speech* (Princeton, NJ: Princeton University Press, 2004), 41.

4. Jody Miller, *Getting Played: African American Girls, Urban Inequality, and Gendered Violence* (New York: New York University Press, 2008), 8; see also Daphne Spain, *Gendered Spaces* (Chapel Hill: University of North Carolina Press, 1992): 18; see also RAINN, "Who Are the Victims?" n.d., http://www.rainn.org/get-information/statistics/sexual-assault-victims.

5. Deirdre Davis, "The Harm that Has No Name: Street Harassment, Embodiment, and African American Women," in *Gender Struggles: Practical Approaches to Contemporary Feminism*, ed. Constance L. Mui and Julien S. Murphy (Oxford: Rowman & Littlefield Publishers, Inc., 2002); see also Sue Wise and Liz Stanley, *Georgie Porgie: Sexual Harassment in Everyday Life* (London: Pandora, 1987), 86; see also Patricia Hill Collins, *Black Feminist Thought: Knowledge, Consciousness, and the Politics of Empowerment* (New York: Routledge, 1990); see also bell hooks, *Ain't I a Woman?: Black Women and Feminism* (Boston, MA: South End Press, 1981).

6. Stereotypes that Asian and Asian American women are submissive also play a role in how men treat and exotify them. Edith Wen-Chu Chen studied and wrote about this in "Sexual Harassment from the Perspective of Asian-American Women," in *Everyday Sexism in the Third Millennium*, ed. Carol Rambo Ronai, Barbara A. Zsembik, and Joe. R. Feagin (New York: Routledge, 1997).

7. Maggie Hadleigh-West, *War Zone*, Film Fatale, Inc., 1998 (71-minute version).

8. David Pilgrim, "Jezebel Stereotypes," Jim Crow Museum of Racists Memorabilia, Ferris State University, n.d., http://www.ferris.edu/jimcrow/jezebel/; see also Deborah Gray White, *'Ar'n't I a Woman? Female Slaves in the Plantation South* (New York: Norton, 1999), 27–61.

9. bell hooks, *Black Looks: Race and Representation* (Boston, MA: South End Press, 1992), 61-65.

10. A. M. (a 2008 survey respondent) e-mail message to author, September 3, 2009.

11. Tiffanie Heben, "Reshaping of the Law: Interpreting and Remedying Street Harassment," *Review of Law and Women's Studies* 4, no. 1 (1994), 197; see also Davis, 219; see also Kimberle Crenshaw, "Race, Gender, and Sexual Harassment," *Southern California Law Review* 65 (1991–1992), 1467–76.

12. Patricia Hill Collins, *Black Feminist Thought: Knowledge, Consciousness, and the Politics of Empowerment* (New York: Routledge,

1991), 174, cited in Melinda Mills, "'You Talking to Me?' Considering Black Women's Racialized and Gendered Experiences with and Responses or Reactions to Street Harassment from Men," Masters of Arts Thesis for Georgia State University, 2007, 49.

13. Cynthia Grant Bowman, "Street Harassment and the Informal Ghettoization of Women," *Harvard Law Review* 106, no. 3 (January 1993), 13.

14. Monique Hazeur and Nijla Mumin, "BACK UP! Concrete Diaries," a documentary that is still in production. The author attended a screening of the documentary in progress in July 2009.

15. Crenshaw, 1470.

16. Fearful, "Anti-Black Woman Harasser in Arlington," Stop Street Harassment, August 7, 2009, http://streetharassment.wordpress.com/2009/08/07/anti-black-woman-harasser-in-arlington.

17. Martha Langelan, *Back Off! How to Confront and Stop Sexual Harassment and Harassers* (New York: Fireside Press, 1993), 32.

18. Author notes from a Street Harassment Summit in New York City, New York, May 5, 2007.

19. Stacey Chan, "Off the Map—Power on the Street," Kirwan Institute Blog, August 13, 2009, http://kirwaninstitute.blogspot.com/2009/08/off-map-power-on-street_13.html.

20. M. S. (a 2008 survey respondent) e-mail message to author, August 18, 2009.

21. A. M. (a 2008 survey respondent) e-mail message to author, September 3, 2009; see also Los Angelista, "No, You Can't Touch My Hair," September 13, 2009, http://www.losangelista.com/2009/09/no-you-cant-touch-my-hair.html.

22. Native American women are 2.5 times more likely to be raped or sexually assaulted than other women, and the men who perpetrate at least 86 percent of reported assaults are non-Native men. This is thought to be because of the federal maze of jurisdictions that make it easier for non-Natives to commit crimes on reservations without penalty. If mostly non-Native men are raping Native women, they are likely the one perpetrating the most street harassment too. Anecdotally, in *Messengers of the Wind: Native American Women Tell Their Life Stories*, Inupiat Florence Kenney said as a teenager she was sent away from her Alaskan village to Anchorage. There was an air base with thousands of Air Force and Army men, and there was a lot of sexual harassment from them in the streets. She noted that she did not recall any time Native men had harassed her this way (p. 39).

23. In all my research, I have yet to come across any mention of Asian American men as harassers.

24. Miller, 3; see also Crenshaw, 1472; see also Margaret T. Gordon and Stephanie Riger, *The Female Fear: The Social Cost of Rape* (Urbana, IL: University of Illinois Press, 1991), 50.

25. Charisse Jones and Kumea Shorter-Gooden, *Shifting: the Double Lives of Black Women in America* (New York: HarperCollins, 2003), 38–39; see also Beverly Grier, "Making Sense of Our Differences: African American Women on Anita Hill," in *Sexual Harassment Issues and Answers*, ed. Linda LeMoncheck and James P. Sterba (Oxford: Oxford University Press: 2001), 159–160.

26. Bowman, 533–534; see also Hawley Fogg-Davis, "Theorizing Black Lesbians within Black Feminism: A Critique of Same-Race Street Harassment," *Politics & Gender* 2 (2006), 24.

27. Fogg-Davis, 64–65.

28. Gardner, 109, 117.

29. Also see Joan Fayer's article "Changes in Gender Use of Public Space in Puerto Rico," in *Voices in the Street: Explorations in Gender, Media, and Public Space*, ed. Susan J. Drucker and Gary Gumpert (Cresskill, NJ: Hampton Press, Inc: 1996).

30. "Antiracism," HollaBackNYC, October 2, 2005, http://hollabacknyc. blogspot.com/2005/10/antiracism.html. All of the HollaBack Web sites use this.

31. Gardner, 109, 117.

32. "Race, Class, and Street Harassment," Feministe, July 20, 2007, http://www.feministe.us/blog/archives/2007/07/20/race-class-and-street-harassment.

33. Martha Langelan, 61; see also C. Dana, "Talking Back to Harassers," *Washington Post* (August 19, 1986) C5; see also "Race, Class, and Street Harassment," Feministe, July 20, 2007, http://www.feministe.us/blog/archives/2007/07/20/race-class-and-street-harassment/; see also Latoya Peterson, "Catcalling Is a Cross Cultural Annoyance," Racialicious, June 29, 2007, http://www.racialicious.com/2007/06/29/catcalling-is-a-cross-cultural-annoyance.

34. Hadleigh-West, *War Zone*, and Girls for Gender Equity's documentary *Hey . . . Shorty* directed by Ashley Lewis and Sala Cyril in 2007.

35. Norma Anne Oshynko, "No Safe Place: The Legal Regulation of Street Harassment," Thesis for Masters of Law in Faculty of Law, University of British Columbia, 2002, 36–37.

36. Heben, 192–193.

37. Fogg-Davis, 58.

38. Gary Comstock, *Violence against Lesbians and Gay Men* (New York: Columbia University Press, 1991), 41, cited in Oshynko, "No Safe Place: The Legal Regulation of Street Harassment," 36.

39. Oshynko, 36.

40. Heben, 193.

41. K. M. (a 2008 survey respondent) e-mail message to author, August 15, 2009.

42. Maria, "Unpleasant Reminder," Stop Street Harassment Blog, May 28, 2009, http://streetharassment.wordpress.com/2009/05/28/unpleasant-reminder.

43. Irving Dejohn and Brendan Brosh, "Two Arrested in Queens Bias Attack on Transgender Female," *New York Daily News*, July 10, 2009, http://www.nydailynews.com/news/ny_crime/2009/07/10/2009-07-10_2_arrested_in_queens_transgender_attack.html.

44. Josh T. "TransFeminism/CisFeminism: Why Can't We Be Friends?" Community Feministing, April 17, 2009, http://community.feministing.com/2009/04/transfeminismcisfeminism-why-c.html.

45. "Transgender Death Statistics 2009," Remember Our Dead, 2009, http://www.transgenderdor.org/?page_id=192.

46. Rebecca Ashling, comment on "Street Harassment," Bird of Paradox, comment posted on August 18, 2009, http://birdofparadox.wordpress.com/2009/08/17/street-harassment.

47. National Center for Transgender Equality, "It's Official: First Federal Law to Protect Transgender People," October 22, 2009, http://transequality.org/news.html#first_law.

48. Langelan, 61.

49. Deborah Thompson, "'The Woman in the Street:' Reclaiming the Public Space from Sexual Harassment," *Yale Journal of Law and Feminism* 1994, 313.

50. Miller, 3.

51. Miller, 36.

52. Jane Pitcher, Rosie Campbell, Phil Hubbard, Maggie O'Neill, and Jane Scoular, *Living and Working in Areas of Street Sex Work: From Conflict to Coexistence* (York, UK: Joseph Rowntree Foundation, 2006), 4, 18–19.

53. R. Barri Flowers, *The Prostitution of Women and Girls* (London: McFarland & Company, Inc., Publishers, 1998), 48–50.

54. Pitcher, 18–19.

55. Marilyn French, *The War Against Women* (New York: Ballantine Books, 1992), 195.

56. Stephanie Golden, "Lady versus Low Creature: Old Roots of Current Attitudes Toward Homeless Women," in *Women: A Feminist Perspective, Fifth Edition*, ed. Jo Freeman (Mountain View, CA: Mayfield Publishing Company, 1995), 489.

57. Golden, 491.

58. Mark C. Weber, *Disability Harassment* (New York: New York University Press, 2007), 17.

59. Ibid., 25.

60. Gardner, 235.

61. Ibid.

62. Ibid., 236.

63. Never That Easy comment on "Blogging against Disablism Day: Street Harassment Edition," Stop Street Harassment Blog, comment posted on May 2, 2009, http://streetharassment.wordpress.com/2009/05/01/blogging-against-disablism-day-street-harassment-edition.

64. Andrea Shettle, comment on "Blogging against Disablism Day: Street Harassment Edition," comment posted on May 18, 2009.

_____ *Chapter 4* _____

Street Harassment
Is a Global Problem

Throughout the world, women's access to public places is more limited than is men's, largely due to gender-based harassment and the threat of male violence. In addition to the other forms of discrimination that limit them, women's inability to safely enter public spaces further impedes their equality with men in public life because it can deter them from attending school, reduce their ability to earn an income, prevent them from participating in political activities, and curtail their exploration of the world. This chapter opens by examining global harassment trends, including the frequency of harassment girls and women face while commuting to work and school and traveling abroad. Next, I examine some of the regionally specific restrictions women face, such as legal ones in countries like Saudi Arabia and Yemen, and ones caused by war or periods of high crime in places like Sudan and Colombia. Last, I highlight three countries that are rapidly gaining a street harassment reputation: Italy, Japan, and Egypt.

GLOBAL HARASSMENT

Studies show that street harassment is a global problem.[1] Stories written by my 2008 informal online survey respondents, which include women from twenty-three countries on five continents, and stories people have submitted to my blog and other anti-harassment blogs (such as Blank Noise in India, Psst in Mauritius, and HollaBack websites in Australia and London) further illustrate this. Here are a few stories from my survey:

Growing up in Tokyo, the subway was a haven for perverts. The subway cars would get very jammed packed with people. [I] felt hands molesting me under my skirt many times. [I] couldn't move to protect myself [and I] felt helpless and very violated. [I] felt men rubbing their erect penis up against me. [I] got off the subway crying most days. My stockings were always run from men's rough hands groping my legs. My breasts were regularly groped also but mainly [there were] upskirt violations.

—30–39-year-old heterosexual Japanese woman in New York City

Recently I was walking home along the route I take every day and I walked past a group of lads who stared and shouted "the pussy here is really good."

—20–29-year-old heterosexual British/Irish woman
in Bristol, United Kingdom

Being stared at/yelled at from a distance (for example, when I'm out running and passing construction sites) is very uncomfortable and completely unacceptable. Many times I've changed my route so as not to pass by construction sites.

—20–29-year-old bisexual Israeli woman

I got off the railway station at 10:30 at night and was walking towards my home which is hardly 2 minutes from the railway station. A group of young men on the road made me feel very unsafe and scared because they made a vulgar gesture and tried to block my path with a bike. There were not many people around and I panicked, but just walked past with a confidence I didn't feel inside, ignoring the cigarette smoke that they blew into my face.

—20–29-year-old heterosexual woman in Thrissur, Kerala, India

I was walking by a construction crew doing some work in the evening time . . . I heard the workers start to call "Hey!" and "Sweetie, c'mere!" and "Looking fine, baby!" I didn't respond, so one of the workers said to another, "Hey, you grab the front and I'll go behind, then we'll see how the bitch likes it." I felt like I couldn't breathe; it was dark, there weren't many other people around, and I didn't know if they were going to act on this. I was so angry and frightened, I thought I was going to start crying right there. I didn't, though; I just turned my music back up and walked away, like most other women would. I felt disgusting.

—20–29-year-old bisexual white woman in Toronto, Canada

One of the more terrifying things is when a group of men follows closely in a car, having slowed to walking pace, making remarks. . . . There are many other stories of sexual harassment, frottage, flashing, and several "minor" sexual assaults (men grabbing breasts, bottom)—overall I consider myself relatively "lucky" based on the fact that I've never actually been raped by a stranger.

—40–49-year-old heterosexual white woman in Perth, Western Australia

A common experience I came across in the survey respondents' stories and in other research I conducted is one of being harassed while simply trying to commute to school or work, especially on public transportation.

Harassed and Groped while Commuting

All over the world, men harass women and girls who walk or take public transportation to places like school and work. For example, in Nepal, everyone who commutes by public transportation vehicles must deal with congestion, but girls and women also must deal with male harassers. Two young women were quoted in an article about this problem in the newspaper *My Republica*. "'We regularly face harassment while using public transport,' says Pratima, a twelfth-grader. 'We don't mind some friendly flirting, but they (boys) don't stop at that and start to talk nonsense.' . . . 'We dread crowded buses, but we have to board them. We cannot miss our college, can we?' her classmate Anita adds, 'The khalasis (helpers/conductors) are always on a lookout for an excuse to get their hands on us.'"[2]

In Mexico, male harassment on public transportation is so common that some cities have resorted to women-only buses[3] and women-only taxi cab services.[4] There is also an ongoing problem of young women disappearing during their commute and being found mutilated, often raped, and killed. As detailed in Teresa Rodriguez's and Diana Montane's book *The Daughters of Juarez* and an ongoing Amnesty International campaign "Take Action for the Women of Juarez,"[5] since 1993, more than 400 women's bodies have been found this way in Ciudad Juarez and Chihuahua, Mexico, and the extensive corruption in the law enforcement system has meant most of the crimes are never solved. Many of the young women were kidnapped on their way to school or work, while waiting for the bus in deserted areas early in the morning or late at night.[6]

In rural Zambia, only 20 percent of children who enter primary school complete twelfth grade because of the long distances they must travel to and from school. Not only is traveling that far tiring, but, for girls, it also includes a risk of sexual assault and rape. One student at Ndapula Community School said in an Inter Press Service article, "I used to wake up at 4 A.M. in order for me and my friends to arrive at school before 7 A.M. when classes start. This journey was especially bad because sometimes you could find bad boys who used to chase us and force those whom they caught to do bad things."[7] Today, students at the Ndapula Community School have bicycles through the Chicago-based World Bicycle Relief organization, which enable them to travel to school in less time and attend more often. Most of the bicycles went to girls because of the additional safety risk they face.[8]

As the stories in Nepal, Mexico, Zambia, and countless other places demonstrate, men harass girls and women as they commute on foot, rickshaws, buses, subways, trains, and taxis to work, school, shops, and places of recreation. Without prompting, around 50 percent the 389 female respondents who wrote about a street harassment incident in my 2008 survey mentioned it happening on a form of public transportation. This is consistent with the findings of several studies cited earlier in the book. In very crowded cities, the sheer volume of people who use public transportation makes it easy for men to harass women, and it also makes it hard for women to identify the harasser and report or confront him. Because young and poor to middle-class women often must rely on walking or public transportation, they are most vulnerable to the harassment and also the least likely to know how to deal with it or have the resources to report it.

Due to high rates of male harassment on public transportation, major cities in more than fifteen countries have implemented women-only subway cars, buses, taxis, and train cars to address the problem. Countries with women-only bus services include Bangladesh, Indonesia, Pakistan, India, the United Arab Emirates, Mexico, and Thailand. Women-only subway cars are found in countries including Japan, Egypt, Iran, Mexico, South Korea, and Brazil.

Women who drive taxi cabs and the women who are passengers also face potential male harassment and assault. As a result, there are women-only taxi services with women drivers in countries such as England, Russia, Australia, Lebanon, Iran, India, Mexico, and the United Arab Emirates. In some of the cultures where women and men who are not related are not supposed to be alone together, a female taxi driver helps increase women's safety and mobility.[9]

Due to requests from its passengers, particularly women, in 2006, Russian Railways introduced female-only and male-only sleeping cars, in addition to the existing mixed-sex compartments, on eight of its overnight train lines connecting the main cities in western Russia. Unlike other European countries, most Russians continue to use trains for long trips instead of planes because of the lower cost. The sex-segregated compartments are only available to passengers who ride in first- and second-class train cars; all third-class cars remain mixed sex.[10]

Sex segregation is better than nothing, and it is an option many women are happy to have when the alternative is harassment in a mixed-sex car. Yet these initiatives are problematic. They are essentially a band-aid solution for women who can use them, and they do not address the root problem: why are men harassing women? Nor do the initiatives hold men accountable for ending the behavior. Instead, the initiatives segregate women away from men to provide them with temporary relief from the harassment. Jessica Valenti, feminist author and founder of the feminist blog Feministing.com, articulates the problem with segregated public transportation in a 2007 *Guardian* article, "While the idea of a safe space is compelling, this international trend—which often comes couched in paternalistic rhetoric about 'protecting' women—raises questions of just how equal the sexes are if women's safety relies on us being separated. After all, shouldn't we be targeting the gropers and harassers? The onus should be on men to stop harassing women, not on women to escape them."[11]

Men will not stop harassing women until what constitutes acceptable social behavior changes and until there is an atmosphere of respect for women and a realization of gender equity. So instead of devoting realistic resources to meet these goals, governments turn to sex segregation as a solution because it is something they can achieve more easily. Then they can point to the initiative as a sign that they take women's complaints seriously. But while sex-segregated public transportation surely offers needed relief to the women who can use it, in the long term, nothing will change until women are respected and men are socialized not to harass and are penalized if they do. Women will not be free to travel and explore the world until this happens either.

Harassment while Traveling

For centuries, men of all social classes have traveled alone or with male friends as a coming-of-age activity. For women, traveling alone or with female friends usually has been viewed as improper and dangerous because of male harassment and assault. Historian Patricia Cline Cohen wrote about women who traveled in the United States between 1750 and 1850, and said that, "men who saw women alone exhibiting freedom of manners, sociability, and splendid dress marked them as disreputable women and treated them accordingly. A woman who wanted to appear reputable, therefore, had to constrain her actions, draw her cloak close, maintain reserve, and accept male escortage wherever possible."[12] Until relatively recently, the only way to achieve the same freedom as men was to dress as a man and act like a man. Nineteenth-century woman's rights activist Elizabeth Cady Stanton wrote the following in 1869:

A young lady in Fifth Avenue dressed in male costume for years, traveling all over Europe and this country. She says it would have been impossible to have seen and known as much of life in women's attire, and to have felt the independence and security she did, had her sex been proclaimed before all Israel and the sun. There are a good many reasons for adopting male costume. . . . A concealment of sex would protect our young girls from these terrible outrages from brutal men, reported in all our daily papers.[13]

Fewer people today view women traveling alone or with other women as improper. According to the Travel Channel, in 2007, 32 million women traveled alone.[14] Male harassment and assault, however, still prevents women from enjoying all the same freedoms as men when they travel, as most travel guides or study abroad advice sheets show.[15] While men and women are targeted for pick pocketing, begging, and forceful sales pitches, women, especially young women, are almost always more at risk for sexual harassment and assault. Thus, many travel guides have a section specifically aimed at women, especially for female students studying abroad. For example, IIEPassport, a college study abroad directory, says on its page with tips for female students:

Female students inevitably will have to fend off unwanted attention more than their male counterparts. And simply because your new surroundings will be unfamiliar to you, you need to be more vigilant than you would be on your home campus or in your hometown. Of course, you will want to avoid taking shortcuts and routes that are off the beaten path, especially late at night. You should also travel around with at least one other person. Cat calls or other unsolicited attention from the locals should remain unacknowledged in these situations. Much of staying safe abroad is common sense.[16]

While several travel Web sites aimed at women travelers, as opposed to students studying abroad, were more encouraging about traveling alone, they all recommended practices that restricted women's freedom in public, such as not traveling alone at night, staying in a busy hotel in a central part of a city, and always being aware of one's surroundings while projecting confidence and attitude.[17]

Encountering harassment while traveling or living outside the United States was a common problem among women I studied. Here are two of their stories.

I have lived overseas, and traveled to countries in Europe and Asia, the Caribbean, and Canada. In Western Europe, I had a few men follow me, one was grabbing his crotch. Other men yelled at me from their cars as they drove past. In Hong Kong, I was approached by quite a few foreign men . . . who were trying to get me to stop and talk to them . . . I am guessing they targeted me because I am a woman and because I was alone. . . . The Caribbean was the only place that I was harassed more than, or equally to, being harassed in the United States. But I believe I was harassed in the Caribbean in part because I am "white."[18]

—30–39-year-old heterosexual mixed-race woman (white and Asian American) from Indiana

When I was studying abroad in Salzburg, Austria, I had a pretty scary experience with a harasser who decided to stalk me. I was in a grocery store, standing in line to check out. A middle-aged man who was in line behind me moved so that he was standing uncomfortably close. . . . I paid for what I wanted, and then left. Rather than checking out himself, he followed me right out of the store. Noticing this, I ducked through a crowd and took a random turn to try and lose him. I took several back alleys, finally ending up on the larger street that I could follow to the tunnel I needed to take to get out of town. I felt a hand grab my hip, and turned to see the man from the store. . . . At that point I ran back to my school. . . . I told my classmates what had happened, and this is the only time I think I've been universally taken seriously when complaining about an incident of street harassment. The cooking professor had to go the same way I did to get home, so she offered to walk with me. This was in broad daylight, maybe 3 P.M."[19]

—20–29-year-old bisexual white woman in Washington, D.C.

In my research, I have come across many women who will not travel alone or who do so with much trepidation because they fear male harassment or assault. Traveling has so many benefits, including the chance to expand one's horizon and to understand other cultures and the world, and it's a shame women can't have the same freedom of mobility to go to new places (or old/familiar places for that matter) as men. The rest of the chapter examines ways in which street harassment can vary by region and country.

LEGAL RESTRICTIONS

There are countries where the laws, as well as male harassment, keep women from having the same access to public spaces as men. One of the worst countries for women's equality in public spaces—and equality in general—is Saudi Arabia. Women are forbidden from leaving their local neighborhood without the company of a male family member or guardian. Women need permission from their male family member or guardian to travel by airplane, check into hotels, or rent apartments.[20] Even mosques and some public streets are reserved for men, and women only have limited access to parks, museums, and libraries.[21]

Women in Saudi Arabia are also prohibited from driving cars.[22] Abdel Mohsen Gifari, a researcher for the country's religious police who has spent much of his career enforcing laws, such as those prohibiting women drivers, told a *Miami Herald* reporter in 2009 that one of his daughters wants to drive. "I told her that driving is allowed in Islam," Gifari said in an interview with a Western reporter. "But it is more of a cultural thing. We already have a lot of problems on the road when it comes to sexual harassment, with guys flirting with girls in the car. If a woman drives, it's only going to bring more problems."[23]

Other countries that legally restrict or legally permit the restriction of women's mobility in public spaces include Kuwait, Yemen, and the United Arab Emirates (UAE). In Kuwait, women must receive male permission before leaving their home at night and in many professions women are forbidden from working at night. Women also must have male permission before traveling abroad.[24] Similarly, women in Yemen often need permission from their husband, father or male guardian to leave the house or to apply for a passport.[25] While UAE laws do not restrict women's mobility in public, they do allow fathers and husbands to prevent their daughters and wives from participating in professional and social life. Men also can keep their wives, minor children, and adult unmarried daughters from leaving the country by withholding their passports or by contacting the immigration authorities.[26]

Veiling

In countries like Saudi Arabia and Yemen, requiring women to veil heavily in public is another way to restrict their autonomy. People justify requiring women to cover their face by citing the Koran, which requires all female and male believers to dress in a "modest fashion." Religious leaders have interpreted this to mean women, and not men, should be veiled when they are in public or in the company of men who are not relatives. Scholars Ramsay Harik and Elsa Marston wrote in their book *Women in the Middle East: Traditions and Changes*:

The most specific instructions in the Koran gives to women as follows: that they should lower their gaze, draw their veils over their bosoms, and reveal their "adornments" only to the men and other women in their own households. . . . The Koran also advises Muslim women to "draw their cloaks around them" when they go out, so that they will be recognized as Muslims and not bothered on the street. Nowhere does the Koran require Muslim women to veil heavily or cover their face.[27]

Indeed, historically, not all women wore such restrictive veils. Only wealthy women use to wear them, and they also stayed home to show that their high social status meant they did not have to work. Harik and Marston note that veiling has "always been largely a middle- and upper-class custom. Peasant women and lower-class urban women usually did not 'cover,' because they had to work in the fields and the streets."[28]

The number of women who wear a veil and how much of their face they cover differs between countries and regions today.[29] For example, legislation requires all women in Saudi Arabia to cover completely when they are in public, which severely limits their mobility and range of vision.[30] In 2008, a Muslim cleric caused controversy by admonishing that women wear a niqab (full veil) that only reveals one eye because, he said, showing both eyes encouraged women to use eye make-up to look seductive![31] In many other countries, there are no legal requirements for veiling, but social pressure, religion, and the belief that it will cut down on male harassment results in many women veiling. In the UAE most women cover their hair with a scarf or veil.[32] In Egypt, about 70 percent of women wear veils,[33] and in Tunisia many women choose to wear a veil in public spaces.[34] Under the Taliban, women in Afghanistan were required to cover from head to foot. While laws no longer require this, the general climate of hostility toward women continues in Afghanistan to the extent that many choose to or are pressured into wearing a veil in public for their own safety.[35]

Today, the justification for heavy veiling is primarily based in religion, but also because it is supposed to keep women "safe" and prevent them from tempting men who would not otherwise be able to control themselves at the sight of a woman's shape and face.[36] One ad campaign in Egypt warned, "A veil to protect, or eyes will molest."[37] This is flawed reasoning. Harassing women and fetishizing body parts like breasts, buttocks, shoulders, ankles, wrists, and eyes are social constructs. If such behavior can be taught, it can be unlearned or not taught at all. But instead of teaching men not to "lose control" and harass women, women have their lives curtailed and their faces and bodies covered.

While wearing a veil may lessen harassment in areas where not wearing one signifies a "bad" woman, it does not necessarily stop harassment. A 2008 Egyptian survey showed that 83 percent of Egyptian women had been harassed by men in public at least once, and nearly half the respondents reported daily harassment, whether they were veiled or not.[38] One woman interviewed for a Cairo Institute for Human Rights Studies article said, "At 15, I was groped as I was performing the rites of the hajj pilgrimage at Mecca, the holiest site for Muslims. Every part of my body was covered except for my face and hands. I'd never been groped before and burst into tears, but I was too ashamed to explain to my family what had happened."[39]

In 2009 in Sana'a, Yemen, a place where most women wear a veil, 90 percent of the 70 interviewees said men had sexually harassed them in public. About 37 percent of the sample said they had experienced physical harassment.[40] While women feel they have to deal with harassment on their way to and from work, 55 percent of the respondents said when they had a choice, they would rather cancel their outdoor activities such as shopping than go out without a companion.[41] Still, the silver lining to being harassed while veiled is that it may reduce the chance that people will blame the women for the male harassment.

During the last several years France and a few other European governments have debated banning the wearing of all veils in public.[42] I disagree with a ban. Women should have the freedom to choose what to wear. Also, even though there is more evidence of gender equity in France than in a country like Saudi Arabia, men still harass women there. Until men stop harassing women in public places, women should be able to do what they can to feel safe in public. I do, however, support ending laws like those in Saudi Arabia that require veiling since women should have a choice.

CONFLICT AREAS

In war zones, conflict areas, and places with high crime rates, both men and women face dangers when they go in public spaces. Because most countries today are led by men, men usually are the main perpetrators of war and violent crimes against other men as they fight for power, money, and resources. Rape is commonly men's weapon of choice against women. In 2008, the United Nations officially recognized it as a war crime.[43]

While soldiers may rape women in their homes, the risk of rape is extremely high for women who leave their homes or leave a refugee camp to enter public spaces. According to the Social Institutions and Gender Index of the Organisation for Economic Co-operation and Development, civil war has made Sudanese women extremely vulnerable to sexual violence in public and displaced women in south Sudan are at a particularly high risk for sexual abuse and rape.[44] In Iraq, recent changes to laws mean women are no longer restricted from being in public, but the on-going war prevents many women from leaving their homes without a male escort for fear of rape or assault.[45]

A 2007 Oxfam International report found that during displacement, men rape and sexually assault women and girls who leave refugee camps for simple tasks. Around 90 percent of rapes among Somali refugees living in Dadaab and Kakuma camps in Kenya occurred when the women and girls were gathering firewood. Women had to walk up to 10 kilometers per day to find enough firewood and during that time sometimes warring clans would rape and beat them.[46] In a 2006 report, the Christian Children's Fund found that girls were the ones most likely to be assigned the task of gathering firewood at refugee camps and that girls were also the most vulnerable to sexual abuse and exploitation.[47] Oxfam also found that the burden of gathering firewood falls upon women and girls not only because cooking-related activities are considered "women's work," but also because of a belief that men and boys would be killed if they went to search for firewood, whereas women and girls might "only" be raped.[48] The dismissal and trivialization of sexual violence is common in countries at peace and is even more common in countries at war or civil unrest.

Rape and sexual assault also are used as weapons in the on-going conflict in Colombia. A 2004 Amnesty International report on violence in Colombia found that throughout the country's 40 year conflict, the security forces, paramilitaries, and the guerilla have used rape "as a method of torture or a means of injuring the 'enemy's honour,' [and] has been a common feature of the conflict."[49] While in many cases the women are targeted because the are a relative of or someone close to a man the assailant wants to kill, random women are killed, too. The report cites an incident in which a young woman was traveling by bus from Dabeiba to Medellín with her boyfriend. Paramilitaries stopped the bus and randomly dragged the young woman out, later raping and torturing her to death.[50]

After decades of civil war, gang violence and drug-related violence is epidemic Guatemala. The judicial system is corrupt, and raping and murdering women is used as a weapon to gain control of areas and to gain status among other men. An article in the *Christian Science Monitor* details the problem: "Members of Mara Salvatrucha 13 and Mara 18, two of the largest gangs in Central America, use rape as a way to gain a reputation. During territory disputes, such as the one in Marisole's neighborhood, they will often target women as a method of instilling fear by which to control areas."[51]

Even jailed gang members in Guatemala still rape women through gang members outside of jail. The *Global Post* quoted a woman who, at age 16, was grabbed by men when she was a few blocks from her house and taken to a jail where two men repeatedly raped her. Then they let her go. A doctor at a clinic in the area was quoted in the same story as saying it is not an infrequent occurrence and that she has treated girls as young as 14 who had been snatched from the streets and raped by men inside the prison.[52] Sandra Moran, a woman's rights activist, told the BBC that men engage in so much sexual violence because women are disrespected and many men believe they can treat them however they want, so they do.[53]

HARASSMENT REPUTATIONS

When I was researching street harassment outside the United States, three countries stood out because of their growing bad reputation for harassment, and I think they are worth highlighting. They are Italy, Egypt, and Japan.

Bottom-Pinching in Italy

In college, I double majored in history and women's and gender studies. I decided to participate in a study abroad program my junior year. My top choice was Italy, a county steeped in ancient history. But the more I talked to people and read about the county, the more I learned about the huge problem of male harassment. Even a family friend who went to Italy and was in her forties at the time had a shopkeeper grope her breasts when she was purchasing an item at his store. At the time, I did not know the term "street harassment" and still believed male harassment was a normal, accepted part of female life, but my fear of it made me realize I did not want to spend a year of my life there. Instead of Italy, I studied abroad for a year in England (where, incidentally, I was still verbally harassed, but at least no one grabbed me).

Emanuela Guano, an associate professor of anthropology at Georgia State University studied and wrote about issues of gender performance in public in Genoa, Italy. She found that Italian streets are definitively a male domain and that it is common to see groups of men congregating in public spaces but not women. She interviewed two young women who decided to establish a "turf" of their own on a stone wall where they liked to hang out, but they soon gave it up because they were inundated with lewd comments from men passing by.[54] While Guano found that street harassment is a big problem in Italy, most Italians, including the women who suffer, largely keep silent on the topic. They see it as a shameful, embarrassing topic.[55]

Bottom pinching is an "old custom" in Italy and one that even taxi drivers indulge in by sticking their hand through a car window and grabbing women walking by.[56] In 2005, the Italian Supreme Court upheld the conviction but suspended the fourteen-month prison sentence of a man who touched the buttocks of a woman as she stood in a public telephone booth making a call. In a groundbreaking decision, the court ruled that "bottom pinching" constitutes sexual assault.[57] This type of groping is so common that many people were outraged over the ruling. One man quoted in an article about the ruling claimed that men who engage in street harassment are just being friendly, and said of the following about the court decision, "If we put every man who touched a woman's bum in jail, there'd be no room for the drug dealers."[58] Unsurprisingly, given the public openness to treating women as objects, Italy is ranked 72nd out of 134 countries by the World Economic Forum for gender equity. One day I hope to visit Italy and see the historical sites and amazing art masterpieces, but the reality of public harassment likely will mean I would enjoy a visit more with a male companion.

Public Sexual Harassment in Egypt

Egypt is another country with fascinating historical sites that is a notorious location for intense street harassment, particularly in Cairo. One young woman interviewed for an article about harassment for the *BBC* said, "I walk home everyday. It only takes me 15 minutes, I cross the bridge. It is usually very loud and busy, but that does not stop men from approaching girls, any girl, good looking or bad looking, covered or not. I remember so many scary harassments. There was this guy who followed me and suddenly grabbed my bottom in front of everyone. I screamed but he ran away and no one interfered."[59]

The Egyptian Centre for Women's Rights (ECWR) surveyed more than 2,000 Egyptian men and women and 109 foreign women about street harassment issues, or, as the Egyptians describe it, public sexual harassment. They published their startling results in 2008: "62 percent of Egyptian men reported perpetrating harassment, while 83 percent of Egyptian women reported having been sexually harassed. Nearly half of women said the abuse occurred daily . . . 98 percent of foreign women had been harassed."[60]

The ECWR received global attention for the report and a few months after its release, an Egyptian man was jailed for three years and ordered to pay 5,001 Egyptian pounds ($895) for sexually harassing Noha Rushdi Saleh, also known as Noha Ostadh. The man repeatedly groped her from his car while she was walking. The ruling was the first time a harasser had been jailed for such an offense, showing a societal shift toward seeing such behavior as unacceptable. At the time of the attack, passersby blamed her and told her not to go to the police. With much difficulty, Ostadh dragged the harasser to the police station to report him where the police initially refused to open an investigation.[61] An end to victim blaming and an increase in police education must happen before women report harassers, but this ruling was still a major victory.

The ECWR report and Ostadh's case have opened up a dialogue on street harassment throughout Egypt. All over Egypt the number of women and girls enrolled in martial arts training classes is on the rise because they are acknowledging that male harassment and assault is a real problem. A young woman quoted in a *BBC* article on self-defense in Egypt said, "I was on my way home from school and I was attacked—I didn't know what to do," Shaza Saeed, 14, said. "But now I have learnt how to defend myself so I am not afraid any more. I think every girl should go to self-defense classes like this."[62]

One of my female coworkers recently vacationed in Egypt, traveling with three female friends in their late twenties. People constantly harassed them for being tourists, but many men also used gendered language in the harassment, such as "Let me see your beautiful eyes," "Show off those legs," and "Talk to me Baby Spice."[63] The experience of my coworker and her friends was par for the course; nearly every foreign woman has been street harassed in Egypt according to the ECWR. A few months after the report was published, the Egyptian Tourism Ministry released a new ad campaign warning men that if they harass foreign visitors (the visitor in the clip I saw was a woman), they are not "the only one who loses. The whole country has to lose."[64] From an economic standpoint, the Egyptian government has recognized that male harassment is bad business for tourism, even if, to date, it does not seem to care if men harass Egyptian women.

But the Egyptian government soon may have an opportunity to show that they do care about Egyptian women. At the time of this writing, Georgette Kellini, a member of Parliament for the ruling National Democratic Party, said she has prepared a draft law for sexual harassment that she will introduce in the next session. The new law would legally define the harassment and would include a number of penalties designed to deter perpetrators.[65] Even with the new law, it will take a long time to see an end to harassment, especially as Egypt is ranked 126th out of 134 countries on the 2009 Global Gender Gap Index, but at least it will signify that such behavior is unacceptable and women will have the ability to press charges against their harassers.[66]

Subway Groping in Japan

Japan, particularly Tokyo, has a lurid history of and contemporary problem with men groping girls and women on the subway. There are so many men who grope that they even have a name: they are referred to by the slang term "chikan," or "idiot man."

A 1994 survey revealed that three-fourths of the women in their 20s and 30s who ride public transportation in Osaka were groped by men.[67] That same year, a self-confessed chikan published a best-selling book, *A Groper's Diary*, in which he wrote about molesting an average of a dozen women and girls a day for 26 years. He said he counted on women being too embarrassed or too afraid of accusing the wrong man to say anything. A convicted groper can be sentenced up to seven years, but few women report the assaults, including, apparently, this man's victims.[68]

In 2000, the Tokyo railway temporarily introduced women-only cars on late-night trains over the holiday season in Tokyo to "address the growing problem of drunken men groping women commuters."[69] After a 2004 survey showed that "chikans" had groped nearly 64 percent of women in their twenties and thirties on public transportation, the public transportation division introduced women-only subway cars again, this time during rush hour.[70] The government also created posters in the subway stations showing young working women scolding red-faced businessmen. The posters say both in English and in Japanese, "No Touching!"[71]

Groping attacks against women commuters continued to increase in 2006, despite the growing number of women-only subway cars.[72] That year, a news article on subway groping stated that "experts say the number of chikan has swelled simply because many do not view their actions as a crime." Yuko Kawanishi, a sociologist at Tokyo Gakugei University said, "More fundamentally, [groping] shows a distinct lack of respect for Japanese women."[73]

Groping continues to be a problem in Japan. In 2008 in Tokyo alone there were 2,000 reported groping cases, though like sexual assault in other urban areas, groping in Japan is a grossly under-reported crime. Most of the attacks occurred during morning rush hour and almost half of the women targeted were in their 20s. More than 30 percent were teenagers.[74] Grown men should (and do) know better than to grope teenage girls on their way to school.

Popular cultural oddities like the Train Café and the video game RapeLay, which allow men to actually and virtually assault young women, do little to increase men's respect for women. The Train Café is—or at least was in 2006—a members-only club for adults near Tokyo's Ikebukuro station where chikans can freely grope young women. Complete with a simulated train, each hour there is an "all-aboard" event where paying male members "board" the train together with young women whom they are free to touch and fondle. Upskirt grabbing is the only type of groping not allowed. Supposedly the establishment provides a safe outlet for men who are otherwise tempted to grope women on subways and helps keep them from doing so.[75] As this isn't a legally sanctioned way of curbing deviant behavior or considered rehabilitative sex therapy, the motive behind this space is questionable at best.

Another "outlet" for male harassment is an infamous Japanese video game called RapeLay. The game begins with a man standing on a subway platform near a girl in a sundress. On the platform, the player can summon a wind that lifts the girl's skirt, causing her to blush. Inside the subway car, the player can use the mouse to grope the girl as they stand among silent commuters. Then the player's character can corner his victim in various locations, such as a station bathroom, and engage in a series of interactive rape scenes.[76] This horrific game is banned in the United States, but not in Japan (although it is legal in the U.S. to assault and kill female prostitutes in the video game Grand Theft Auto). Unsurprisingly, in 2009, Japan was ranked number 75th in the Global Gender Gap Index.[77]

CONCLUSION

All over the world, public spaces are more restricted to women than to men. In large part, this is due to the number of men who harass women who are commuting to work or school or who are traveling or studying abroad. In some countries, there also are legal restrictions for women, while in others, a heightened risk of rape because of war or crime keeps many women inside. Last, even in "developed" countries, and ones with centuries-old recorded history, like Italy, Egypt, and Japan, street harassment can occur at alarming rates. Until street harassment ends, women will not be free to explore their world, let alone commute to school or work safely in their own community.

NOTES

1. One possible exception is Scandinavian countries. I have not come across any studies showing that street harassment occurs there (where women have the most gender equity throughout the world), nor did anyone who took my survey say they had been harassed there. I did, however, come across articles about women's fear of rape in public in Sweden and Finland. Anecdotally, an American friend who has lived in Denmark for over a year has not experienced street harassment. In the United States, men often harassed her. From my own experiences of traveling in Denmark, Sweden, and Norway (at times I was alone, other times with a female friend, and sometimes I was with my male partner), I can attest to not being harassed there.

2. Prem Dhakal, "The Sorry Side of Public Transport," My Republica, February 16, 2009, http://www.myrepublica.com/portal/index.php?action=news_details&news_id=173.

3. *USA Today*, "Mexico City Debuts Women-Only buses," January 24, 2008, http://www.usatoday.com/news/world/2008-01-24-mexicpcity-buses_N.htm.

4. MSNBC, "Mexico's Pink Taxis Cater to Fed-up Females," October 19, 2009, http://www.msnbc.msn.com/id/33385984.

5. Amnesty International, "Take Action for the Women of Juarez," n.d., http://www.amnestyusa.org/artists-for-amnesty/bordertown/take-action-for-the-women-of-juarez/page.do?id=1101544.

6. Amnesty International, "Take Action for the Women of Juarez"; see also Teresa Rodriguez, Diana Montane, and Lisa Pulitzer, *Daughters of Juarez: A True Story of Serial Murder South of the Border* (New York: Atria Books, 2007).

7. Lewis Mwanagombe, "Education-Zambia: Bicycles Help Girls Go Further," IPS, September 7, 2009, http://ipsnews.net/news.asp?idnews=48349.

8. Ibid.

9. Holly Kearl, "Want a Female Taxi Driver?" AAUW Dialog, January 8, 2009, http://blog-aauw.org/2009/01/08/want-a-female-taxi-driver.

10. Radio Free Europe, "Russia to Introduce Women-Only Train Compartments," November 15, 2006, http://www.rferl.org/content/Article/1072739.html.

11. Jessica Valenti, "Is Segregation the Only Answer to Sexual Harassment?" *Guardian*, August 3, 2007, http://www.guardian.co.uk/lifeandstyle/2007/aug/03/healthandwellbeing.gender.

12. Patricia Cline Cohen, "Safety and Danger: Women on American Public Transport, 1750–1850," in *Gendered Domains: Rethinking Public and Private in Women's History*, ed. Dorothy O. Helly and Susan M. Reverby (Ithaca, NY: Cornell University Press, 1992), 121.

13. Catherine Smith and Cynthia Greig, *Manly Maidens, Cowgirls, and Other Renegades, Women in Pants* (New York: Harry N. Abrams, Inc, 2003), 114.

14. Mei-Ling McNamara, "Travel Tips for Women Travelers: Safely Experience the Freedom of the Unaccompanied Female," TravelChannel.com, n.d., http://www.travelchannel.com/Travel_Ideas/Girlfriend_Getaways/ci.Travel_Tips_for_Women_Travelers.artTravelIdeasFmt?vgnextfmt=artTravelIdeasFmt.

15. Sara Savage, "Study Abroad Safety Tips for Female Students," IIE-Passport, n.d., http://info.iiepassport.org/tipsforfemalestudents.html; see also David S. Katz, "Personal Safety for Women Traveling Abroad on Business," WITI, 2004, http://www.witi.com/careers/2004/travelsafety.php; see also "Safety Tips for Students Studying Abroad," University of Chicago, n.d., http://study-abroad.uchicago.edu/safety.html; see also "A Woman's Guide to Safe Travel," Authentic Ireland Travel, n.d., http://www.authenticireland.com/womens+guide+to+safe+travel.

16. Savage, http://info.iiepassport.org/tipsforfemalestudents.html.

17. McNamara, http://www.travelchannel.com/Travel_Ideas/Girlfriend_Getaways/ci.Travel_Tips_for_Women_Travelers.artTravelIdeasFmt?vgnextfmt=artTravelIdeasFmt.

18. J. S. (a 2008 survey respondent) e-mail message to author, August 18, 2009.

19. L.G. (a 2008 survey respondent) e-mail message to author, August 18, 2009.

20. Social Institutions and Gender Index, "Gender Equality and Social Institutions in Saudi Arabia," n.d., http://genderindex.org/country/saudi-arabia.

21. E.A. Doumato, Women's Rights in the Middle East and North Africa: Citizenship and Justice – Saudi Arabia Country Report (Washington, DC: Freedom House Inc., 2005), cited on "Gender Equality and Social Institutions in Saudi Arabia."

22. Ibid.

23. Associated Press, "Saudi Arabia's Religious Police Undergoes Change Slowly," July 7, 2009, http://www.miamiherald.com/news/world/AP/story/1138310.html.

24. Social Institutions and Gender Index, "Gender Equality and Social Institutions in Kuwait," n.d., http://genderindex.org/country/Kuwait.

25. Social Institutions and Gender Index, "Gender Equality and Social Institutions in Yemen," n.d., http://genderindex.org/country/yemen.

26. Social Institutions and Gender Index, "Gender Equality and Social Institutions in United Arab Emirates," n.d., http://genderindex.org/country/united-arab-emirates.

27. Ramsay M. Harik and Elsa Marston, *Women in the Middle East: Tradition and Changes* (New York: Franklin Watts, a Division of Grolier Publishing, 1996), 123–124.

28. Ibid., 124.

29. Ibid., 127.

30. Doumato, http://genderindex.org/country/saudi-arabia.

31. The BBC, "Saudi Cleric Favours One-Eye Veil," October 3, 2008, http://news.bbc.co.uk/2/hi/middle_east/7651231.stm.

32. "Gender Equality and Social Institutions in United Arab Emirates."

33. Social Institutions and Gender Index, "Gender Equality and Social Institutions in Egypt," n.d., http://genderindex.org/country/egypt-arab-rep.

34. Social Institutions and Gender Index, "Gender Equality and Social Institutions in Tunisia," n.d., http://genderindex.org/country/tunisia.

35. Revolutionary Association of the Women of Afghanistan, "On the Situation of Afghan Women," n.d., http://www.rawa.org/wom-view.htm; see also John W. Warnock, "The Status of Women in Karzai's Afghanistan," Global Research, April 14, 2009, http://www.globalresearch.ca/index.php?context=va&aid=13184; see also Social Institutions and Gender Index, "Gender Equality and Social Institutions in Afghanistan," n.d., http://genderindex.org/country/afghanistan.

36. Harik and Marston, 133–134.

37. Ellen Knickmeyer, "In Egypt, Some Women Say That Veils Increase Harassment," *Washington Post,* August 17, 2008, http://www.washingtonpost.com/wp-dyn/content/article/2008/08/16/AR2008081602063_pf.html.

38. Ibid., see also Cynthia Johnston, "Two-thirds of Egyptian Men Harass Women?" *Reuters,* July 17, 2008, http://www.reuters.com/article/email/idUSL1732581120080717; see also Magdi Abdelhadi, "Egypt's sexual harassment 'cancer,'" The BBC, July 18, 2008, http://news.bbc.co.uk/2/hi/middle_east/7514567.stm.

39. Manar Ammar and Joseph Mayton, "A Majority of Cairo Women Face Street Harassment," Alternet.org, October 21, 2008, http://www.alternet.org/reproductivejustice/103130/a_majority_of_cairo_women_face_street_harassment.

40. Ali Saeed and Nadia Al-Sakkaf, "Sexual Harassment Deters Women from Outdoor Activities," *Yemen Times,* January 21, 2009, http://www.yementimes.com/article.shtml?i=1226&p=report&a=2.

41. *Ibid.*

42. Lizzy Davies, "Why Not Ban Full Veil, Says French Government Spokesman," *Guardian*, June 19, 2009, http://www.guardian.co.uk/world/2009/jun/19/veil-burka-france-muslim-women; see also The BBC, "Viewpoints: Europe and the Headscarf," February 10, 2004, http://news.bbc.co.uk/2/hi/3459963.stm.

43. "Security Council Demands Immediate and Complete Halt to Acts of Sexual Violence," United Nations Security Council, June 19, 2008, http://www.un.org/News/Press/docs//2008/sc9364.doc.htm.

44. Social Institutions and Gender Index, "Gender Equality and Social Institutions in Sudan," n.d., http://genderindex.org/country/sudan.

45. Social Institutions and Gender Index, "Gender Equality and Social Institutions in Iraq," n.d., http://genderindex.org/country/iraq.

46. Sarah K. Chynoweth and Erin M. Patrick, "Sexual Violence during Firewood Collection: Income-Generation as Protection in Displaced Settings," in *Gender-Based Violence*, ed. Geraldine Terry and Joanna Hoare (Oxford: Oxfam Great Britain, 2007), 44–45.

47. Ibid., 46.

48. Ibid., 45.

49. Amnesty International, "Colombia: 'Scarred Bodies, Hidden Crimes": Sexual Violence against Women in the Armed Conflict," 2004, http://www.amnesty.org/en/library/asset/AMR23/040/2004/en/eeb9c46a-d598-11dd-bb24-1fb85fe8fa05/amr230402004en.html.

50. Ibid.

51. Ezra Fieser, "Guatemala Slowly Confronts Widespread Rape of Women," *Christian Science Monitor*, November 20, 2009, http://www.csmonitor.com/World/Americas/2009/1120/p90s01-woam.html.

52. Ezra Fieser, "Guatemalan Gangs: Swagger, Tattoos, But No Rules," *Global Post*, November 23, 2009, http://www.globalpost.com/dispatch/the-americas/091109/guatemala-gang-culture-rape?page=0,1.

53. Adam Blenford, "Guatemala's Epidemic of Killing," *BBC*, June 9, 2005, http://news.bbc.co.uk/2/hi/americas/4074880.stm.

54. Emanuela Guano, "Respectable Ladies and Uncouth Men: The Performative Politics of Class and Gender in the Public Realm of an Italian City," *Journal of American Folklore* 120 (475), 54–56.

55. Ibid., 52–57.

56. Julia Llewellyn Smith, "If We Put Every Man Who Touched a Woman's Bum in Jail, There'd Be No Room for the Drug Dealers," *Telegraph*, July 13, 2003, http://www.telegraph.co.uk/news/worldnews/europe/italy/1435997/If-we-put-every-man-who-touched-a-womans-bum-in-jail-thered-be-no-room-for-the-drug-dealers.html.

57. Jason Horowitz, "World Briefing, Europe: Italy: Court Rules 'Bottom Pinching' Is Assault," *New York Times*, January 20, 2005, http://query.nytimes.com/gst/fullpage.html?res=9507E3DB1038F933A15752C0A9639C8B63.

58. Smith.

59. Lina Wardani, "Egypt Voices: Sexual Harassment," *BBC*, September 3, 2008, http://news.bbc.co.uk/2/hi/middle_east/7593765.stm#nancy.

60. Cynthia Johnson, "Two-thirds of Egyptian Men Harass Women?" *Reuters*, July 17, 2008, http://www.reuters.com/article/email/idUSL17325 81120080717.

61. The BBC, "Egyptian Sexual Harasser Jailed," October 21, 2009, http://news.bbc.co.uk/2/hi/africa/7682951.stm.

62. Christian Fraser, "Egyptian Women Learn to Fight Back," *BBC*, March 18, 2009, http://news.bbc.co.uk/2/hi/middle_east/7936071.stm.

63. Kate Farrar, "Baby Spice to Burkas," AAUW Dialog, September 24, 2009, http://blog-aauw.org/2009/09/24/baby-spice-to-burkas.

64. Julie Marquet, "Fighting Sexual Harassment in Egypt," *The Observers*, April 14, 2009, http://observers.france24.com/en/content/20090414-fighting-sexual-harrassment-egypt-women-rights.

65. Bikya Masr, "Egypt: Sexual Harassment Law Coming?" Bikya Masr, November 2, 2009, http://bikyamasr.com/?p=5417; see also Joseph Mayton, "Egypt Puts Tougher Sex-Harassment Law on Agenda," *Women's E News*, February 4, 2009, http://www.womensenews.org/story/the-world/090204/egypt-puts-tougher-sex-harassment-law-agenda.

66. World Economic Forum, "Global Gender Gap Index 2009," http://www.weforum.org/pdf/gendergap/rankings2009.pdf.

67. Mari Yamaguchi, "Japanese Women Must Run Gantlet—Gropers are Common In Crowded Train Cars," *Seattle Times*, October 23, 1994, http://community.seattletimes.nwsource.com/archive/?date=19941023&slug=1937419.

68. *Ibid.*

69. "Tokyo Trains Tackle Groping Problem," *BBC News*, December 5, 2000, http://news.bbc.co.uk/2/hi/asia-pacific/1055599.stm.

70. "Japan Tries Women-Only Train Cars to Stop Groping," *ABC News*, June 10, 2005, http://abcnews.go.com/GMA/International/story?id=803965&CMP=OTC-RSSFeeds0312.

71. Veronica Chambers, *Kickboxing Geishas: How Modern Japanese are Changing Their Nation.* (New York: Free Press, 2007), 9–10.

72. James, "Train Molesting Remains a Major Problem!" Japan Probe, August 22, 2006, http://www.japanprobe.com/?p=413.

73. Mariko Sanchanta, "Train Operators Fight Groping by Creating Women-Only Cars," *Los Angeles Times*, January 2, 2006, http://articles.latimes.com/2006/jan/02/business/ft-subways2.

74. Takahiro Fukada, "In Anonymous Packed Train Lurk Gropers," *Japan Times*, August 18, 2009, http://search.japantimes.co.jp/cgi-bin/nn2009 0818i1.html.

75. Terry Ng, "Japan's Simulated Train Café—Groping Allowed," Kineda, January 25, 2006, http://www.kineda.com/japans-train-cafe-groping-allowed/; see also "Chikan Choo Choo," Japundit Blog, September 28, 2006, http://blog.japundit.com/archives/2006/09/28/3627.

76. Leigh Alexander, "And You Thought Grand Theft Auto Was Bad," Slate.com, March 9, 2009, http://www.slate.com/id/2213073.

77. World Economic Forum, "Global Gender Gap Index 2009," http://www.weforum.org/pdf/gendergap/rankings2009.pdf.

_____ *Chapter 5* _____

Women's Views: Harassing or Complimentary Behavior?

Street harassment, by definition, is unwelcome behavior. It encompasses actions and comments by unknown men that make women feel annoyed, insulted, threatened, and scared in public. But a complicated aspect of street harassment and efforts to end it is that the exact actions and comments make women feel harassed can vary by person and even by scenario. As two women who took my 2008 survey wrote:

There are certain behaviors that are always unacceptable (e.g., flashing, masturbating, making racist/sexist/homophobic comments), but other interactions can be acceptable or unacceptable depending on the context, intent, and persons involved.
                    —20–29-year-old heterosexual white woman in Texas

I will be honest and say that if a man is very attractive and he is excessively staring at me I am not offended but flattered. If he is a guy I am not attracted to especially an older man and he is staring and says hello I am offended. But what is always unacceptable for me attractive or not is when they whistle or make comments about my appearance.
                    —30–39-year-old heterosexual Latina in Bronx, New York

Thus, a comment that may seem sexist to one woman may not to another and actions by one man in a specific scenario may feel threatening or annoying to a woman while the same actions in a different scenario may not to the same woman.

Humans are complex, and there are numerous factors that contribute to how a woman views men's attention in public. Factors such as racial dynamics and a woman's sexual orientation impact women's views; for example, a lesbian is less likely than a heterosexual woman to view male attention as complimentary, while a white woman who has internalized racist stereotypes is more likely to interpret comments from a man of color as harassment than if they came from a white man. If the harassing man is handsome or appears wealthy or is of a woman's same race and class (or a "better" one), a woman may feel his comments or actions are complimentary or at least inoffensive compared to the same or similar comments by men who are not. Similarly, age differences between harassers and the woman can change how she feels about comments, and she may see an interaction as creepy if the man is much older or disturbing if it is a young boy compared to someone her age. A woman's past experiences with physical assault also can impact her views.[1]

In her study of street harassment in Indianapolis, Carol Brooks Gardner also found that women who viewed male harassment as a legitimate form of courtship and men's natural behavior toward attractive women tended to be apolitical and traditional.[2] Meanwhile, women who had a feminist or political framework toward street harassment tended to view it as unacceptable and similar to the sexual harassment women experience in school or in the workplace.[3] They saw violence in the street on a continuum with violence women experience in the home.[4]

This chapter explores four other significant factors that contribute to how a woman views the attention of men in public and whether or not she sees it as harassment: the type and severity of the man's actions or comments, the frequency of harassment a woman regularly experiences, the woman's feelings of safety at the time, and how they interpret men's motivation for the actions. At the end of this chapter, acceptable versus unacceptable behavior will be clearer.

TYPE AND SEVERITY

The type and severity of men's actions and comments affect how women view them. In her research, legal scholar and author of journal article "A Radical Reshaping of the Law: Interpreting and Remedying Street Harassment," Tiffanie Heben found that women interpreted physical acts, sexually explicit references, and racial or homophobic slurs as severe behaviors that upset them most; sexual innuendoes as moderately severe behaviors; and unnecessary comments and stares as the least severe behavior and those which upset them the least.[5] Through my research, I found that the majority of women view smiles, hellos, and gender-neutral comments, such as a remark on the weather, as acceptable and even enjoyable. On the other end, I have yet to find a woman who views insulting or threatening language, stalking, masturbation, or touching as flattering or acceptable behavior. As to the actions and comments that fall in between, women generally do not like sexually explicit language, and many women do not like their looks being evaluated—positively or negatively—by a stranger in public, be it through comments, kissy noises, whistles, or honks. One heterosexual teenage white woman in Columbus, Ohio, who took my 2008 survey wrote, "There have been multiple times when someone has honked at me when I was walking down the street. It always makes me feel like I'm a piece of meat, and not a human being. I've never noticed men getting honked at."

One of the questions of my 2008 informal online survey asked people how they felt about twenty-five specific forms of interactions in public with strangers. Respondents could select emotions such as flattered, grateful, happy, neutral, annoyed, ashamed, scared, and angry. Respondents could choose as many emotions as they wanted per action to recognize that any given action may elicit multiple feelings, as well as to acknowledge that the circumstances may prompt different feelings; therefore the percentages do not add up to 100. Just over 800 women answered this question. Here are six of the more commons forms of interactions with strangers and how women tend to view them:

- Smiles at them: 49 percent felt happy, 48 percent were neutral, 22 percent were flattered, and 18 percent were annoyed

- Says hello to them: 52 percent felt neutral, 45 percent were happy, 20 percent were annoyed, and 10 percent were flattered

- Makes small talk with them (i.e. about the weather): 58 percent felt neutral, 38 percent were annoyed, and 29 percent were happy

- Whistles at them: 62 percent felt annoyed, 40 percent were angry, 26 percent were insulted, 12 percent were scared, and 8 percent were flattered

- Tries to get their attention or a date or phone number: 62 percent felt annoyed, 23 percent were flattered, 21 percent were angry, 16 percent were neutral, and 10 percent were insulted

- Comments on their appearance: 52 percent felt annoyed, 37 percent were angry, 28 percent were insulted, 21 percent were flattered, 16 percent felt ashamed/guilty, 16 percent were neutral, and 13 percent were scared.

Having someone smile, say hello, or make small talk about a topic like the weather were the actions that made the most women feel happy, flattered, or neutral and the least annoyed. These actions also made fewer than 5 percent of women feel scared. Also of note, actions like having a door held open for women, being offered help with a heavy bag or box, and having someone offer to give up their seat on a bus or subway made most women feel grateful (around 50 percent for each), happy (20 to 33 percent for each), and neutral (19 to 33 percent for each); less than 1 percent of women felt angry.

On the other hand, most women reported feeling annoyed or angry at evaluative behavior, such as whistling or comments on their appearance. A portion of respondents felt it could be flattering, though they often indicated that they drew the line before sexually explicit language. So while "You look beautiful" was acceptable to them, "Nice tits" or "Great ass" was not. Notably, 81 percent of women respondents had been the target of sexually explicit comments (and 59 percent had been the object of the comments more than five times), and most said it made them angry, scared, insulted, and annoyed. Less than 1 percent said sexually explicit comments made them feel happy or flattered.

Several women who took my survey were clear about this distinction when they said what they liked. A heterosexual Asian American woman in her thirties in Chicago, Illinois, said, "I don't mind smiling, hellos, chatting, compliments, or even flirting. However when the flirting gets to be aggressive (i.e., kissing noises, staring) that's when I find it starts getting offensive." Another survey respondent, a heterosexual white woman in her twenties in New York City, said, "If I think someone is good-looking and I'm attracted to them, then I might feel happy if they flirt with me or make a suggestive comment. If I'm clearly uncomfortable or scared, or don't respond, then I think it becomes unacceptable to continue making comments. It depends on the nature of the comment too: 'nice ass' is very different than 'You have a nice smile' or something."

Several women wrote comments to a 2008 CNN article on catcalling about what evaluative male behaviors they felt were complimentary. Importantly, they too, noted other behavior they had experienced that was not complimentary. One woman, Lisa wrote, "A while back a guy drove by me in the Target parking lot and yelled, 'I think you're beautiful, will you marry me?!' I couldn't help but laugh and feel flattered and he kept driving and there was no harm. (Wearing a wool coat by the way) . . . There's definitely a difference between expressing admiration in a flattering way versus threatening sexual advance. I just try to ignore most of it and be aware of my surroundings."[6] Another woman, Brenna said, "It's not harassment unless they touch you. I like the compliment. I get tired of being the smart girl all the time."[7]

Very few women (less than 10 percent, if at all), said that behaviors like leering, vulgar gestures, sexually explicit comments, masturbators, stalkers, or sexual touching, made them feel a positive emotion such as flattered or happy. Instead, nearly all women picked angry, annoyed, scared, or insulted for those actions. Here are a few examples of stranger interaction:

- Being followed: 68 percent felt scared, 43 percent were angry, 17 percent were annoyed, and 10 percent were insulted.
- Being leered at: 56 percent felt angry, 46 percent were annoyed, 46 percent were scared, and 25 percent were insulted.
- Having an explicit comment made to them: 62 percent felt angry, 35 percent were scared, 33 percent were insulted, 31 percent were angry, and 13 percent were ashamed.
- Having a sexist comment made to them: 69 percent felt angry, 40 percent were insulted, 36 percent were annoyed, and 15 percent were scared.
- Having a vulgar gesture made to them: 61 percent felt angry, 32 percent were annoyed, 32 percent were insulted, and 27 percent were scared.
- Being touched or grabbed in a sexual way: 50 percent felt angry, 44 percent were scared, 18 percent were insulted, 16 percent were annoyed, and 12 percent were ashamed.

Here are two stories women shared in my survey illustrating these feelings from women who took my survey:

A couple of times walking to the train station I have been flashed by these nasty, hobo looking white men. When one guy took off his underwear and waved hello at me . . . the incident left me feeling more angry than scared. It was disgusting.

—30–39-year-old heterosexual African American
woman in Bronx, New York

I went to the Dollar Store to do some shopping . . . and noticed two men following me around the store. I finished my shopping . . . as I walked to leave the store, they cut across the aisle and also headed for the door. I thought to myself, "What the hell? Are these fuckers really going to follow me out?" Sure enough they did. They followed me to my car, one in front of the other. . . . This story stands out the most because it was the time that I was the most scared. I was totally preparing myself to experience and defend myself in an assault in that parking lot.

—20–29-year-old heterosexual white woman
in Raleigh, North Carolina

While I think very few people would argue that severe forms of male harassment are complimentary, more than a few people may not realize how often those more severe forms of harassment occur or how much just one bad harassment or assault incident can impact a woman's whole sense of safety in public and the strategies she uses to try to stay safe. When a man first approaches a woman or calls out to her, in many circumstances she does not know if he will say something and leave or if he will then try to touch her or follow her or ask her personal questions. For example, in CNN commenter Lisa's story above, she said that since the man who hollered at her drove on, no harm was done. But clearly she was worried he would not drive on and would do something. Since he did not, she felt comfortable saying it was flattering.

Also of note, there are many men that become insulting if a woman does not react the way the men want, as these two stories from commenters to my blog Stop Street Harassment show. One woman wrote, "I'm tired of the street harassment and especially the 'fuck you then, bitch' comments that follow me ignoring them. . . . I don't respond to horns honking and I'm not going to walk over to your car. I'm not going to yell back across streets to respond to you."[8] Another woman said, "I remember when I was about 17, me and my girlfriends were walking home. These guys were in the schoolyard playing ball. One of the guys tried talking to us. We were not interested and kept walking. Well we got called all kinds of bitches and hoe's. We just kept walking."[9]

The inability to gauge the total severity of an incident until after it is over may make some women simultaneously feel flattered at the attention, but also worried that it may go further. If it does not go further, then women may be relieved and say that it was a harmless compliment. The reality of severe street harassment and the chance that "complimentary" harassment can escalate into severe harassment must be taken into consideration; it reveals that overall street harassment is not as harmless as it appears if one only considers the stereotype of a man yelling, "Hey Gorgeous," out his car window to a woman in a skirt walking by. The sheer amount of harassment women experience also affects how they view it.

FREQUENCY OF HARASSMENT

Why are some women harassed daily while others are only harassed a few times in their life? I believe that there are a number of contributing factors. If a woman lives in a community where she knows everyone, she will not experience street harassment there, since street harassment occurs between strangers. A woman in a rural area probably will experience less frequent street harassment than a woman in a city because she will encounter far fewer people on any given day. Older women tend to face less harassment than younger women, perhaps because they are seen as less vulnerable and because they are not as sexually objectified. Women who are not in public often or who are not often alone there will experience less harassment than women who are in public often or who often are alone. Women who drive are usually harassed less than women who walk or take public transportation; however, they can still face harassment walking to or from their car or at stop lights. Women who experience other forms of harassment, such as racism or homophobia or transphobia also may experience an increase in street harassment compared to women who do not. Last, women who live in areas with more gender equity likely will face less harassment than those who live in places with less gender equity.[10]

My informal survey results suggest a direct correlation between how often women are harassed and how they view it. Since "comments on one's appearance" is the type of harassment most commonly in contention, I filtered my survey responses through that experience to see how the volume of such comments affected how women viewed them. Two hundred and five women said that strangers comment on their appearance on a daily or weekly basis. The most common response—and they could select more than one—for how those comments made them feel was angry (55 percent). A close second was annoyed (54 percent), followed by insulted (31 percent), flattered (19 percent), ashamed (18 percent), scared (15 percent), and happy (10 percent). Notably, this question does not ask them which emotion they feel the most, which would further illuminate how women felt. The majority of these women also experienced many other forms of harassment on a daily/weekly basis, including excessive leering (72 percent), whistling (55 percent), kissing noises (51 percent), sexist comments (49 percent), and sexually explicit comments (25 percent). About 73 percent had been sexually touched at least once and 43 percent had been assaulted. The most commonly selected emotion for how respondents felt about these other behaviors also was angry, followed by annoyed or scared for behaviors like sexual touching and assault. Less than two percent of women said any of these behaviors were flattering, except for whistling, which seven percent deemed flattering.

On the other end of the spectrum, 89 women said strangers had commented on their appearance as few as one to five times. The most common response among these women, as it was among women who frequently experience such comments, was annoyed (48 percent), and followed by flattered (24 percent), angry (22 percent), insulted (20 percent), scared (15 percent), and ashamed (13 percent). In contrast with other women, very few women experienced other forms of harassing behavior on a daily, or weekly or even monthly basis. Only 1 percent said they were leered at daily or weekly, while 38 percent said they had experienced that one to five times. Only four percent had been whistled at daily/weekly, while 43 percent said that happened one to five times. No women said they were the target of sexually explicit comments daily or weekly, while 58 percent said they had never been the target of it. About 26 percent had been sexually touched and eight percent had been assaulted.

For another example, 153 women said they were whistled at by strangers on a daily or weekly basis. They felt annoyed (62 percent), followed by angry (51 percent), insulted (34 percent), scared (16 percent), ashamed (12 percent), and then flattered (6 percent). In contrast, 111 women said strangers have whistled at them only one to five times. Of these women, the most common feeling was still annoyance (58 percent), followed by anger (31 percent), and insulted (16 percent), but over twice as many women said they felt flattered (14 percent) than the women who were regularly whistled at.

These comparisons suggest that women who are regularly harassed— be it daily, week or monthly—are less likely to see comments on their appearance or whistling as flattering compared to women who have had it happen a handful of times. Annoyance, however, is always among the most commonly cited responses.

SENSE OF SAFETY

Whether or not women feel safe when a man approaches them or calls out to them significantly impacts how they feel about it. What can initially feel harmless can become menacing if a woman realizes there is no one else around and it is getting dark. She may then wonder why she was singled out and if she can get away safely. A story submission to my street harassment blog from a young woman in Morgantown, North Carolina, illustrates this point. The woman was leaving a movie theater in broad daylight when a car full of men started shouting at her: "HEY GIRL HEY HEY HEY HEY WHAT'S YOUR NAME HEY LET ME HIT IT." At first she laughed at them, she said, but then she realized the parking lot was empty and so she picked up her pace and held her keys as a weapon as she went to her car. She said, "I've never been followed before, but I've also never been catcalled while completely alone outside with not a soul in sight. It was scary, but I felt like I at least had daylight on my side. I got in my car and locked the doors and felt better after that. . . . It was funny at first, then scary when I realized I was so alone."[11]

In one 2008 survey question, I asked respondents to mark what factors on a scale of one (nonthreatening) to seven (most threatening) made interactions with unknown men in public feel threatening versus non-threatening. Of the 623 women responses, by far the most threatening circumstances were being alone—73 percent marked a seven (94 percent marked at least a five)—and being in a deserted area—74 percent said a seven (92 percent said at least a five). A man approaching a woman when she is alone in a deserted area will likely make her feel threatened. Of course, if he does not end up threatening or hurting her, she may relax, but at the initial approach or at the thought of what could happen, she likely will feel threatened.

Other factors that made interactions more threatening to women included:

- Darkness (58 percent marked that as a seven, and 34 percent more marked it as a five or six).
- If the person is larger than them (50 percent marked it as a seven, and 42 percent more marked it as a five or six).
- If they are in an unfamiliar area (40 percent marked it as a seven and an additional 43 percent marked it as a five or six).
- If the person is older than them (83 percent said at least a four).
- If the person is in a car while they are on foot (57 percent marked at least a five).

Women, however, felt less threatened when faced with the opposite circumstances. For example, most of them said they feel less or not threatened if they are with several friends (80 percent marked a one, two, or three), with their significant other (66 percent marked a one, two, or three), or if they are in a populated area (68 percent marked a one, two, or three). One woman who took my 2008 survey wrote, "Once when I was on the subway a man revealed himself to me. . . . This was pretty scary. I'm so happy I was with my friend and not all alone!"

As many girls and women know, harassers tend to target them when they are alone and when the man is in a position of power (such as being bigger than his target or in a car while she is on foot). In my survey I asked respondents to indicate on a scale of one (least) to seven (most) in what circumstances men harass them the most: 92 percent of women said they are harassed the most when they are alone (80 percent said a seven and another 12 percent said a five or a six). Combined then, my informal survey results show most women experience harassment when they are alone, and about 94 percent say that being alone makes street harassment feel very threatening. It also shows that since men tend to harass women who are alone, most male allies do not know that other men routinely harass women, and many women may not realize that other women are harassed either.

INTENT OF THE MEN

Women tend to interpret men's motives for harassment two ways: Either the men are complimenting the woman's attractiveness or they are disrespecting women and purposely harassing them. CNN commenter Laura said, "As a woman, I have absolutely no problem with non-lewd catcalls. . . . In fact, I find being whistled at very flattering. I take the time to look good, and when someone takes notice, why shouldn't I appreciate it? . . . Just keep it clean and you'll never hear women like me whine about it."[12] On the flip side, a heterosexual Latina in her thirties in New York City, who took my 2008 survey, wrote, "It's not really about any one incident, but about the constant, daily wearing away of your sense of safety. Every day I am reminded that we live in a world where women are a commodity, because every day, I am treated like a piece of public property."

There are many reasons why women may interpret men's actions as being driven by her attractiveness and several street harassment scholars have theorized on the topic. For example, scholar Deirdre Davis wrote in an article "The Harm that Has No Name: Street Harassment, Embodiment, and African American Women" that women may interpret men's harassment as complimentary or harmless because society tells them that it is.[13] In her legal thesis for the University of British Columbia, Norma Anne Oshynko wrote about how women are made into sexual objects when men harass them and consequently, women are forced to see themselves as sexual objects. Women thus may accept that their worth is based on how attractive they are, and positive male attention in public makes women feel attractive and therefore worthwhile.[14] When studying whether or not people in the California Bay Area supported the regulation of offensive public speech, legal scholar Laura Beth Nielsen found that people generally understood that there is no permissible reason for racially charged speech, but some argued that sexual banter on the street between strangers may lead to a romantic relationship and should be allowed, implying such speech is complimentary.[15]

The results of a 2007 report by the American Psychology Association (APA) Task Force on the Sexualization of Girls further theorize on the topic. The Task Force found that, overwhelmingly, girls are sexualized by every form of media, parents and teachers, their peers, and themselves. Such sexualization can help women believe that that is where their worth lies. "Girls and young women are repeatedly encouraged to look and dress in specific ways to look sexy for men, a phenomenon labeled 'costuming for seduction.' . . . Repeated attempts are made, in the form of advice about hairstyles, cosmetics, diets, and exercise, to remake the reader [of women's magazines] as an object of male desire. Nearly everything girls and women are encouraged to do in the line of self-improvement is geared toward gaining the attention of men," the report stated.[16]

The Task Force also found severe consequences to the sexualization of girls. It noted, "Frequent exposure to media images that sexualize girls and women affects how girls conceptualize femininity and sexuality. Girls and young women who more frequently consume or engage with mainstream media content offer stronger endorsement of sexual stereotypes that depict women as sexual objects. They also place appearance and physical attractiveness at the center of women's value."[17] Street harassment, for better or worse, is male attention, so if that is a woman's goal she may interpret such actions as testament to her attractiveness.

All over mainstream media, harassment is portrayed as driven by men's intent to compliment a woman's looks. From Michael Jackson's "The Way You Make Me Feel" to Katy Perry's video for

"Starstrukk," street harassment is depicted as complimentary and something women seek out or at least like. Even cartoons I saw growing up did this, from the girl mouse in Tom & Jerry to the girl dog in Pluto, to the nurse in Animaniacs, the female characters are portrayed as voluptuous and made-up, they'd walk suggestively and look like they enjoyed the male's whistles and calls of "Helloooo nurse." Not all female characters liked the harassment, but it was still portrayed as occurring due to the female's attractiveness, like the female cat who is constantly chased by the skunk Pepe Le Pew and the women in Jim Henson's Muppets whom the character Animal chased.

Numerous women who now do not find harassment complimentary might have used to because of the strength of our socialization. In her anti-street harassment documentary, filmmaker, producer, and social justice activist Maggie Hadleigh-West said, "For as long as I can remember, strange men and boys have said things to me on the streets." She said she used to think it was flattering, but later she came to see it as a judgment and resented them imposing themselves into her life.[18] Similarly, one of my 2008 survey respondents wrote, "I used to smile and wave when I was honked/whistled at, because I thought I should take what I can get, but after getting some self-confidence, I realized that those kinds of interactions aren't worth shit, and they're damaging. That's not the kind of attention I want or deserve. I flip them off now."

This brings me to women who interpret the intentions of men who harass them as driven by disrespect. Many street harassment scholars hold this point of view themselves. Bowman, Fogg-Davis, and Langelan have each argued that the intention of men who street harass is power, as with sexual harassment at work or school, not a desire to compliment a woman's attractiveness.[19] Langelan makes the point that the difference between sincere compliments and harassment is the use of power by saying, "When the recipient has no choice in the encounter, or has reason to fear the repercussions if she declines, the interaction has moved out of the realm of . . . courtship into the ugly arena of intimidation and aggression. Labeling sexual harassment as an inept form of courtship is a convenient fabrication to mask the abuse of power involved, a way to cloud and obscure the real dynamics of harassment."[20]

In Nielsen's study of street harassment in the Bay Area of California, 78 percent of the women surveyed reported that sexually suggestive comments constitute a social problem and they often connected the speech to "broader systems of gender hierarchy in society. They see this kind of speech as an aspect of a larger social problem."[21]

Because few men are street harassed because of their gender; whistled at; hounded for their phone number, name, or a date; or touched, or raped in public, while many women are, street harassment is a sign of gender inequality. Many men who harass women say their intent is to compliment them, but why do they usually not "compliment" women who are accompanied by other men and often only do it when a woman is alone? Why do they tend to object to other men "complimenting" their female significant other (if applicable), female friends, or female family members? Why do some men grow hostile and violent when women do not thank them and act flattered? Why do they feel compelled to compliment women at all? Rarely are they expecting a date. Many times they do not even wait to see a woman's reaction as they fly by in their car or as they turn to start harassing the next woman. They are doing it to exert their power, to entertain their friends, to relieve boredom, or to demonstrate that they can evaluate a complete stranger to her face, just because she is a woman.[22]

Numerous women who took my 2008 survey spoke to issues of gender equality and the disrespect men show them when they discussed their views of men's attention. Here are a few of their thoughts.

For me, a strange man treating me differently than he would if I were accompanied by a man/older person/etc., i.e. someone he would respect and not view in a sexual way is street harassment. A woman should be treated the same as a man when it is someone the man does not know on the street.

The line is drawn [between what is acceptable and not] when I make it clear that I am not interested in sexual advances and that is not respected. Or [the line is drawn] when I am treated differently because of my assumed race or sex.

I hate always being harassed by men on the street: staring at me, making comments, even trying to grab me. I feel like an animal. I hate it, and hate that people think it's acceptable.

It's the everyday stupid comments, kissy noises and Hey, sweetheart's that wear me down and create a culture where I don't feel comfortable striking up a pleasant conversation with a stranger on the bus.

Various bloggers have written eloquently on this topic too, including the following:

I feel like only in a culture where women are taught that the way they look is their main worth, would anyone call heckling from a random dude you don't know on the street, a compliment.[23]

—Feministing.com

It is not a "compliment" to be cat-called, to be reduced to a walking sexual object that requires only a whistle of appreciation before its panties drop and its legs spread. You want to give me a compliment? Have a damn *conversation* with me.[24]

—Heartless Doll

[Harassing men] will do it to you no matter what you're wearing, because it's not a compliment. I can understand why this woman [someone cited in a CNN article who believes catcalls are complimentary] is deluding herself—it's both flattering to imagine you're so hot men are inspired to passion by the mere sight of you and it also helps protect the brain from realizing how many men out there just really hate you—but I'm sure she's not unaware of those times when the cat-calling occurs when there are no other people around and you find yourself grabbing for a weapon or your cell phone. Because it's a threat in many cases, or at bare minimum a reminder to random women that the cat-caller feels entitled to control their experience of being outside the house.[25]

—Alternet.org

This is something mainly done to women who are on their own, and frequently who are on their own at night. Put slightly differently: It's not an all-purpose, if somewhat crass, appreciation of beauty. It's only done when women are most vulnerable, and the guy—often in a group—is utterly safe. It's about intimidation, and, more fundamentally, changing the power balance of a non-interaction."[26]

—The American Prospect

I agree. Most men engage in harassment without any intent of complimenting the woman or of complimenting her in a respectful way. And telling a woman she has beautiful legs or whistling at her is not a respectful compliment. It is treating the woman like a sex object that anyone has the right to evaluate just because she is in public.

CONCLUSION

How and why women view street harassment—and what they feel constitutes harassing behavior—is one of the most contentious points in street harassment debates, and it is an area in which much more research is needed to better understand the issue. Most women do not like most forms of street harassment, but actions like sexist comments, touching, and following are not often discussed. From my research, I have found that the media—and society in general— tend to suggest that street harassment such as comments on one's appearance, whistling, and being asked for one's phone number is complimentary to women and, unless a woman comes to another conclusion, either through her experiences or from learning more about issues like women's rights, she may hold that view her whole life. Many men hold it, too. But even among the women who say those actions can be flattering, they still usually feel less flattered if comments happen a lot or in conjunction with more severe forms of harassment (such as touching or following) or if it happens when they feel unsafe. Later chapters discuss guidelines for interactions with strangers that take these factors into consideration.

NOTES

1. Tiffanie Heben, "Reshaping of the Law: Interpreting and Remedying Street Harassment," *South California's Review of Law and Women's Studies* 4, no. 1 (1994), 190–192; see also Carol Brooks Gardner, *Passing By: Gender and Public Harassment* (Berkeley, CA: University of California Press, 1995), 112–119; see also Deirdre Davis, "The Harm that Has No Name: Street Harassment, Embodiment, and African American Women," in *Gender Struggles: Practical Approaches to Contemporary Feminism*, ed. Constance L. Mui and Julien S. Murphy (Oxford: Rowman & Littlefield Publishers, Inc., 2002).

2. Gardner, 161, 174, and 179.

3. Ibid., 160.

4. Ibid., 183.

5. Heben, 187–188.

6. Lisa, comment on "Catcalling: Creepy or a Compliment?" CNN, comment posted on May 14, 2008, http://www.cnn.com/2008/LIVING/personal/05/14/lw.catcalls/index.html (accessed May 14, 2008).

7. Brenna, comment on "Catcalling: Creepy or a Compliment?" comment posted on May 14, 2008, (accessed May 14, 2008).

8. Nia, comment on "You Think You're Better than Me?" Stop Street Harassment Blog, comment posted on June 13, 2009, http://streetharassment.wordpress.com/2009/06/12/you-think-youre-better-than-me/#comments (accessed June 13, 2009).

9. Black woman, comment on "You Think You're Better than Me?" comment posted on June 13, 2009, (accessed June 13, 2009).

10. Martha Langelan, *Back Off! How to Confront and Stop Sexual Harassment and Harassers* (New York: Fireside Press, 1993), 37; see also World Health Organization, "Violence Prevention the Evidence," 2009, http://www.cph.org.uk/showPublication.aspx?pubid=574 (accessed December 29, 2009).

11. D.W. "Going to the Movies is Soooo Fun," Stop Street Harassment Blog, September 10, 2009, http://streetharassment.wordpress.com/2009/09/10/going-to-the-movies-is-soooooo-fun.

12. Laura, comment on "Catcalling: Creepy or a Compliment?" comment posted on May 14, 2008, (accessed May 14, 2008).

13. Deirdre Davis, "The Harm that Has No Name: Street Harassment, Embodiment, and African American Women" (1994) 4 *UCLA Women's Law Journal* 133, 153, cited in Norma Anne Oshynko, "No Safe Place: The Legal Regulation of Street Harassment," Thesis for Masters of Law in Faculty of Law, University of British Columbia, 2002, 76.

14. Oshynoka, 16.

15. Laura Beth Nielsen, *License to Harass: Law, Hierarchy, and Offensive Public Speech* (Princeton, NJ: Princeton University Press, 2004), 95–96.

16. American Psychology Association, "Report of the APA Task Force on the Sexualization of Girls," 2007, http://www.apa.org/pi/women/programs/girls/report.aspx?item=2, 7.

17. Ibid.

18. Maggie Hadleigh-West, *War Zone*, Film Fatale, Inc., 1998 (71-minute version).

19. Langelan, 41.

20. Ibid., 40.

21. Nielsen, 78.

22. Cheryl Benard and Edith Schlaffer, "The Man in the Street: Why He Harasses," in *Feminist Frameworks*, ed. Allison M. Jaggar and Paula S. Rothenberg (New York: McGraw Hill, 1984), 71; see also Gardner, 100–108; see also Langelan, 37–74.

23. Samhita Mukhopadhyay, "Catcalling is Creepy," Feministing.com, May 20, 2008, http://www.feministing.com/archives/009231.html.

24. Andrea Grimes, "Street Objectification: A Call against Cat-Calling," Heartless Doll, June 17, 2009, http://www.heartlessdoll.com/2009/06/italian_women_tired_of_italian_objectification.php.

25. Amanda Marcotte, "Catcalling is NOT a Compliment," Alternet.org, May 16, 2008, http://www.alternet.org/blogs/peek/85566.

26. Ezra Klein, "Catcalling," *American Prospect*, May 15, 2008, http://www.prospect.org/csnc/blogs/ezraklein_archive?month=05&year=2008&base_name=catcalling.

Chapter 6

Strategies Women Practice to Avoid Harassment

> Men get to own the whole wide world, and women have to work so hard to find little spots to feel safe in.[1]

Outside of war-torn areas or areas with high crime, most men do not think twice about entering and being in public spaces. For many women, however, going out in public anywhere requires some level of planning because of male street harassment and the threat of male violence. When women are in public, particularly if they are alone or if they do not believe they have adequate physical strength, many women feel like they must be on guard and wary of men. This limits their peace of mind and freedom.[2] One white woman in her twenties in Kalamazoo, Michigan, wrote in my 2008 online survey, "Pretty much every time I'm out, street harassment is on my mind. I try to cover up when I'm walking on the street. I always walk in a group."

As this chapter will explain, many women are told to and "choose" to—subconsciously and consciously—engage in strategies like going out in public with a companion, avoiding places after dark, or scowling or avoiding eye contact to try to reduce their chances of being harassed or attacked by male strangers.[3] I say choose with quotation marks because these choices are forced ones; the other option is only better than being harassed. Furthermore, the unpredictability of how harassers will act if a woman responds to them can make it easier to try to avoid them altogether, as the latter half of the chapter details. Women most often practice "on guard" strategies in public, like constantly assessing their surroundings or glaring, but many also restrict their access to public spaces by avoiding certain neighborhoods or only going in public with a companion. Some women even change jobs or hobbies to avoid harassment. Individually and collectively, the outcome of these choices is a more limited public and social life for women, less peace of mind, and a denial of the same right to go in public that most men enjoy.[4]

SOCIALIZATION

My mother used to always tell me to beware of strangers, and probably when I was around 10 or 11 I realized that she actually meant men.[5]
—Maggie Hadleigh-West, filmmaker and producer of the anti-street harassment documentary, *War Zone*

Parents, guardians, teachers, and other adults often teach children not to talk to strangers and to be wary of people they do not know. As children, girls and boys report engaging in similar amounts of precaution in public places to stay safe. Around puberty, however, girls begin to report engaging in more precautions than boys.[6] This is notable because boys, who are socialized to be more aggressive and violent than girls, are at more risk for nonsexual violence and harassment in public. Girls, on the other hand, are socialized to be passive, polite, and to fear public places.

While adults may advise teenage boys not to drive too fast, use drugs, or engage in other personally reckless behavior, teenage girls are more likely to be given advice about how to avoid other people who are engaging in inappropriate behavior. Concerned adults may warn teenage girls not to go in public alone after dark or not to go certain places alone, to wear shoes they can run in, to carry a cell phone, and to ignore men who try to approach them. As one of my survey respondents said, "My parents can't seem to reiterate that I not go out alone and at night enough." Another one said people have told her "don't make eye contact, don't say hi to men on the street."

I can relate. When I was a teenager, I attended a week-long cross country summer camp for girls and boys ages 12 to 18 at a university. The girls and boys were together for all of our runs, hikes, clinics, and social activities, except for one. Boys participated in another activity while the girls attended a special clinic to hear a woman runner talk about safety. She advised us not to go running after dark or in deserted areas alone. She also emphasized that we should not become predictable in our routes and the time of day we ran. A man attacked her during a run, she said, because she had a regular routine, and he figured it out and waited for her. The boys did not receive this advice, which told me that if I were a boy, I would be able to run whenever, wherever, and however I wanted without facing the risk of assault.

Each August, the Rape, Abuse, and Incest National Network (RAINN) publishes "Back-To-School Tips for Students" for college students. While the language is gender-neutral, the organization notes at the beginning that college-aged women are at the highest risk for sexual assault and that "being aware of this risk is often the first step in staying safe." Their list includes tips like "avoid being alone or isolated with someone you don't know well," "form a buddy system when you go out. Arrive with your friends, check in with each other throughout the night, and leave together," "try not to go out alone at night," and "don't let your guard down."[7] Many colleges give out similar advice to women on "how to reduce their risk of assault," instead of focusing on keeping people from assaulting. One of my 2008 survey respondents wrote, "During my freshman year at college, we were so indoctrinated with the fear of night that I didn't participate in any social activities at night, unless a large group was going. I knew I wasn't supposed to go anywhere alone at night, but trying to find a buddy further reminded me how vulnerable I was, so I just stayed in."

While advice from parents, guardians, and other concerned adults may be well intentioned, it teaches girls that public spaces are unsafe for them. Following this advice means that young women have to constrict their lives in ways men usually do not. The advice also suggests that it is not men's responsibility to stop harassing and assaulting women, but that instead it is women's responsibility to try to "avoid" those men and to generally learn how to read men's minds to know which ones will harass and assault them and when. Since that is impossible, it can be easier and feel safer for girls to choose to stay home or to only go out in groups. While such restrictions may cut down on harassment, they may not cut down on assault. Esther Madriz wrote in her book *Nothing Bad Happens to Good Girls: Fear of Crime in Women's Lives* that there is almost no difference in the rate of assault of women who purposely take precautions to avoid it and those who do not.[8] (On the other hand, Sue Wise and Liz Stanley write in their book *Georgie Porgie: Sexual Harassment in Everyday Life* that one reason why more women are raped by people they know than people they do not know could be because they take so many precautions to avoid stranger rape.[9])

Furthermore, short of telling women to stay home, advice like avoiding eye contact or wearing baggy clothing does not always work at deterring harassers.[10] For example, one of the 2008 online survey respondent who answered follow-up questions in 2009 wrote that people have told her to "Ignore it [male street harassment], which doesn't deter anyone since it's what I already do." Another respondent said, "I've been told that the best way to avoid street harassment is by not dressing provocatively. I disagree with this because I've been harassed wearing sweatpants." More alarming is the following comment to a post on the Shakesville blog: "The guy who assaulted me was a friend that had offered to walk me home because it was dark, and he wanted to make sure I got home 'safe.' Then, the fucker raped me. He wanted me to be safe from all those other rapists, I guess."[11]

Adding to the advice from adults, girls and women see images in the mass media and stories in the news that portray them as vulnerable to aggression and attack by unknown men in public. While women are more likely to be raped by someone they know, movies and television shows are less likely to show this type of assault, and when they do, they are less likely to present it as rape.[12] The news also disproportionately focuses on rapes carried out by strangers and rapes that end in murder, even though in reality the latter only happens in about 3 percent of all cases.[13] One only need read or watch cable news outlets like CNN and FOX for a few weeks to see how often there are stories about young women—usually attractive, white women—who go missing and are found brutally raped and murdered by a stranger.[14] One of the main points of Madriz's book *Nothing Bad Happens to Good Girls* is that instilling a fear of crime in women, who are less frequently the target of violent crimes than men, perpetuates gender inequalities, such as keeping women home more than men and alone in public less often than men.[15]

Unfortunately, too many girls and women also learn from experience or from hearing about their friends' or family members' experience that they are at risk of harassment and assault when they are in public.

EXPERIENCING HARASSMENT AND ASSAULT

Most women experience harassment in public at least a few times in their life. Given rape culture, a shocking number of women also are sexually assaulted, though usually by someone they know. According to the National Institute of Justice and the Centers for Disease Control and Prevention, one in six women will be a victim of an attempted or completed sexual assault (as will one in thirty-three men), but mixed-race women stand a one-in-four chance and Native American women one-in-three.[16] The U.S. Department of Justice numbers show that strangers perpetrate about 27 percent of the attacks.[17] In my informal online survey in 2008, 639 selected various ways people had harassed them in public. Exactly 25 percent said they had been assaulted in public. Of the nearly 300 women Carol Brooks Gardner interviewed for her street harassment study in Indianapolis, Indiana, sixty-six women volunteered the information that they had been assaulted and/ or raped by a stranger. This is about 22 percent, but since Gardner did not directly ask the respondents this question, the figure is probably higher.[18]

Young women ages 16 to 19 are four times more likely than the general population to be the target of rape, attempted rape, or sexual assault, and women and girls face the most risk from ages 12 to 34.[19] Incidentally, these are the years in which women begin experiencing street harassment and tend to face the worst of it. Scholar Hawley Fogg-Davis wrote in "A Black Feminist Critique of Same-Race Street Harassment," that "most girls first experience street harassment by boys and men at or even before puberty, and thus learn to see their bodies as sources of sexual danger; their sexual vulnerability to boys and men becomes an inescapable and constant condition of being female."[20] Of the more than 800 women who took my informal online survey in 2008, the majority reported first being street harassed around the time of puberty: 22 percent said it happened by the time they were 12, and 87 percent by the time they were 19. Three women wrote, "Street harassment made my life out in public a living hell from age 12 right through my 30s. For my daughter, it started at age 9." "This has been going on since middle school," and "Honestly, I've been harassed so much that I can't remember my first experience. It really feels like the minute I grew boobs it started happening."

Finnish scholar Hille Koskela has spent years studying the gendered fear of violence in Finland, particularly as it relates to urban settings. She found that there are several factors that can prompt a woman who was brave regarding movement in public spaces to become fearful, at least in some circumstances. These factors include violent and threatening experiences, growing up (becoming more fearful as one ages), and changes in life situations (such as developing a disease or ailment that makes one feel more vulnerable).[21] My research findings support the first circumstance. Numerous women who took my survey in 2008 or answered follow-up questions in 2009 mentioned how a particularly bad harassment or assault experience impacted their actions going forward.

When I was younger (middle and high school), based on a previous experience I had, I would not make eye contact with people I saw on the street.

I try to avoid construction sites because I've had negative experiences walking by these sites and so have many of my friends.

One guy had touched my leg when I was buying something at the corner store. I never went to that store ever again after that incident.

I no longer take the subway train late at night or even with a girl friend. We always add a cab ride into our budget whenever we go out at night. We've all had past experiences of being physically accosted, verbally harassed, and followed and we've all decided it's just NOT worth it.

Hearing about other women being harassed or assaulted in public also can cause women to begin fearing certain circumstances or places in public, even though that suspicion and fear did not previously influence their choices.[22]

Also, women's experiences with trying to respond to harassers can make them decide it is better to try to avoid them, especially when many harassers startle women and give them no time to respond or react. When women have time to respond to a harasser, many factors cause the vast majority of them to ignore (or pretend to ignore) the harasser or humor him by smiling and saying thank you.[23] In addition to perhaps not having the energy to respond to every harasser one encounters, women and girls may do so because they are typically socialized to be polite, nice, and not make a scene. They may fear the man will escalate into more severe harassment or assault if they appear to challenge his behavior through an assertive or aggressive response.[24] They may have tried other responses without success. They also may feel that giving any other response would give the harasser the satisfaction of getting a rise out of them. Some of my survey respondents explain:

I find that typically any attempt to engage only increases the harassment. I'm not interested in being a single crusader against people with no concept of how to live in harmony. I ignore them as best as possible, and try to walk away.

I try to be nice because I don't want the person to hurt me but I don't ever give out my number.

Always best to ignore it so you don't antagonize the situation.

No way of dealing with street harassment is foolproof. While I think appearing preoccupied (talking on the phone, etc.) or appearing unfriendly, angry, and otherwise inaccessible can help to prevent harassment, it's never 100% effective. I don't know of any good way to deal with the emotional fallout of street harassment and the fear it creates.

I just ignore it as much as possible. I assume they are looking for a reaction and I am not about to give them one.

In my survey I found that only once a man touched or assaulted a woman did the majority of them take action instead of ignoring or trying to avoid the harasser.

I was once followed home from the subway by two men making sexually explicit comments and suggestions. I ignored them until one grabbed me from behind, at which point I turned around and started to scream profanity at them. That convinced them to leave, since it was crowded.

Ignore it unless it gets to a point of extreme discomfort. Then, call a friend or the police in certain circumstances.

The best advice for women is to ignore it unless it crosses a line into threats or touching.

I usually ignore it. It depends on the situation. But if someone crosses the line, flashes someone else, touches them at all, follows them or the harassment is habitual, I would yell or hit them (if they touch me), or call attention to the person (if they're flashing or masturbating in public).

No matter whether a woman ignores a harasser or flips him off, the harasser can escalate to verbal insults and violent behavior. If she humors him, he may think she wants the attention and continue to pester her. As several of my survey respondents noted, there is no foolproof solution, though later in the book there are ideas for assertive responses for those who would like to use them. Ultimately, men need to stop harassing women; it should not have to be the woman's burden to decide in a split second which response to a harasser will keep her the least victimized.

Women's socialization from puberty to fear public spaces—combined with the reality of harassment and assault and a lack of a foolproof, all-purpose response to every type of harassment—causes women to limit their access to public spaces at least sometimes. The rest of the chapter details specific ways in which women restrict their public lives.

WOMEN'S STRATEGIES IN PUBLIC

There are numerous adaptive strategies most women use from time to time to reduce their chances of encountering street harassment and assault, to find those "little spots" of the world in which to feel safe. Some of these strategies relate to being on guard when they are in public. Others relate to planning when and where to go in public. More severely but less frequently, some women use drastic strategies, like moving homes or gaining weight. Of note, a handful of women in my survey specifically said they did not alter their life and refused to be anyone's victim, but even among them, there was a tendency to say that it was an attitude they consciously chose or that they tried not to change their habits because of the threat of harassment "if at all possible."

I found that women who were harassed the most and/or had been assaulted often practiced the most adaptive strategies, while women who were only occasionally harassed or had not been assaulted engaged in adaptive strategies far less. For a quick example, of the 205 women who had strangers comment on their appearance on a daily or weekly basis (and who also experienced several other forms of harassment that often) 77 percent said they always constantly assessed their surroundings and most engaged in numerous other adaptive strategies at least on a monthly basis. In contrast, of the eighty-nine women who had men comment on their appearance one to five times (and almost none were harassed on a daily or weekly basis period) 52 percent said they always constantly assessed their surroundings but otherwise they engaged in few other restrictive behaviors on even a monthly basis.

To illustrate the strategies most women use, I cite statistics from two studies. Most of the statistics are from my 2008 survey and are women's responses to the question, "Have you done/do you do any of the following because of actual or feared interactions with strangers in public? (Please check all that apply.)" The multiple choice question had twenty-one options. Around 800 women and 90 men responded. The other set of statistics comes from a study conducted by Margaret Gordon and Stephanie Riger for their 1991

book *The Female Fear: The Social Cost of Rape*. They phone surveyed and interviewed in person thousands of people in San Francisco, Boston, and Chicago about how frequently they engaged in
particular activities. Not every strategy I discuss was asked in their
survey, so their statistics will not inform every section.

Most of the stories I include in the rest of the section to illustrate
the statistics come from the open-ended sections of my 2008 survey
and from follow-up questions I asked ninety women in 2009. A
few come from a thread of 435 comments to a 2008 Shakesville
blog post in which blogger Melissa McEwan asked, "In what ways
has the idea of sexual assault and/or street harassment affected your
daily movements?"[25] Those comments have an endnote to distin-
guish them from my survey respondents.

On Guard

The most common restrictive behaviors women said they regularly engaged in related to being "on guard" while in public, particularly when they are alone. Of the 21 options for my multiple
choice survey question, "constantly assessing their surroundings"
was the option that women selected "always" for the most and
"never" the least (see Table 6.1).

I used to live in Germantown. I didn't realize how uptight I was about
living there (constantly assessing environment, constantly the brunt of
stares/comments) until I moved and I could literally feel my whole body
relax.

Table 6.1
Constantly Assessing Their Surroundings

	Women Respondents	Men Respondents
Always	62 percent	42 percent (37 percent of heterosexual males)
At least monthly	80 percent	52 percent (47 percent of heterosexual males)
Never	4 percent	19 percent (23 percent of heterosexual males)

Table 6.2
Crossing the Street or Taking Another Route

	Women Respondents	Men Respondents
Always	18 percent	3 percent
At least monthly	50 percent	20 percent
Never	5 percent	23 percent

Trying to have a blank or angry look on my face, taking alternate routes, leaving a party late with a friend or calling a cab rather than going alone, always assessing surroundings.

As part of being on guard in public, there are several specific actions and behaviors women said they do to avoid harassment or deter harassers, such as crossing the street or taking a different route (see Table 6.2), scowling (see Table 6.3), avoiding eye contact (see Table 6.4), wearing headphones (see Table 6.5), and talking on a cell phone (see Table 6.6).

Gordon and Riger asked this question too, and they found that 52 percent of women regularly crossed the street when they saw someone who looked "strange or dangerous," compared with 25 percent of men.[26]

I've crossed the street to avoid walking past groups of men. I run to/from my car at night.

I have driven places that are very close to my house because I don't feel like having to be harassed while I'm walking down the street. Sometimes I will just stay home instead of walking to the coffee shop or will take a longer route to avoid the main street where guys are more likely to be hanging around in groups and harassing women when they walk by.

I scowl, assess surroundings, walk quickly, [and] avoid certain areas. I don't keep my money in one place.

Table 6.3
Scowling

	Women Respondents	Men Respondents
Always	19 percent	8 percent
At least monthly	49 percent	17 percent
Never	20 percent	57 percent

Any time I walk down the street, I keep my head up and constantly look around me, especially if it's dark or getting dark. I tend to scowl at anyone who shouts at me from a passing car.

Once I learned to avoid eye contact, look as if I know exactly where I'm going, walk fast, and wear a permanent grimace in public, it mostly stopped.

In general, in areas where I experienced A LOT of sex harassment (which was pretty much all of NYC), I would try to avoid eye contact as much as possible. It was, obviously, not easy to do.

I keep my iPod charged at all times in order to avoid any sort of potential harassment.

I wear headphones when walking during the day so I can pretend I don't hear them.

Table 6.4
Avoiding Eye Contact

	Women Respondents	Men Respondents
Always	33 percent	8 percent
At least monthly	70 percent	38 percent
Never	8 percent	26 percent

Table 6.5
Wearing Headphones

	Women Respondents	Men Respondents
Always	15 percent	7 percent
At least monthly	38 percent	15 percent
Never	37 percent	68 percent

Table 6.6
Talking on a Cell Phone

	Women Respondents	Men Respondents
Always	15 percent	7 percent
At least monthly	38 percent	15 percent
Never	37 percent	68 percent

On a monthly basis, I definitely pretend to be on the phone or cross the street. I'll also walk absurdly fast if I feel like someone might be following me, so that I could tell (it would be difficult/annoying to keep up the speed).

If I'm feeling nervous or afraid, I will open my cell phone so it's look like I'm on the phone with someone, or I will call someone to talk (my mom, my boyfriend, my grandma).

Having to be on guard to try to deter and avoid male harassers is tiring and distracting, and it prevents peace of mind. These kinds of restrictive behaviors result in many women feeling less safe and welcome when they are in public than most men, particularly white, heterosexual, cismen.

Careful Planning

While not quite as common across the board as the "on guard" behaviors, numerous women said they regularly make planning decisions about being in public based on the threat of interactions with strangers. Always avoiding going out after dark was a common planning strategy (see Table 6.7).

Similarly, in Gordon and Riger's survey, 26 percent of their female respondents said they always avoid going out after dark, compared with 9 percent of men. Only 25 percent of women said they never restrict themselves in this way, compared with 72 percent of men.[27]

I try my best not to be out alone past 10 P.M. I don't walk in alleys at night. I ride the CTA in the closest car near the operator . . . and try to find populated cars.

There are definitely routes I avoid in the dark, and when I used to have a car, there were times I would unnecessarily drive somewhere to avoid

Table 6.7
Avoiding Being Out after Dark

	Women Respondents	Men Respondents
Always	11 percent	3 percent
At least monthly	45 percent	12 percent
Never	17 percent	49 percent (58 percent of heterosexual men)

Table 6.8
Avoiding Going Out Alone

	Women Respondents	Men Respondents
Always	8 percent	1 percent
At least monthly	40 percent	6 percent
Never	19 percent	53 percent (60 percent of heterosexual men)

having to walk through dark, especially unsafe areas of town at night. It wasn't even that they *were* unsafe. It was based on how I felt.

Trying to avoid ever going out in public alone period was another specific planning step women said they took (see Table 6.8).

This strategy was common in Gordon and Riger's survey too. Strikingly, 51 percent of women said they always go in public "with a friend or two as a protector," compared with 4 percent of men. Ten percent of women said they never engaged in this strategy, compared with 50 percent of men.[28]

I think I was pretty good at feeling comfortable in public for a long time, but recently I just don't go out much. I rarely go out alone unless I can't avoid it.

I've allowed it to take over my life. I've turned into a hermit, and only go out when I absolutely have to. I always have my pepper spray on me, and even find myself avoiding passing by any man on the street if I am alone. It's both an enraging and depressing subject for me.[29]

Avoiding specific neighborhoods (see Table 6.9), purposely wearing clothes they think will attract less attention (see Table 6.10), and exercising at a gym instead of outside (see Table 6.11) are examples of three other common planning strategies women engaged in because of the fear of interactions with strangers in public.

Table 6.9
Avoiding a Specific Neighborhood

	Women Respondents	Men Respondents
Always	27 percent	12 percent
At least monthly	57 percent	28 percent
Never	5 percent	15 percent

I live in Sunset Park and the way this neighborhood is I feel from one block to the next can be much nicer than others. I'm now a stay at home mom but when I worked my husband would pick me up at the bus on 48 and 5 to walk home to 48 b/w 7 and 8 just because some blocks are so dark and creepy I didn't want to walk alone. . . . Now I avoid taking my children around the neighborhood due to these same reasons.

I wear different shoes, try to hang out in groups at night, avoid certain neighborhoods.

A couple of years ago, my grandmother moved into assisted living, and it was my job to help clean out her house. I ended up with a lot of her clothes and started wearing them all the time, in part to be funny and hip, but also in part to keep unwanted attention at bay. A granny shirt seems to get a few less hollers than a short skirt.

I've started wearing baggy clothes, not wearing makeup, and looking ragged in certain areas I'm forced to be in.

I love to run and exercise outside (hiking etc) . . . sadly for a good part of the year the only viable time to do this is at night. Obviously that makes it rather hard as I certainly don't go out after dark to run along the streets or at a track by myself. Why? Well of course, because I am a woman, and face harassment during the day when I go running, let alone what would happen at night! It honestly frightens me. . . . So, sadly, I confine myself to a gym most of the time, where some weirdo will still ogle me, but at least I have the safety of numbers.[30]

Table 6.10
Purposely Wearing Clothes You Think Will Attract Less Attention

	Women Respondents	Men Respondents
Always	10 percent	2 percent
At least monthly	37 percent	11 percent
Never	19 percent	65 percent

Table 6.11
Exercising at the Gym Instead of Outside

	Women Respondents	Men Respondents
Always	10 percent	0 percent
At least monthly	23 percent	5 percent
Never	54 percent	89 percent

It is hard for women to have equality with men when they spend so much extra time planning and worrying about going in public and restricting their access in consequential ways to try to be safe and unharassed. Women may not take night classes, work night shifts, or attend community meetings or forums at night because they fear being outside after dark, and they may avoid other community or public activities if they do not have someone with whom they can go.

Significant Choices

While fewer in number, there were women who said they have made significant life choices as a result of their fear of stranger interactions in public. For example, about 10 percent of the women who answered the multiple choice question said they had gained or kept on weight at least once specifically because of stranger interactions in public.

God, there are many incidences. . . . Basically, I've gained about 60 lbs in the last 10 years and I'm FINALLY invisible to all but the loneliest.

Every time I lose weight, I am shocked at how it completely changes the way people interact with me . . . I honestly feel happier and safer as "the fatty.". . . I do not get nearly as much unwanted attention this way.[31]

Around 9 percent of women, compared with 1 percent of men, said they had changed jobs at least once because of harassment near their workplace or during their commute.

I used to work in Lincoln Park but I lived in Roger's Park; about an hour long commute by El/Bus. I would often get home from work around 1 A.M. and have to walk several blocks to my apartment. One night as I was walking home, I was surrounded by a group of 6 or 8 young men who all made vulgar comments about the "things they would do to me." Needless to say I was terrified, so I got out my mace, and my cell phone and I called my boyfriend and tried to pretend I didn't notice them. Thankfully they went away a few minutes later, but it was enough to make me decide to quit my job. I was often harassed in other instances in that neighborhood so I moved away shortly after.

I've changed my walk to work twice because of street harassment. I've worked nights off and on for years. The thing that made me quit my job working nights at a gas station wasn't either of the two times I was robbed . . . but the group of asshole men who would show up outside at night in a car and start taking photos of me at work. That's it, I was done.[32]

A woman on the Shakesville blog said she decided not to take a job because of her fear of harassment and assault in public, "I didn't take a job once because it would have required me to leave work after dark and was in an area with several bars that I would have to walk past."[33]

Several women who answered the open-ended questions in my survey and posted stories on the Shakesville blog post talked about other significant choices they have made because of harassment and the threat of male assault. A common one was paying more for transportation in an effort to be safe. In the long run, this is a financial drain for women.

When it's later at night and I am alone I will take a cab, no matter how expensive it may be.

I rode buses for years. I think public transport is an environmentally sound choice, the price made sense, and I liked having the time for reading and reflecting. Then I was waiting at a bus stop one day and was forced into a car at knife point, raped, and left for dead at the side of the road. Now I drive. I look at buses wistfully, but I can't count on having someone I trust waiting with me at the bus stops.[34]

I live about a mile from my work . . . If it's after dark, I NEVER walk alone. My husband picks me up, or I take a cab, which costs $9 including tip for a 1-mile ride.[35]

Similarly, in their survey, Riger and Gordon found that 40 percent of women always opt to drive instead of walk because they fear being harmed, compared with 13 percent of men. Only 18 percent of women had never engaged in that strategy compared with 56 percent of men.[36]

Stopping or restricting specific hobbies because of male harassment or the threat of assault was another common theme I found. This was one I had not considered before, but I think it helps explain why there may be more male hikers and cyclists or even more astronomers than women. So not only does harassment restrict the types of hobbies women can have, but it also can impact what career field one chooses.

I love the outdoors and feel bereft of them because of my fear and loathing of attacks—whether verbal, visual, or physical.

A friend of mine in grad school took large scale landscapes with a beautiful one of a kind view camera. She was a fiercely independent woman from

Germany who had travelled all over the world. On one photo taking excursion she set up her camera in broad daylight in a huge field outside of Albuquerque. A car with two men was driving by on a dirt road stopped and began harassing her. . . . Before she knew it the men had jumped her and had her pants off holding her on the ground. Luckily for her there was a telephone repair person who was up on a pole who . . . ran to help her. The two men ran off. She was shaken to the core—sold the camera—now only works in small format and never ventures alone into those wild places that formerly gave her such peace and solace.[37]

If surviving attacks by humans weren't an issue, I'd be going for solo rambles in the woods daily, often in the small hours of the morning. I'd spend a lot of time out in the middle of nowhere alone with a telescope.[38]

Another common outcome of street harassment and the threat of violence I noticed in women's stories was how women would leave somewhere earlier than they wanted or intended. This not only makes them have to stop what they are doing and perhaps enjoying but also can deter them from doing the same thing in the future, or at least may make them wary of it.

I went to see a movie. I was alone. I was intent on the movie and then noticed movement beside me, only to look over and see that the man one seat away was staring at my breasts and masturbating. I shouted out my disgust and made a big, noisy scene as I left.

A man once very obviously followed me around a grocery store. I still needed a few more items, but I decided to check out and pay early, anyway.

Last, street harassment and the threat of male violence can lead some women to distrust any male stranger. It relates to a quote from feminist writer Marilyn French about how half of the population "bears the guise of the predator, in which no factor—age, dress, or color—distinguishes a man who will harm a woman from one who will not."[39] Consequently, nonharassing men are negatively affected because they are treated as untrustworthy and a threat.

I usually try to avoid walking in my neighborhood, luckily I drive, but I still get harassed going to my car. I have started walking around w/pepper spray, in case of anything. Men have asked me to approach their car b/c they need direction, I either point or say I don't know. I don't trust ANY MAN in public and it's sad.

Depressingly, the major thing that life has taught me is not to help men. During my first term at uni [college] in London I was making the five-minute trek from my flat to the campus (at 11 in the morning, I might add), when a bus pulled up beside me and the driver asked me to come and help because he was lost. Naively, I got on the bus to look at his map, and he asked . . . if he could have my number. When I said no he shut the doors and drove off down the road with me. He had to stop at a traffic light at the bottom of the road and I managed to press the emergency button and jump out.[40]

Individually, any one of these strategies and restrictions may not seem like a big deal. Collectively, however, the long list of ways women tend to change their lives is extensive (and still does not include everything) and illustrates the commonality among women's experiences in public. It shows the extent to which women strategically plan and work to try to stay safe and unharmed in public, spaces where men can largely roam freely without much thought to their safety or chance of being approached by a stranger.

A Human Rights Issue

In October 2008, feminist blogger Echidne of the Snakes wrote a powerful blog post titled "The Right to Go Out" about how women's fear of public spaces is seen as "just how things are" and not a human rights issue.

The difference in our ability to go out, alone and fairly safely, is highly dependent on whether we are men or women. . . . In most societies women . . . are seen as prey. So women adjust to this, accommodate themselves to this, stay at home, and agree to live lesser lives because of their sex.

I have never met a woman who isn't aware of this difference, who isn't used to carefully mapping out routes to new places, who isn't cautious about going anywhere at night on her own. But despite this and all those take-back-the-night marches the idea that women should somehow have the right to go out alone and not be at any greater risk than anyone else is—what? A stupid idea? Impossibly idealistic? Whatever it is, it is also a human rights issue. But for some reason we have lost sight of that.[41]

She is right. The ways most women are told to and "choose" to restrict their lives are myriad and often so ingrained that we may not even realize why we do them anymore. Instead of collectively being outraged about this as a human rights issue, most men live in ignorance and most women are not aware of the connection between why they do not feel safe going to the corner store alone at night or walking through a deserted parking lot to their vehicle and the continuation of gender inequality around the world. Instead, women tend to adapt, try not to think about why they cannot have the same freedoms as men, and say, as Echidne put it, "It's just how things are." Silence and inaction on this topic must end.

NOTES

1. AnnieF, comment on "Feminism 101," Shakesville Blog, comment posted on October 18, 2008, http://shakespearessister.blogspot.com/2008/10/feminism-101. html#disqus_thread (accessed October 10, 2009).

2. Carole J. Sheffield, "Sexual Terrorism," in *Women: A Feminist Perspective, Fifth Edition*, ed. Jo Freeman (Palo Alto, CA: Mayfield Publishing Company, 1995), 12.

3. Sue Wise and Liz Stanley, *Georgie Porgie: Sexual Harassment in Everyday Life* (London: Pandora, 1987): 98–99.

4. Gerd Bohner and Norbert Schwarz, "The Threat of Rape: Its Psychological Impact on Nonvictimized Women," in *Sex, Power, Conflict: Evolutionary and Feminist Perspectives*, eds. David M. Buss and Neil M. Malamuth (Oxford: Oxford University Press, 1996), 173.

5. Maggie Hadleigh-West, *War Zone* documentary, 1997.

6. Margaret T. Gordon and Stephanie Riger, *The Female Fear: The Social Cost of Rape* (Urbana: University of Illinois Press, 1991), 53–54.

7. RAINN, "RAINN's 2009 Back-To-School Tips for Students," August 10, 2009, http://www.rainn.org/news-room/sexual-assault-news/2009-back-to-school-tips.

8. Esther Madriz, *Nothing Bad Happens to Good Girls: Fear of Crime in Women's Lives* (Berkeley, CA: University of California Press, 1997), 2.

9. Wise and Stanley, 1987, 171.

10. Gordon and Riger, 45.

11. Carleigh, comment on "Feminism 101," comment posted on October 18, 2008, (accessed October 10, 2009).

12. Marilyn French, *The War Against Women* (New York: Ballantine Books, 1992), 190; Gordon and Riger, 67–69.

13. Gordon and Riger, 2, 9, 68–69.

14. Alex Johnson, "Damsels in Distress, If You're Missing, It Helps to Be Young, White, and Female," MSNBC, July 23, 2004, http://www.msnbc.msn.com/id/5325808. For example, when I was writing my master's thesis on street harassment, CNN.com covered two of these stories as the lead stories within 24 hours: "Police Arrest Suspect in Teen's Abduction, Slaying," June 7, 2007, http://www.cnn.com/2007/US/06/07/missing.teen/index.html and "Missing Girl Found Hidden under Staircase," June 6, 2007, http://www.cnn.com/2007/US/06/06/conn. kidnap/index.html.

15. Madriz, 2.

16. RAINN, "Who Are the Victims?" n.d., http://rainn.org/get-information/statistics/sexual-assault-victims.

17. U.S. Department of Justice, 2005, National Crime Victimization Study, cited on "The Offenders," Rape, Abuse, and Incest National Network, n.d., http://rainn.org/get-information/statistics/sexual-assault-offenders.

18. Carol Brooks Gardner, *Passing By: Gender and Public Harassment* (Berkeley: University of California Press, 1995), 7.

19. RAINN, "Who Are the Victims?" n.d., http://rainn.org/get-information/statistics/sexual-assault-victims.

20. Hawley Fogg-Davis, "Theorizing Black Lesbians within Black Feminism: A Critique of Same-Race Street Harassment." *Politics and Gender* 2 (2006): 20–21.

21. Hille Koskela, "'Bold Walk and Breakings': Women's Spatial Confidence versus Fear of Violence," *Gender, Place and Culture* 4, no. 3 (1997), 301–319.

22. Gordon and Riger, 44.

23. Wise and Stanley, 169; see also Gardner, 148–157; see also Kimberly Fairchild and Laurie A. Rudman, "Everyday Stranger Harassment and Women's Self-Objectification," *Social Justice Research* 21, no. 3 (2008), 344.

24. Oshynoka, 55.

25. Melissa McEwan, "Feminism 101," Shakesville, October 18, 2008, http://shakespearessister.blogspot.com/2008/10/feminism-101.html#disqus_thread.

26. Gordon and Riger, 17.

27. Ibid., 16.

28. Ibid., 16.

29. ThedaBara, comment on "Feminism 101," Shakesville Blog, comment posted October 19, 2008, http://shakespearessister.blogspot.com/2008/10/feminism-101.html#disqus_thread (accessed October 10, 2009).

30. Brandy, comment on "Feminism 101," comment posted on October 18, 2008 (accessed October 10, 2009).

31. Kemp, comment on "Feminism 101," comment posted on October 18, 2008 (accessed October 10, 2009).

32. Anna, comment on "Feminism 101," comment posted on October 18, 2008 (accessed October 10, 2009).

33. Ajoye, comment on "Feminism 101," comment posted on October 18, 2008 (accessed October 10, 2009).

34. Hilleviw, comment on "Feminism 101," comment posted on October 18, 2008 (accessed October 10, 2009).

35. Scrappy, comment on "Feminism 101," comment posted on October 18, 2008 (accessed October 10, 2009).

36. Gordon and Riger, 16.

37. Gwyllion, comment on "Feminism 101," comment posted on October 18, 2008 (accessed October 10, 2009).

38. HelenHuntingdon, comment on "Feminism 101," comment posted on October 18, 2008 (accessed October 10, 2009).

39. French, 197.

40. Jen, comment on "Feminism 101," comment posted on October 19, 2008 (accessed October 10, 2009).

41. Echidne of the Snakes, "The Right to Go Out," October 16, 2008, http://echidneofthesnakes.blogspot.com/2008_10_01_archive.html#401984367 2375903459 (accessed October 20, 2008).

Part Two

Strategies for Ending
Street Harassment

_____ *Chapter 7* _____

Educating Men and Engaging Male Allies

Street harassment will not end until men stop behaving inappropriately toward women they do not know in public spaces. Since most men who harass women do not think they are doing anything wrong—or they do not care that they are—and men who do not harass women tend to not know it occurs or else also do not think it is wrong, ending the behavior is challenging and will require a multilayered, comprehensive approach. The layers I propose include educating men to respect women and to intervene when they see other men harassing women, empowering women to know street harassment is not their fault and equipping them with assertive responses they can use against harassers, raising public awareness that street harassment is a problem, and working to make street harassment an issue the way sexual assault or workplace sexual harassment is, including lobbying for anti-street harassment laws.

To get to the heart of how to solve street harassment, we must find out why men harass women in public spaces. There are people who use sexist rationales to explain why, saying it is due to men's natural, animal instincts and they "can't help it" when they see a beautiful woman.[1] Since not all men harass women, this is false reasoning, especially as some men who are not sexually attracted to women still harass them. Street harassment, instead, is learned behavior.[2] In both informal surveys I conducted, education was the suggestion most commonly given by people for how to stop street harassment. I agree with this assessment. Education must play a key role in helping men unlearn harassing behaviors. First, education should be used to teach boys and men healthy definitions of masculinity, respect for women, and how to appropriately interact with women in public. Second, education should be used to teach male allies how to educate other men about street harassment and how to intervene when they see harassment occur. Before addressing the education initiatives, this chapter opens with an exploration of why men harass women.

MASCULINITY AND WHY MEN HARASS

Why some men harass women in public is an under-researched topic. To truly be able to address street harassment, scholars and community activists must study it further to know what educational initiatives will be the most useful and effective in stopping it. From what we do know about why men harass, several of the major reasons are connected to harmful definitions of masculinity and its rigid framework. These are the reasons I will discuss.

In the United States, some of the main characteristics that comprise the cultural definition of masculinity and what it means to be a man are aggression, violence, and power. As a result, far more men than women engage in all forms of violence, harassment, and otherwise aggressive behaviors.[3] This definition is reinforced in countless ways, including in video games; sports like football, wrestling, and boxing; pornography; comic books and action movies; and in deadly forms like hunting, gang activity, and war; all activities that have mostly male audiences or participants. Men can engage in aggressive and violent activities to prove their "manhood," but speaking out against these activities can make a man seem weak or "feminine." The peer pressure to be masculine keeps many men who disagree with violence, aggression, harassment, or other negative behavior silent so they will be accepted by other men.[4]

Gender, unlike sex, is not biologically determined, and what it means to be a man or a woman is constantly in flux and varies across cultures. Proving one belongs to a specific gender can be a constant struggle, particularly when the construct is narrow. Part of proving one's masculinity is "othering," devaluing, and even harming everything that is not considered masculine.[5] Even though most societies are male dominated, because of the devaluation of "feminine" traits and pursuits, men tend to face a more rigid gender role than women. Many "masculine" traits are perceived as good, such as being adventurous and athletic, so girls and women who exhibit them may be praised or endearingly called "tomboys" (or vilified if they threaten men, like being called a bitch for being an assertive boss). On the other hand, many feminine traits are perceived to be negative. For example, if a boy shows sensitivity, he may be called a "sissy," a "wuss," or a "fag." Boys and men may be called "girls" when they are being made fun of or bullied.[6] There even are women who devalue, objectify, and distance themselves from feminine traits as they strive to be "one of the boys."[7]

The "tough guise" men are required to wear at all times the strict adherence to traditional masculine traits are unhealthy and harmful—to men and to women. In his book *Messages Men Hear: Constructing Masculinities*, scholar Ian Harris wrote about how traditional definitions of masculinity contribute to men's shorter life expectancy and higher rates of alcoholism, drug abuse, assault, incarceration, and homelessness compared to women.[8] Another scholar, Joseph Peck, wrote in his article "Men's Power with Women, Other Men, and Society: A Men's Movement Analysis" how patriarchy is a dual system: one that oppresses women and one through which men oppress each other and themselves through harassment and assault as they enforce gender roles and gender power structures.[9] For example, because members of the LGBQTI community generally defy traditional gender roles, they face a lot of harassment and assault from men who feel threatened by their gender fluidity or "deviance." Men who commit hate crimes seem particularly threatened by openly gay men and transwomen because these biological men do not adhere to traditional masculinity gender constructs.[10]

The efforts to try to live up to and enforce unhealthy versions of masculinity help explain why men harass women in public spaces.[11]

Purposely Exerting Power

Power is a cornerstone of traditional masculinity, and some men harass women to exert power and to put them in "their place" because they can. No matter how accomplished, smart, or witty a woman is, a man can instantly—and with virtually no consequences—reduce her to her body parts through whistles, comments, and groping, or exert power by demanding her attention.[12] Cheryl Benard and Edith Schlaffer, professors at the Institute of Political Science of the University of Vienna, asked sixty men who harassed Benard and Schlaffer why they did so, and 15 percent of the men admitted they were specifically trying to anger or humiliate the two women. These were the men who tended to use sexually explicit comments and threats.[13]

When studying street harassment in Washington, D.C., Martha Langelan found that some migrant workers, working-class white men, and Black and Hispanic men who harassed women said they specifically targeted those who were white and middle and upper-class as a way of expressing hostility to the racial or class privilege the women represented. The ability to harass women was the only power they felt they had in a racist, classist, and sexist society.[14] Some of the migrant laborers and construction workers Benard and Schlaffer interviewed also admitted they would harass a well-dressed middle-class woman because of the "snobbish, privileged class she symbolizes to them."[15] Thus, some men harass women to show that even in a racist and classist society, they have power over women.

Disrespecting Women

Most men who engage in street harassment are not consciously trying to exert power over women. Instead their behavior is a byproduct of a general culture of disrespect for women and of male privilege, meaning the reality of stranger rape and gender inequality women live with is largely invisible to them as men. When questioned about why they harassed women, by Benard and Schlaffer and by Maggie Hadleigh-West for her anti-street harassment documentary *War Zone* and the Girls for Gender Equity (GGE) interns for their documentary *Hey . . . Shorty*, most men were at a loss to explain why they engaged in the behavior. No one had questioned them before, and it was hard for them to think about why they actually did it. When pressed, men told Benard and Schlaffer that it "relieved boredom," was "fun," and "doesn't hurt anybody." Some, as will be discussed shortly, said they did it to show off for or entertain their male friends.

Other men's reasoning suggests they believe their actions are an appropriate way to greet a woman. For example, one man Hadleigh-West questioned about why he whistled at her said he was, "Just saying hi."[16] Another man she engaged with in a dialogue about his behavior said he had made a sexual face at her because "I wanted your attention. I wanted to let you know that I appreciate your beauty." When Hadleigh-West asked him on camera what he thought he would do with her attention, he said, "Oh, I'm presently involved, but say hello, and probably make a new friend." When she pushed him further by asking, "So do you think that women enjoy it when you do things like that?" He said, "I think they are genuinely offended by it." He became visibly embarrassed when he said that, as though he was considering the woman's point of view for the first time.[17]

When asked by Benard and Schlaffer, Hadleigh-West, and the GGE interns how they think their actions make women feel, many men had not even considered women's feelings before. In the documentary *War Zone* one man said, "I don't care what they think; I do what I want to do."[18] Most men in the documentaries visibly appeared to have trouble comprehending why women would not want strange men to comment on their looks or ask for their phone number. They, and most of the men I have encountered who engage in street harassment, claim women enjoy the attention. One man Benard and Schlaffer interviewed told them he "specialized in older and less attractive women to whom, he was sure, his display of sexual interest was certain to be the highlight of an otherwise drab existence."[19] The hostility many men showed on the films when asked how they would feel if another man "complimented" their female significant other, sister, or daughter, however, shows that at some level they know it is not complimentary behavior.

Proving Heterosexuality

Proving male heterosexuality to themselves and to other men by objectifying women's looks and being a sexual player is an important component of masculinity, too. It can cause men of all sexual orientations to whistle at or comment on unknown women's looks. For example, doctoral student Amit Taneja wrote about how when he was in college, the guys in his building said they hated "fags," and since Taneja was gay, he decided to hide that by objectifying and harassing women. He wanted men's respect and acceptance so much that he tried to gain it at the expense of women (and by denying his own identity).[20] Similarly, a commenter on a *Guardian* news article about street harassment wrote, "This is all about peer pressure. Notice that it is always a group of males. It's a sign that they are not GAY and therefore have nothing to fear from their mates. Usually the GAY bloke will be the first to exhibit this sign so as to deny his sexuality in front of STRAIGHTS. . . . Male bonding, that's all."[21]

Unfortunately, there are women who contribute to this mindset, too. In Carol Brooks Gardner's study of street harassment in Indianapolis, among women who believed street harassment was complimentary, there were several who said they thought a man must be gay if he did not harass her.[22] Or, as bell hooks wrote in an article "Seduced by Violence No More," there are women who are so used to men being aggressive, violent, and "macho," that if a man is not, they assume he is gay.[23] Then, men who try to treat women with respect—but see women go for the "bad boys" anyway—may throw their hands in the air and decide to be more aggressive to prove their manhood and heterosexuality to women, as well as to men.

Proving male heterosexuality and manliness also can make men feel pressured to have many sexual conquests (a concept absent in many rape-free societies). This pressure can cause men to engage in the "numbers" game and hope that if they ask one hundred women for their phone number, they will get at least one number and score (without caring how annoyed or upset the other ninety-nine women who ignored them or glared at them felt).[24]

Impressing Friends

Similarly, some men use women in their efforts to impress male friends and to belong in the group. In his article "Staring at Janae's Legs," Hugo Schwyzer wrote about homosociality, which is the idea that men are more eager to please other men than women and thus they use women in front of each other as pawns to prove their masculinity. Schwyzer specifically cites men catcalling to women as an example of homosociality: the women are the object of the men's jokes or harassment so the men can show off or bond with their friends.[25]

Many men harass women when they are in groups. In the anti-street harassment documentaries *War Zone* and *Hey . . . Shorty*, most of the men interviewed were with other men and several said they harassed women to "get a rise" out of their friends and bond with them. Benard and Schlaffer found that while many men harassed women both while in groups or alone, about 20 percent said they only harassed women when they were in the company of male friends and otherwise left women alone.[26] Only in a culture where women are disrespected could this be acceptable male-bonding behavior.

The pressure to impress other men and to be accepted also prevents most men from speaking out against street harassment, gender violence, and gender discrimination.[27] Anti-gender violence activist Jackson Katz has written in great length about how men may feel pressure to participate in or stand quietly by while their friends participate in sexist and even violent behaviors in order to be accepted. He said, "Many men simply learn to keep their discomfort to themselves . . . emotional detachment, competitiveness and the sexual objectification of women are often the criteria by which men judge each other. When men do not 'measure up' in those terms—and many do not—they often keep their objections to themselves so as not to threaten their standing in the group."[28]

Also of note, most men do not harass women who are accompanied by men because they do not want to risk confrontation with the men. On the occasion when men do harass women that are accompanied by men, it may be in such a way that the man she is with does not realize it, or it may be done in a backhanded way, such as a compliment to the man on having an attractive girlfriend or wife—just as he may compliment him on having a nice car.

Men are socialized to be aggressive and violent and to pursue women. Street harassment is a way they can do all three to gain or maintain power and to prove their masculinity. This behavior is learned, and so it can be unlearned or not taught at all.

EDUCATING MEN

Educating men to stop harassing women will require several approaches. I will touch on some of the important ones and highlight them by using current programs operating around the nation. First, men need to be taught healthy definitions of masculinity and to respect women. Men also need to be taught specific messages about street harassment so that they understand why women do not like it and so they will be more likely to stop or never engage in the behavior. In the last section I discuss how, because of homosociality and gender discrimination, men tend to respect and listen to other men more than women. As a result, we must have male allies lead the way in education efforts. We also need them to stop street harassment by preventing their friends from engaging in it and intervening when they see it occurring. Confronting other men, even if they are colleagues or friends, can be hard to do. The chapter ends with suggestions and success stories for how to do so.

Healthy Definitions of Masculinity

Providing men with healthy definitions of masculinity is an essential component to ending street harassment. Men need to be able to perceive themselves as masculine while displaying sensitivity, caring, and respect. For the last several years, there has been a growing movement among men's anti-violence groups to do just that, including showing men they do not need to use or condone violence or harassment to be men. The Washington, D.C.-based nonprofit Men Can Stop Rape (MCSR) is an example of a group working on this messaging in several ways.

Using a media campaign, "My Strength Is Not for Hurting," MCSR is working to change the definition of masculinity by emphasizing how men can be strong without violence. An example of this is a poster with one young man staring at the viewer and "My Strength Is Not for Hurting" printed at the top. MCSR also has worked with other organizations, such as the U.S. Department of Defense and the California Coalition against Sexual Assault to create tailored public education campaigns. MCSR offers a no-cost initial consultation to any interested group about how to use a positive message that reframes masculinity for young men.[29]

One of MCSR's most successful programs, and the premiere primary prevention program for male youth in the United States, is the Men of Strength (MOST) Club. Through the MOST Club, MCSR provides high school age young men with "a structured and supportive space to learn about healthy masculinity and redefine male strength."[30] During the 16-week program, young men discuss masculinity, male strength, and how traditional definitions of masculinity contribute to gender violence and harassment. The young men learn about healthier, nonviolent models and visions of manhood and how they can be leaders among men and allies with women to promote gender equality and end male violence.[31] Since 2000, over 2,000 men at more than one hundred schools in seven states and Washington, D.C., have been involved with MOST Clubs. Since 2008, MCSR has started clubs at the middle school and college level. Each year, MCSR holds several trainings for individuals interested in bringing the program to their school. Visit www.men canstoprape.org to learn more.

Respecting Women

Teaching boys and men to respect women is another way to help end street harassment. Unfortunately, there are a lot of barriers to doing so.

In American society—and in most societies—few women are leaders or are in positions of power, and in general, instead of being valued for their intelligence or talents as men are, women often are valued for their looks. Women are commonly portrayed as silent, submissive sexual objects in all forms of media, from music videos and movies, to comic books and video games.[32] The more people see these depictions without a larger number of positive images of women to counterbalance them, the easier it is for men and women to sexually objectify and disrespect women.[33]

Hopefully in time there will be more women in power and more positive female figureheads. In the meantime, teaching men to recognize the disconnection between the women they see in movies and advertisements and the women they know and respect can help remind them that in the flesh, women are not sexual objects, but full human beings. When they see an attractive woman, reminding them that she is more than her looks and has other attributes to her personality is important.

Hugo Schwyzer, a professor of gender studies, gave a good example of how to remind youth of this. In his article "Staring at Janae's Legs" one girl, Janae, at a youth group event was wearing revealing, tight clothing. When the youth were divided up by sex, the boys kept talking about how hot she was and how they wanted to "hit that." Schwyzer asked them what it feels like when a girl like her is showing a lot of skin and the boys enthusiastically said it was awesome and they couldn't stop looking. Schwyzer challenged this asking if they really couldn't control their eyes. Some of the boys realized it is a choice to look and how long to do so. Schwyzer said to them:

I don't think there's anything wrong with noticing girls. . . . I do think there's something very wrong when your focus on their bodies makes it impossible for you to see them as people, as friends, as human beings. When you find yourself noticing a girl's body and staring at her skin, I don't want you to beat yourself up. But I don't want you to objectify her, either. . . . Next time you're looking at Janae's legs, I want you to remind yourself that she is more than just her body.[34]

If men remember that all women they see in public are more than sexualized bodies, they may be less apt to tell them they have nice legs or that they are "looking good." Reminding them to think about how they would feel if a woman they respect was being harassed by a stranger when they were just walking down the street can help them realize that no woman deserves to be treated so disrespectfully. Several women who took my 2008 survey offered advice for men about what acceptable behavior is:

- If you would get mad if someone did it to your mom or your sister, don't do it to a stranger.
- If you wouldn't say it in front of your mother, your sister, your daughter, or a good friend then don't say it. Show women the respect and courtesy you would show any person.
- If you wouldn't do it to a member of your own sex (or whatever gender(s) you aren't sexually attracted to) you shouldn't do it to me.
- Treating me like a human being is acceptable.

Explaining Street Harassment

One barrier to men understanding the inappropriateness of street harassment is male privilege, which can keep men from realizing or understanding women's point of view and make them defensive when the topic is brought up.[35] Getting them to view street harassment from a woman's perspective is an important part of educating men about street harassment. Having a woman they care about talk to them about their street harassment experiences and how it makes them feel is one option. In an informal survey of eighty-five male allies, 95 percent said this was the best idea for informing men about street harassment and educating them that this is a problem. The onus should not be on women to have to tell them, though, but on men to ask them if they would be willing to share their stories and discuss how street harassment makes them feel. Seeing the personal connection to an issue helps people care about it and take action.

Putting the scenario in a framework that is understandable to men can help them better understand it, too. For example, trying to show how threatening and insulting it is to women by placing men in the women's role: asking men how they would like it if other men who were larger than them regularly interrupted them to tell them to smile, comment on their looks and body parts, ask for their name, touch them, follow them, or start masturbating in front of them. Help men see the issue from a woman's perspective and realize that all many women are trying to do is simply go about their day.

Informing men about the facts of street harassment is another important approach. Anyone trying to talk to a man who does not believe the problem can cite the studies listed in the first several chapters of this book and direct them to sources in the bibliography.

Men and women may have different views about what is an appropriate way to approach and interact with a stranger in public given their different perspectives and place in a society with gender equity. Thus, it is important to teach men appropriate ways to interact with women that will be the least offensive or threatening. The following tips can guide any interaction with women in public (and if they sound too dumbed down, I agree, but doing so seems to be necessary given some men's attitudes about commenting on and harassing women in public):

- Treat women like human beings, with respect and dignity.
- If you want to say hello to a woman, just smile and nod or say hello. Do not whistle, honk, or make kissy noises at her. Do not say, "Hey

baby," or "Hi cutie." Those are disrespectful and inappropriate actions and terms to use with a stranger.

- The way a woman is dressed does not tell you if she wants to be commented on. If she looks dressed up, do not assume it is to gain the admiration of all men she sees and that you should say something to her. She may enjoy dressing up, she may be dressed up for an event, or she may be dressed up to gain the admiration of a specific person or persons. Unless she has a sign on that says, "Please comment on my looks," do not do it.

- Stranger rape and harassment are real threats for women. If you find yourself alone with a woman in a deserted parking garage, road, or park, especially at night, keep a respectful distance and do not approach her.

Unless the comments or actions of men who want to flirt or meet a woman in public to date or "hook up" with are welcome by the woman, they constitute harassment. Here are several things to teach men so they can avoid being a harasser:

- Do not assume all women are single, heterosexual or bisexual, or interested in male attention or in forming a relationship.

- Differences or similarities in race, class, and age between you and the woman and the woman's sexual orientation can cause her to interpret attention a certain way.

- Women deserve the same right to privacy in public that most men enjoy, and many women will view a man who approaches her for a reason other than a gender-neutral one, such as asking for directions, the time, or to offer assistance, as violating their privacy, and they may be rude or hostile.

- Most of the time, women do not want to be approached for a date by a man in public places like the street or at a bus stop. Women are usually in public for a reason: to commute to school or work, to run errands, or to get exercise, not to meet men. There are times when a woman may be open to meeting someone in public, but they are rare, so keep in mind that chances are great that if you approach a woman, she will not want to meet you to form a relationship.

- If you do approach a woman, try not to do so if it is dark out, if it is a deserted area, if there are no other people around, or if you are with your friends while she is alone. All of these factors can make women feel threatened by any man approaching them.

- Never follow a woman without a good reason, like she dropped her wallet and you are trying to return it. Aside from assault, being followed is the behavior women feel the most threatened by when they are alone in public.

- Only approach a woman when she does not appear to be in a hurry or preoccupied. Initiate the interaction by smiling at her and/or saying hello. If, and only if, she smiles and/or says hello back and then does not hurry away, look away, or otherwise try to ignore you, then you can say something else to her that is respectful and polite, including non-sexually explicit flirtatious remarks.

- If you say hello and/or smile and the woman hurries away, ignores you or responds rudely, leave her alone. She may not have the time or desire to talk, so be respectful of her schedule and feelings. She may have had a bad harassment or assault experience and now is wary of all men who approach her. You may be the third or fourth person to approach her that day and even if done politely, it can become wearisome and annoying.

- If a woman initiates a conversation with you, be polite and respectful in your responses. If at any point during a conversation a woman looks uncomfortable, gives you one word answers, looks away, or tries to leave, follow her cues and stop talking. If she does not resume the conversation, leave her alone.

- If in any doubt about your behavior, ask yourself the following questions, adopted from Dr. Bernice Sandler's guide "How Men (and Women) Can Tell if Their Behavior is Sexual Harassment"[36]:

  o Would I mind if someone treated my spouse, partner, girlfriend, mother, sister, or daughter this way?

  o Would I mind if this person told my spouse, partner, girlfriend, mother, sister, or daughter what I was saying and doing?

  o Would I do this if I was with my spouse, partner, girlfriend, mother, sister, or daughter?

  o When a person objects to my behavior do I apologize and stop, or do I get angry instead?

  o Is my behavior reciprocated? Are there specific indications of pleasure and not "she didn't object"?

MALE ALLIES

We need male allies. Because men listen to other men and look to other men for approval, having men tell other men not to harass and intervene when they see harassment occurring can, sadly, be a more effective way of educating men not to harass women than if women talk to them.

Among the eighty-five male allies I informally surveyed in late 2009 (see www.stopstreetharassment.com/book/surveys), 82 percent said they would be willing to talk to their male friends and family members about street harassment to help end the problem. In an open-ended question, several of them suggested messaging that men can use with other men, including:

- Street harassment is vastly more common than men think. It happens to almost all women at some point.

- Women deserve respect and have the same right to exist in public spaces as men.
- Think about what you are REALLY doing. Street harassment to the harassed is really scary and a person could have fear of bodily harm.
- Making men empathize with the harassed or imagine themselves in women's place.
- Casting street harassment in terms of how many of their male friends might be problems, and how many female friends suffer from it.
- These people [being harassed] are your mothers, sisters, wives, girlfriends, coworkers, fellow citizens.
- We have a choice to not harass people on that street, and the power to do so, and we should exercise that choice and power. Also, this is not saying you are not allowed to appreciate a beautiful woman on the street, but you must stop doing so in a way that invades her space and makes her feel unsafe . . . Men can still look at women, just do so without comment or a leer that suggests that you own that woman's body or have the right to consume it.

There are many barriers that keep people, especially men, from preventing and intervening in street harassment incidents as often as they could. For example, if there are several other people around, the "bystander effect" may mean that each person expects the other to respond or that if no one responds, there is no need to or it must be inappropriate to do so. The following are some of the barriers that the 85 male allies mentioned:

- A bystander may not be sure if what is happening is unwelcome by the woman or if it constitutes inappropriate behavior.
- He or she may not want to assume the woman cannot handle the situation herself and feel that intervening is disempowering to the woman.
- A shy person may not want to draw any attention to him or herself or may be too scared to attempt to intervene.
- A bystander may not know what to even do or say that will help the situation.
- A bystander may fear the perpetrator's reaction and not want to become the target of his anger at being challenged.

Groups such as Men Can Stop Rape (MCSR) and Mentors in Violence Prevention (MVP) know this and so their programming includes bystander intervention. The MCSR programming allows men to brainstorm and role play ways they can intervene when they hear sexist talk and witness gender-based violence or harassment. They also discuss issues of masculinity and the importance of speaking out. They emphasize that chances are, there are other guys who feel the same way but are too scared to speak out unless someone else does first. The MVP program, a leadership training program that motivates male student-athletes and leaders to play a primary role in preventing men's violence and harassment of women, holds workshops on bystander training.

In the opening of the trainings, usually done in all-male groups, the facilitator asks everyone to visualize a scenario in which a woman close to them is being harassed or assaulted by a man. The facilitator then asks them to imagine there is another man in the room who has the power to stop what is happening but chooses not to, either by silently watching or leaving. When asked how the scenario made them feel, men usually react with anger that the bystander did nothing and express feelings of powerlessness and sadness over what happened. The point of the exercise is to get them to think about the role and responsibility of a bystander. Then they discuss less clear-cut harassment and assault scenarios and the moral responsibility of the bystander even when they may face barriers to intervening.[37]

Following the opening exercise, the facilitator creates realistic harassment and assault scenarios using typical experiences young people face at high school and college. Then the group discusses ways a bystander could intervene before, during, or after an incident. As most people immediately worry about their own safety and the high cost of intervening, they discuss those barriers and brainstorm nonviolent and nonthreatening options. The overall MVP model is to stimulate dialogue and critical thinking about the choices bystanders face and the costs and benefits of action and inaction.[38]

Brian Martin, professor of social sciences at the University of Wollongong, Australia, offers additional suggestions to men who wish to intervene in street harassment but are unsure how:

Suppose you are with men who are harassing women (or anyone else):

- Refuse to join in. Do not make any comments yourself.
- Discourage others from doing so. Tell them the person is not enjoying it or tell them to leave the person alone.
- At a suitable time, raise the issue about public harassment with your friends and explain why it is inappropriate to treat people that way.

Suppose you see a man/men harassing women (or anyone else):

- If it looks like a man is bothering a woman, ask her, "Is someone bothering you?" That question alone may deter a harasser who believes no one will intervene. If she says yes and the harasser does not leave or persists harassing, tell the harasser to stop or call for assistance (from police, a transit authority worker, or other people nearby).

- If a woman in a crowd says she has just been harassed or had someone touch her inappropriately, call out a supportive comment such as, "Whoever did that, it is not welcome," or "We do not tolerate that behavior."
- If you see a woman who has been verbally or physically abused, you can ask her if there is anything you can do to help. If she says no, leave, because you do not want to be another person intruding on her space. If she says yes, try to help her as best you can.[39]

Martin points out that being a man may lead to hostility from the woman you are trying to help. She may be suspicious of your motives. She may be wary of all men who approach her in public because of her experiences. Make sure to approach her in as non-threatening a way as possible and try not to take offense if she treats you rudely.[40]

Most of the male allies I surveyed (82 percent) said they would be willing to intervene when they see someone harassing a woman, 17 percent said they had intervened once, and 46 percent said they had intervened more than once. Here are tips some of them offered to other men who are unsure how or are afraid to intervene:

- I've found that distractions and indirect interventions help best. Asking for directions, asking for the time, or other innocuous questions can often be enough of a distraction for a harasser to go away and move on, without causing a big scene or putting anyone in physical danger.
- I do not address the man/group harassing the female. I simply offer my presence.
- You don't have to be loud and physically confrontational. You can simply distract the harasser by saying "waddup" or you can just stay in open view so it won't escalate to a rape scenario.
- Where possible, intervene by giving control to the target of the harassment (e.g. "is he bothering you?" or "are you okay?").
- Just do the right thing. I think there are times when a harasser may be intimidating even to other males, but you have to find the intestinal fortitude to stand up for women in these situations. Otherwise, it's as if we are giving the harassers tacit approval to continue their behaviors.
- Go in fast and loud and willing to do just about anything.
- Be aware of the situation, know what your advantage is, and if confronting a group situation, make sure you are interacting with the leader, and have contacted the police.

- Don't turn a blind eye, confront them even if it's awkward, even if it's not socially acceptable, do it anyways. . . . Remember that many women are not in the situation where they are safe speaking up for themselves.

Many of the suggestions that do not directly challenge a harasser, such as asking the woman if she wants help or asking the harasser what time it is, are excellent to use when one is not sure if it is harassment that is occurring, if they do not want to dis-empower the woman, or if they fear becoming the target of the harasser's inappropriate behavior themselves. Something as simple as clearing one's throat or coughing can help defuse a situation too, particularly if a harasser does not notice other people are around (such as on a dark street). To further illustrate tactics; here are a few stories from my survey of male allies about times they helped stop street harassers:

A young woman was on a metro train and a couple of teenagers started to tell her in explicit and profane language what they wanted to do to her. I told them they needed to leave her alone. . . . They did and moved on. I was happy to see that a couple of other men surrounding us on the train told me that they had my back should things have gone violent.

A woman was being leered at out of a car as she crossed the street (in front of the car). I was walking just behind her. . . . My intervention was rather quiet— I interposed my body between her and the car, falling somewhat behind her as we neared the other side, in order to stay between her and the men.

On public trains if I see a man staring down a woman and she seems scared I have locked eyes with him and started a conversation with the woman so she won't seem alone. My intervening has more so been making my presence as a third party known.

I've berated on numerous occasions coworkers, usually during lunch time, for harassing women walking down the street.

I've intervened with guys who thought rape jokes were funny. Also my brother and I were at a public event when some guy said something ugly about how a young lady looked. My brother said he knew that guy would not allow someone to talk that way if she was a family member. So why did he think it was ok to say such things? Well the guy was shocked and said nothing more about that girl.

WHAT CAN WE DO?

Each of us can stop supporting unhealthy definitions of masculinity, promote respect for women, and educate men about street harassment by:

- Not encouraging or condoning violence in any form, especially men's violence against women. That means not watching music videos, movies, or pornography or playing video games in which violence against women is glorified or sexualized. This also includes not supporting companies that use violent imagery to sell products.

- Not putting pressure on friends to "score," not rewarding men for having multiple sexual partners (or penalizing women who do), and not mocking men who have not had a sexual partner or who have had only one.

- Not describing women as body parts or referring to them only as sex objects instead of as complete human beings with a personality, interests, and talents. Reminding people who do rate women solely by their looks that they have other attributes.

- Not buying products from companies that portray only women's body parts or portray them as sex objects and not watching movies, pornography, or music videos in which women are portrayed as objects that exist for men's pleasure.

- Not penalizing men or women who act outside their gender norms.

- Eliminating language like "pussy," "wuss," "fag," and "girl" as insults used to punish men who are not being "macho."

- Eliminating language that portrays men and things that are masculine to be positive, while women and things that are feminine are negative (e.g., men think rationally while women feel emotionally).

- Not penalizing, mocking, or dismissing men and women who speak out against violence, inequality, and disrespectful behaviors.

- Talking to men about street harassment.

- Brainstorming and role playing ways to intervene in a harassment incident: either before it occurs when our friends are the would-be perpetrators, or when we see it occurring.

- Encouraging people to always stand up for other people, for human rights, for human dignity, even if they think it will make them unpopular. And doing the same ourselves.

NOTES

1. David M. Buss, "Sexual Conflict: Evolutionary Insights into Feminism and the 'Battle of the Sexes,'" in *Sex, Power, Conflict: Evolutionary and Feminist Perspectives*, ed. David M Buss and Neil M. Malamuth (Oxford: Oxford University Press, 1996); see also Barbara Smuts, "Male Aggression against Women: An Evolutionary Perspective," in *Sex, Power, Conflict: Evolutionary and Feminist Perspectives*, ed. David M. Buss and Neil M. Malamuth (Oxford: Oxford University Press, 1996); see also Felicia Pratto, "Sexual Politics," in *Sex, Power, Conflict: Evolutionary and Feminist Perspectives*, ed. David M. Buss and Neil M. Malamuth (Oxford: Oxford University Press, 1996).

2. Cynthia Grant Bowman, "Street Harassment and the Informal Ghettoization of Women," *Harvard Law Review* 106, no. 3 (January

1993): 517–580; see also Elizabeth Grauerholz, "Gender Socialization and Communication: The Inscription of Sexual Harassment in Social Life," in *Conceptualizing Sexual Harassment as Discursive Practice*, ed. Shereen G. Bingham (Westport, CT: Praeger, 1994); see also Martha Langelan, *Back Off! How to Confront and Stop Sexual Harassment and Harassers* (New York: Fireside Press, 1993); see also Catherine MacKinnon, "The Social Causes of Sexual Harassment," in *Sexual Harassment: Confrontation and Decisions*, ed. Edmund Wall. (Buffalo, NY: Prometheus Books, 1992); see also Catherine MacKinnon, "Sexual Harassment as Sex Discrimination," in *Sexual Harassment: Confrontation and Decisions*, ed. Edmund Wall (Buffalo, NY: Prometheus Books, 1992).

3. Pacific Lutheran University, "World Expert Addresses Masculinity, Violence," April 11, 2008, http://news.plu.edu/node/2507.

4. Jeanine Prime and Corinne A. Moss-Racusin, "Engaging Men in Gender Initiatives: What Change Agents Need To Know," Catalyst, May 2009, 15.

5. Michael Kaufman, "The Construction of Masculinity and the Triad of Men's Violence," in *Men's Lives* (second edition), ed. Michael S. Kimmel and Michael A. Messner (New York: Macmillan Publishing Company, 1992): 40.

6. Prime and Moss-Racusin, 3–4.

7. Ariel Levy, *Female Chauvinist Pigs: Women and the Rise of Raunch Culture* (New York: Free Press, 2005).

8. Ian M. Harris, *Messages Men Hear: Constructing Masculinities* (London: Taylor & Francis, 1995): 19.

9. Joseph H. Pleck, "Men's Power with Women, Other Men, and Society: A Men's Movement Analysis," in *Men's Lives* (second edition), ed. Michael S. Kimmel and Michael A. Messner (New York: Macmillan Publishing Company, 1992): 25; see also Kaufman, 43.

10. Charles M. Blow, "Two Little Boys," *New York Times*, April 24, 2009, http://blow.blogs.nytimes.com/2009/04/24/two-little-boys.

11. Marilyn French, *The War Against Women* (New York: Ballantine Books, 1992), 181.

12. Sue Wise and Liz Stanley, *Georgie Porgie: Sexual Harassment in Everyday Life* (London: Pandora, 1987): 80.

13. Cheryl Benard and Edith Schlaffer, "The Man in the Street: Why He Harasses," *Ms. Magazine* (May 1981), 18–19.

14. Langelan, 61.

15. Benard and Schlaffer, 18–19.

16. Maggie Hadleigh-West, *War Zone*, Film Fatale, Inc., 1998.

17. Ibid.

18. Ibid.

19. Benard and Schlaffer, 18–19.

20. Amit Taneja, "From Oppressor to Activist: Reflections of a Feminist Journey," in *Men Speak Out: Views on Gender, Sex and Power*, ed. Shira Tarrant (New York: Routledge, 2008): 155.

21. Brucibaby, comment on "So Angry I Could Strip!" *Guardian*, comment posted on May 28, 2008, http://www.guardian.co.uk/commentisfree/2008/may/28/soangryicouldstrip (accessed July 30, 2008).

22. Gardner, 179.

23. bell hooks, "Seduced by Violence No More," in *Transforming a Rape Culture*, ed. Emilie Buchwald, Pamela R. Fletcher, and Martha Roth (Minneapolis, MN: Milkwood Editions, 1993), 356.

24. Mitchell Duneier, *Sidewalk* (New York: Farrar, Straus, and Giroux, 2000), 189–216; see also Global Action Project, "Crossed Lines," July 9, 2007, http://www.youtube.com/watch?v=oW0dViXyS1o.

25. Hugo Schwyzer, "Staring at Janae's Legs," in *Men Speak Out: Views on Gender, Sex and Power*, ed. Shira Tarrant (New York: Routledge, 2008).

26. Benard and Schlaffer, 18–19.

27. Prime and Moss-Racusin, 15.

28. Jackson Katz, *The Macho Paradox: Why Some Men Hurt Women and How All Men Can Help* (Naperville, IL: Sourcebooks, Inc., 2006), 123.

29. Men Can Stop Rape, "Strength Mediaworks," n.d., http://www.mencanstoprape.org/info-url2698/info-url_list.htm?section=Hire%20Us%20to%20Create%20Your%20Media%20Campaign.

30. Men Can Stop Rape, "Strength Training," n.d., http://www.mencanstoprape.org/info-url2696/info-url.htm.

31. Men Can Stop Rape, "Youth Development: The Men of Strength (MOST) Club," n.d., http://www.mencanstoprape.org/info-url2696/info-url_show.htm?doc_id=697523.

32. American Psychology Association, "Report of the APA Task Force on the Sexualization of Girls," 2007, http://www.apa.org/pi/women/programs/girls/report.aspx?item=2.

33. Elizabeth Landau, "Men See Bikini-Clad Women as Objects, Psychologists Say," CNN, April 2, 2009, http://www.cnn.com/2009/HEALTH/02/19/women.bikinis.objects/index.html.

34. Schwyzer, 74–75.

35. Alas, A Blog, "The Male Privilege Checklist," n.d. www.amptoons.com/blog/the-male-privilege-checklist.

36. Bernice Sandler, "How Men Can Tell if Their Behavior is Sexual Harassment," n.d., http://www.bernicesandler.com/id18.htm.

37. Katz, 212–213.

38. Ibid., 221.

39. Brian Martin, "Men: Help Stop Public Harassment," in *Perspectives on Social Problems, Volume 9: Public Harassment*, ed. Carol Brooks Gardner (Greenwich, CT: JAI Press, 1997): xiii–xvii.

40. Ibid., xiii–xvii.

_____ *Chapter 8* _____

Empowering Women

Ultimately, to end street harassment, the onus is on men to stop harassing women, but achieving that will take time. In the short-term, it also is important to empower girls and women to lead less fearful and restricted public lives by teaching them that street harassment is not their fault, equipping them with a range of ideas for how they can deal with harassment, and, if they want, tactics they can use that could make the harasser think twice about harassing women again. Engaging in tactics that hold harassers accountable is action that women who want to work to end street harassment can do, through verbal responses and by reporting the harasser to persons of authority. In the spirit of female empowerment, this chapter is filled with advice on these topics from female experts and from "regular" women through their success stories.

IT'S NOT YOUR FAULT

In general, most societies trivialize men's harassment of women by dismissing it as a problem and by saying it is a woman's fault due to her attractiveness, what she wore, or where she went. As a result, victim blaming, including self-blame, is rampant. If a woman thinks she is at fault, she may think it is something she has to put up with and, as a result, she may not speak about it or work to end it. She may tell other women it is complimentary or no big deal. She may change her appearance or habits or try to avoid being alone in places where she could be harassed.[1]

One of the most important messages for girls and women, then, is that any street harassment they experience is not their fault, no matter what people may tell them. Women are not at fault because of what they wore, where they went, or what time of day or night they were in public, nor because they looked "too attractive" or "too vulnerable." Men who harass are at fault. They are the ones acting inappropriately. They are the ones with the problem. Women should have the right to walk down the street or wait for a bus without being the target of unwanted sexual or sexist attention or the recipient of insults.

The messages that street harassment is not girls' or women's fault and is not something they must put up with are important ones that several groups that work with young women emphasize. Joanne Smith, founder and executive director of Girls for Gender Equity (GGE) in New York City focuses on female empowerment in all of her programs. She says about street harassment, "One of the things that we teach our girls is that it's not your fault, and that you don't have to accept this as a way of life. We help the girls to be more assertive, to follow their gut instinct."[2] Through GGE, young women are empowered to address street harassment in their community. They created a 20-minute documentary called *Hey . . . Shorty* and organized a free street harassment summit for interested members of their community.

The volunteer-led grassroots nonprofit HOTGIRLS (Helping Our Teen Girls in Real Life Situations) in Atlanta, Georgia, founded by Dr. Carla Stokes, is another example of a group of young women working to teach other young women that street harassment is not their fault. In 2005, the Teen Advisory Board of HOTGIRLS collected stories about girls' experiences with street harassment. Using these stories, they developed educational materials to raise awareness about the impact of street harassment on girls and women. The Teen Advisory Board then organized a summit for predominantly African American girls ages 13 to 19 to discuss street harassment, to share ideas for how to respond to harassers, and to discuss how images of black girls and women in the media and hip hop culture contribute to street harassment. They developed materials to educate harassers, targets, and allies about street harassment and to help combat the "denigrating stereotypes about black women and girls that contribute to harassment and disrespectful treatment on the streets and in other settings."[3]

Members of the youth-driven Rogers Park Young Women's Action Team (YWAT) organization in Chicago also work to share empowering messages among their female peers. In 2003, YWAT members interviewed 168 girls ages 13 to 19 about street harassment, and 53 percent felt there was nothing they could do about the harassment they experienced. Founding YWAT member Jonnae Taylor said that their activism on the issue became focused on addressing that finding. She said, "a lot of teens [we surveyed] felt like [street harassment] was their fault and we want to tell them it is not your fault you are being harassed . . . and there's something you can do to stop it or at least help lessen it."[4] Another founding member, Ronnett Lockett, said, "We want to empower young women not to be afraid to tackle issues."[5]

To help empower young women, YWAT members engage in many initiatives. They regularly hold anti-street harassment workshops at high schools, conferences, and community events to educate both boys and girls about the problem. During the workshops they lead discussions about what street harassment is and how it makes its targets feel. They emphasize to girls that anything that makes them feel uncomfortable is harassment and that "men may not feel like they are attacking us—but we feel attacked."[6] They perform a spoken word piece about how Little Red has to navigate through the Hood while dodging insults from the Big Bad Wolf. They hand out tips they created for how to respond to harassers.[7]

Letting girls and women know that street harassment is not their fault and not something they must put up with is something we can all do by not engaging in victim blaming, not framing street harassment as a "women's" problem but instead as a men's problem, and by teaching girls and women a range of ways to respond to harassers.

RESPONDING TO HARASSERS

When they are harassed, women are put in the difficult position of having to decide very quickly how to respond and their responses typically vary depending on the situation. Overall, most women ignore, walk away from, or humor their harassers. The reasons for their response may include fearing for their safety, being socialized to be polite and not make a scene, not knowing what other response to have, not having the time or energy to address the harasser, and trying not to give the harasser the satisfaction of any response.[8] Depending on the circumstances, these responses may be necessary, but they also can be problematic. Not responding assertively or reporting a harasser rarely deters harassers from continuing their behavior and these responses can leave women feeling disempowered and frustrated.[9] Two of my survey respondents wrote about this:

The standard advice, "Ignore it," doesn't work. It only causes the harassers to escalate. It's better to confront the harasser directly. Sometimes he will stop. Even if he doesn't, you keep more of your dignity.
　　　　　　　　—40–49-year-old gay white woman in Berkeley, California

I've tried everything from ignoring it, to talking to the person, to taking their photo, to yelling back. There is no foolproof method. I find that if I say something or take their photo, at least I feel like I fought back a little. If I ignore it, I get out of the situation more quickly, and feel a bit safer, but I also feel more beaten down, I feel like I let that person walk all over me.
　　　　　　　　—30–39-year-old heterosexual Latina in New York City

Ignoring harassers also can be harmful to women's self-esteem and health. At Rutgers University, psychology scholars Kimberly Fairchild and Laurie A. Rudman studied street harassment and women's self-objectification. Self-objectification means seeing oneself through the eyes of others. In the case of street harassment, it means seeing oneself through the eyes of the men who harass. Studies show that girls and women who self-objectify are more prone to depression, low self-esteem, and eating disorders. A preoccupation with their looks can keep them from having as much energy and time for other pursuits.[10] In Fairchild and Rudman's study of 228 college women, the women who ignored or denied harassment reported higher rates of feeling self-objectified compared with women who responded to the harasser, reported him, or discussed the experience with friends.[11] Taking action against harassers, when possible, may be better for women.

Last, despite a common belief that ignoring a harasser is the best way to stay safe, it is not always true. Unfortunately, there is no foolproof way to stay safe. As the woman from Berkeley previously quoted noted, some harassers escalate their harassment into vicious words ("stuck up slut," "racist bitch," "you're an ugly fat ho anyway,") or assaults when women ignore them. They may do the same when a woman tells them to stop. It is a situation in which women can be "damned if they do and damned if they don't," so, if they want, they should say something since they may be called names regardless. One woman who took my survey said, "I used to ignore it. Sometimes that made it worse. Now I yell back, which seems to scare them away more often. However, it is also scary . . . you never know when you might anger someone who is dangerous, so I sort of play it by ear."

More importantly, crime reports show that women who have the highest success rate in escaping sexual assault are those who use a combination of early verbal and physical resistance, so if a fear of rape is keeping women silent against harassers, it is usually better for them to speak up.[12] The former Executive Director of the Washington, D.C. Rape Crisis Center, Martha Langelan, noted that there are men who use street harassment as a rape test, and they may attempt rape depending on how a woman responds to street harassment. If she is assertive and forceful, they will leave her alone, but if she cowers or humors them, they may attempt rape.[13] Furthermore, self defense instructor and founder of the nonprofit organization Defend Yourself, Lauren R. Taylor wrote an article for the *Washington Post*, saying that "confronting harassment builds your 'self-defense muscle.'. . . If you don't resist harassment and other low-key forms of violence, you will be 'out of shape' should you ever have to deal with a more serious situation with an abusive partner or a rape attempt. Being assertive with harassers helps you learn how to take care of yourself at work, in school, in relationships and in the rest of life."[14]

Women who are concerned about safety should consider other options besides ignoring a harasser. Men who harass with the intent to physically harm a woman are probably expecting that she will be passive and not fight back. Fighting back by yelling or using physical force can throw them off guard and help keep one safe.

There is no overall "best" way to respond to every harasser in every circumstance, and women are the only ones who can determine what the best way is for them to respond in any given incident so they will feel both safe and empowered. The more informed they are about options for responding, the better they can be at making that decision. In this context, if a woman knows a range of options for how she can respond to a harasser and still decides to ignore him, then she has at least made an informed decision.[15] As ignoring, humoring, or yelling at a harasser are responses most women know, the rest of this chapter focuses on other options for dealing with harassers.

HOLDING HARASSERS ACCOUNTABLE

When a woman is deciding how to respond to a harasser, actions like calling him out on his behavior or reporting him are options many do not know, or they are ones they are not comfortable using. To better equip women who want to help end street harassment, this section explores a range of ideas for responses women can use that hold harassers accountable for their behavior, starting with responses women can say to the harasser and finishing with ways to report harassers.

Verbal Responses

Each spring, Lauren R. Taylor, a native of Washington, D.C., and a long-time activist on gender-based violence issues, teaches a community class on street harassment and self-defense. She teaches many self-defense classes through her organization Defend Yourself and began offering this class specifically because many women said they were negatively impacted by street harassment but did not know how to deal with it.

In her workshop, Taylor talks about how street harassment is part of the spectrum of gender-based violence and teaches attendees assertive responses to it. Attendees practice saying "no" in an assertive tone of voice, while standing in a confident, strong stance with an assertive facial expression. Attendees practice telling the harasser what they want, such as, "Stop it!" "I don't like that," "Leave me alone," and "Stop touching me." They also role play different harassment scenarios, taking turns playing a harasser and harassee and responding on the fly to the harassment vignettes. Most of the attendees in the workshop I attended in 2009 said they felt they had been socialized to be polite and nice and so even practicing saying these assertive, "not nice" phrases was challenging, but empowering. Finally, the class offers a few simple physical self defense moves for the times when the harassment escalates. These moves include pushing the palm of the hand to the nose or chin of a harasser, throwing an elbow to their throat, stomping on their feet, and elbowing someone standing behind while yelling, "No!" Taylor's take away messages at the end of the class are (1) don't be afraid to say something; (2) be clear about what you want when you respond; (3) you have several choices for how to respond; and (4) you can contribute to stopping street harassment in any circumstance.[16] She also acknowledges that any situation can escalate to violence, and women must always think about what response will make them feel and be the safest. That may be ignoring or walking away from the harasser, which is fine, as long as that is their choice.[17]

The following section contains suggestions for verbal responses women can use when they feel safe enough. They are a compilation of my own suggestions, as well as many from street harassment and sexual harassment experts including Langelan,[18] Taylor,[19] and Dr. Bernice Sandler.[20] Since a street harassment incident can be startling and throw women off balance, practicing these responses aloud and role playing scenarios can help women feel better able to actually use them.

How to talk to a harasser:

- Always use strong body language: Look the harasser in the eyes; speak in a strong, clear voice. Using your voice, facial expressions, and body language together, without mixed signals, show assertiveness and strength.

- Project confidence and calm. Even if you do not feel that way, it is important to appear calm, serious, and confident.

- Do not apologize, make an excuse, or ask a question. You do not need to say sorry for how you feel or what you want. Be firm. Instead of saying, "Excuse me . . ." "I'm sorry, but . . ." or "Please . . .", say directly, "Stop doing X."

- Do not get into a dialogue with the harasser, try to reason with them, or answer their questions. You do not need to respond to diversions, questions, threats, blaming, or guilt-tripping. Stay on your own agenda. Stick to your point. Repeat your statement or leave.

- Do not swear or lose your temper: This type of reaction is the most likely to make the harasser respond with anger and violence and it also can make you seem like the one who is crazy or wrong when the harassment happens among a group of people, but no one sees what the harasser did to you.

- Decide when you're done. Success is how you define it. If you said what you needed to say and you're ready to leave, do so.

Ideas for what you can say to a harasser:

- Name the behavior and state that it is wrong. For example say, "Do not whistle at me, that is harassment," or "Do not touch my butt, that is sexual harassment."

- Tell them exactly what you want. Say, for example, "move away from me," "stop touching me," or "go stand over there."

- Use statements, not questions if you tell them to leave you alone. For example, say, "Leave me alone," not "Would you please leave me alone?"

- Make an all-purpose anti-harassment statement, such as: "Stop harassing women. I don't like it. No one likes it. Show some respect." Speak it in a neutral but assertive tone.

- Use an A-B-C statement (and be very concrete about A and C).

  A. Tell the harasser what the problem is;

  B. State the effect; and

  C. What you want.
     Here is an example: "When you make kissing noises at me it makes me feel uncomfortable. I want you to say, 'Hello, ma'am,' from now on if you want to talk to me."

- Identify the perpetrator: "Man in the yellow shirt, stop touching me." (This is especially useful if you and the harasser are together somewhere with other people around.)

- Attack the behavior, not the person. Tell them what they are doing that you do not like ("You are standing too close") rather than blaming them as a person ("You are such a jerk"). Avoid cursing, name-calling, put downs, and other actions that may escalate the situation unnecessarily.

- Use the "'Miss Manners' Approach" and ask the harasser something like, "I beg your pardon!" or "I can't believe you said that," or "You must have me confused with someone to whom you think you can speak that way," combined with strong facial expressions of shock, dismay, and disgust.

- Ask a Socratic question such as, "That's so interesting—can you explain why you think you can put your hand on my leg?"

- If the harasser is in a car, write down the license plate of the car. Even if you can't see it, pretending to write it down can scare the perpetrator into stopping. If the harassers are aggressive or threatening and you do write down the license plate number, you can report them to the police.

- Buy a notebook and write in bold letters on the cover "Street Harassment." Take out the notebook when you are harassed and ask the harasser to repeat himself so you can write it down. Make a big show of asking for the date, time, checking the place you are at, etc. If they ask why you're writing things down, you can say you are keeping a record of harassment.

- Tell the harasser that you are conducting a street harassment research project or survey. Take out a notebook and start asking them questions such as, "How often do you do this?" or "How do you choose which people to harass?" or "Are you more likely to do this when you are alone or when you're with other people," or "Do you discuss people you harass with your mother, sister, or female friends?"

- Hand the street harasser a business-size card with messages about not harassing women. The Street Harassment Project (www.streetharassment project.org/flyers) and Stop Street Harassment (www.stopstreetharassment. com/strategies) have several examples of ones you can use.

Stories from people who took my survey or submitted them to anti-street harassment Web sites illustrate these and other verbal tactics women have used to confront their harasser(s) and hold them accountable for their actions. These tactics worked in the particular circumstances these women were in, and may not work in all circumstances, but learning from each other's successes can generate more ideas for dealing with harassers and empower every woman to have more options for how she can respond. Only the stories submitted to blogs have endnote citations, the rest are from my surveys.

Once when I was walking at night a guy stepped in front of me. Then when I moved over he did as well. I was freaked out, but I . . . asked him how he would feel if I was his sister or girlfriend. He then apologized.[21]

Living in France, I often felt harassed and didn't know how to deal with the harasser/language and culture barrier. One night while walking home, a group of young men who often whistled at me or called at me began their usual routine. I usually ignored them, but this time the ringleader slapped my butt as I walked by. I turned around and in French said to him, "Congratulations. Is that the first time you've touched a woman?" I turned around and walked away while his friends laughed at him. I felt that I had really turned their game against them, and they never bothered me again.

A couple of times I have told the people around me (on a bus, on the street) what that guy just did (groped or wouldn't leave me alone). This made the harassment stop and made the guys embarrassed so they left immediately.

I was walking my dog when an SUV with two teenage boys catcalled me. . . . They got stuck behind a bus when it was taking on passengers. I strolled up to the side of their vehicle and asked them if they'd speak to their mother like that and that they should be ashamed of themselves. They looked scared shitless and could barely make words.

Waiting at a bus stop with a man who was making me nervous and threatened, I stood up on the park bench, started twirling, and picked imaginary bits of dust out of the air. He assumed I was crazy (which was my intent) and he moved on.

I was walking along in Covent Garden in broad sunshine in a top and long skirt, when a very well-dressed man in his 50s came up close behind me and hissed, "Oooh, Sexy," in my ear. I wheeled on my heel, gave him a hard stare and said (very loudly) "EXCUSE ME! WHAT DO YOU THINK YOU ARE DOING?" in my best teacher voice. Everyone on the street stared at him and he very shamefacedly muttered something and slunk off. One woman in her late 50s actually congratulated me and said she would never have dared say that![22]

I pulled into a Walgreens [drugstore] on Thursday afternoon. I parked near a truck with a man in it. As I was walking into Walgreens I heard a whistle and a comment. I whirled around. The man looked uncertain as to what would happen next. As if no one has ever confronted him before. I have to say, what happened next made my day and absolutely encouraged me to keep confronting street harassers. I walked to his truck and asked him if he whistled at me. He said yes and what amounted to several more harassing comments. I then whipped out my camera phone and started to snap away. He began to squirm, literally, in the passenger's seat of the truck . . . I told him if he did not like unwanted attention, he should not force it on others. I was forceful, confident. He was caught off guard, squirming. The power dynamic changed. It was a good feeling.[23]

I always make comments like, "What do you think you have the right to do that for?" or "Don't you realize how intimidating that is to women?" These questions are usually met with that, "Duh—does not compute look" that I am sure we all know! I think if you keep it to questions and credit them with SOME intelligence (even though you think they don't have much)—sometimes they think more about it and you can enter into a dialogue.[24]

Several women offered general advice, including these three survey respondents:

Let people know that they're being inappropriate and help others out when you see them being harassed.

Don't be afraid to be rude if someone is bothering you. Just because you've been socialized to smile and nod and keep your mouth shut doesn't mean you have to take shit from people.

Get verbal. It's not enough to ignore it; otherwise people won't realize it's unwanted. Tell people to stop, or if you're uncomfortable with that, tell an authority figure (transit worker, police officer, etc). Speak up, even if your voice shakes.

When applicable, reporting a harasser to a police officer, transit authority, or their employer is another response women can practice both for personal empowerment and to hold men accountable for their behavior.

Reporting Harassers to the Police

If the harasser is threatening, touching or following you, flashing or masturbating at you, or persisting in more benign forms of harassment, you can report him to the police or a security officer. Since you do not know his name or where he lives, taking down a physical description or snapping a picture of him and a description of where it occurred will help your case if you report it. If there are other people nearby, make sure they realize the man's behavior is unwelcome and harassing and see if they would be willing to be a witness to your story for the police. While I have read stories of women who had police officers tell them things like "what did they expect?" or to "get a gun," there are many women who have had success with this tactic. Here are several examples.

I was molested on the W train between Lexington/59th St. and Queensboro Plaza. I wasn't able to collect my senses and get off to report the crime or report it immediately after, but I reported it to the NYC sex crimes hot line two days later and was able to go to the precinct and actually identify the perpetrator out of a mugshot. Turns out he was arrested once before, three years ago, for a sex crime. I encourage women to report the crimes, no matter how small you may think they are.[25]

This happened twice by the same jerky guys. I was walking around my college campus and two guys sped passed me in their car and screamed "whore" at me. That was uncomfortable. The second time I was with friends, so that was less uncomfortable, and we told campus police. The campus police eventually caught the guys and threatened to arrest them if they were found on campus again (they weren't students). That was cool.

I was alone and waiting for my mother to come home. I was outside without a key to the house. A strange man drove back and forth in front of the house. Next thing I know he gets out of the car totally naked and while looking at me starts to masturbate. . . . I finally tried the back door of the house because I was frightened and did not know what this stranger would do. It was unlocked, thanks Mom! I went in and he took off. I called the police and they came out. This stupid man kicked out his wallet upon exiting the car and didn't know it. The police caught him and I pressed charges. This stupid man was an exhibitionist. He had done this before.

I'm a patroller at my school, so one day when we were patrolling, we just did the usual and stopping traffic so students can cross. I blew the whistle once and our signs went out. . . . I was checking to see if anymore cars were coming and then this old, beat up car came blowing down the hill and four or five 19-year olds made kissy noises and said, "hey beautiful" to me. Well I am 11, but the good part was that they went through a stop sign so we wrote down the license plate and the driver's description and reported them to the constable and they got a ticket. HA![26]

On Friday night I was on the blue line bus and as always, everyone was squished like sardines. Some guy directly behind me started touching me inappropriately and I called him out on it. I reported it to the police and he was fortunately caught and charged.[27]

I was in the Pima County Library in Tucson, Arizona one night, and another patron (an older man), approached me and commented on my underwear. He was talking so loud that the other patrons could hear the whole conversation. I was so mad; I called security to have him removed for harassment.

I was walking down Roosevelt Ave. in Jackson Heights when I heard a guy behind me saying . . . something like this: "Yes, your body, I can be inside your body."

I turned around and asked him, "You talking to me?"

"Oh yes, yes."

"Well, you better shut the fuck up, buddy, or I'll have you arrested," I said. I did not know how I was going to have him arrested. "You better stop talking to me like that."

Of course, he did not stop. Despair set in. Then, miracle of miracles! I saw a cop crossing the street. I flagged her down and told her about the harasser. He was trying to hide behind the telephone booth, but we found him. She and I started scolding him, "You don't talk to women like that." He played dumb and denied everything, but the officer wasn't having any of it. To add insult to his injury, every time I tried to talk to the officer the harasser interrupted me. Which caused the officer to yell "shut up" at him over and over. It was quite fun to watch the officer put him in his place. . . . The officer told me she would give the guy a summons. I left them on the corner and went about my merry way.[28]

Reporting Harassers to a Transit Authority Worker

If the harasser is at a bus stop, subway station, or train depot, or if he is on any form of public transportation, report him to the transit authority employee or file a complaint through an online or phone-based system (most major transit organizations have such a form or 800 number). In New York City, you can call NYPD's Sex Crimes Report Line at 212.267. RAPE to report any form of sexual harassment experienced on the transit system. Here are stories from two women who reported their harassers.

I once had a young man enter my el train car sit next to me, stare at me and touch himself through his pants. I wanted to call him out on it, but I was alone (besides him) in the train car and feared assault. I pretended not to notice and got off at the next stop. I reported the incident to the station attendant, giving a detailed description of the man's dress and my train car's number. I am assuming the station attendant reported the incident, but I am unsure if the man was caught. The man was well dressed and seemed stable, but his behavior was very intimidating and his eye contact was intentional and disturbing. I knew my discomfort was turning him on.

I had a person masturbating next to me on the bus. I told the driver and he kicked him off. I contacted bus authorities afterwards about it.

Reporting Harassers to Their Employer

If the harasser works for an identifiable company, call or write the company to let them know that their employees are harassing women on the job. If possible, let them know the location and the time of day that the employee was harassing you so they can better identify which employee it is and hold the employee responsible for his actions. Here are a few success stories illustrating how one can do this.

I was recently shouted at by two men in a ConEdison truck. I reported them to ConEdison (as they were using work hours and a ConEd vehicle to harass women), and when I thanked the operator for taking my complaint seriously, she said, "It is my PLEASURE to write this incident report—we take this very seriously as a company, and I take it very seriously as a woman." She was awesome. The creepy old men in the truck? Not so much. . . . The guys got reamed by their employer, and a woman from corporate called me to let me know about it.

There was a security guy at a construction site at my university. He would sit/stand at a narrow pathway that I had to take to my lab every day (I'm a PhD student). He seemed a bit intimidating and stared a bit but I ignored him or took other paths to my lab sometimes. He was a bully to male university staff too sometimes. One time as my fiancé and I were walking through the path he told me that I looked like Heidi Fleiss. Later that day he got in an argument with my fiancé and told him to go "Fuck your Heidi Fleiss girlfriend in the ass." I was afraid to take that path after this incident and would get very anxious walking to my lab. I went straight to the university authorities and after trying to give me useless solutions (just take another path, etc.), they got rid of him.

After getting a free ice cream from Ben & Jerry's, at M & 31st [in Washington, D.C.], I had to crouch down to pull my umbrella out of my bag since it started raining. A UPS driver was waiting at the light, and he had to say something to me, "Ooh, girl! You don't need to finish that all by yourself!" When I told him that it was tacky and classless for him to hit on me in uniform, he started cracking up. Oh yes, sexual harassment is sooo funny! I am never one who takes harassment lightly. . . . I got the UPS driver's license plate number. As soon as I got home I called UPS to report him, and the woman who took down the information was sympathetic and apologetic and said she'd have someone get in touch with me about it.[29]

In the early '80s at an Ivy League college where I was a lecturer, I was harassed when my daily route took me past a university construction site. I took note of the date, time, place, exact occurrence, and the fact that I felt demeaned and unsafe (that is very important). I noted the name of the contractor (usually posted on a sign at the site). I then went to talk to the head of Buildings and Grounds for the university—the people who let the contracts for buildings—and told him of the incidents. I made it clear that I was determined to put an end to this for myself and female students. I had to go no further; the harassment came to an immediate halt. I still remember walking past those guys at the university construction site immediately after my meeting. They silently looked at me; they were now fearful of saying a word. In a few days women passing by were simply ignored, just like the men passing by.[30]

WHAT CAN WE DO?

Women are not at fault for men's harassment. Until men stop harassing women, it is important for women, especially young women, to know this, to know they have a right to be in public spaces unharassed, and that, if they want, they can take action against harassers. At an individual level, we can all empower girls and women by:

- Refraining from engaging in victim blaming, including self-blame. This includes wondering what the girl or woman was wearing when a man harassed or assaulted her, saying she shouldn't have been out alone, and saying she should have responded a certain way. It also includes saying she was targeted for being "pretty" or for "looking too vulnerable."

- Explaining to people who make victim blaming comments why such comments are inappropriate.

- Teaching girls or young women that men who harass or hurt them are the ones with the problem, not them.

- Brainstorming with girls and women a range of responses one can use against harassers, including thinking about the type of harassment one experiences the most and making a list of several possible responses one could have to them.

- Practicing and role playing a range of responses to various types of harassment so one becomes more comfortable with them and can more easily choose which to use when one is harassed.

- Reading and sharing books like Martha Langelan's *Back Off! How to Confront and Stop Sexual Harassment* (1993) and Sue Wise and Liz Stanley's *Georgie Porgie: Sexual Harassment in Everyday Life* (1987).

- Attending or encouraging girls and women to attend some kind of self-defense class. While most people will not be assaulted by a stranger in public, knowing what to do if they are can lead to more confidence in public spaces. It can make women feel more able to hold harassers accountable for their actions because they will be less fearful of being physically hurt.

NOTES

1. Martha Langelan, *Back Off! How to Confront and Stop Sexual Harassment and Harassers* (New York: Fireside Press, 1993), 99.

2. National Public Radio, "Young Women in Brooklyn Fight for Respect," July 2, 2007, http://www.npr.org/templates/story/story.php?storyId=11654299.

3. HOTGIRLS, "Anti-Street Harassment Campaign," n.d., http://www.helpingourteengirls.org/programs/street_harassment_campaign.htm.

4. "MO'Talks" Channel 25, March 2005, http://www.youtube.com/watch?v=Vw9n4x8VeqM&feature=player_embedded#.

5. Annie Slezickey de Sanches, "Rogers Park YWAT Also a Peace-Builder," *Rogers Park 2000*, Fall 2009, http://www.rogerspark.org/images/September_2009.pdf.

6. Amaya N. Roberson, "Anti-Street Harassment," *Off Our Backs*, May–June 2005, page 48.

7. Ibid.

8. Carol Brooks Gardner, *Passing By: Gender and Public Harassment* (Berkeley, CA: University of California Press, 1995), 148–157; see also Kimberly Fairchild and Laurie A. Rudman, "Everyday Stranger Harassment and Women's Self-Objectification," *Social Justice Research* 21, no. 3 (2008), 344; see also Sue Wise and Liz Stanley, *Georgie Porgie: Sexual Harassment in Everyday Life* (London: Pandora, 1987), 169.

9. Langelan, 102.

10. Caroline Heldman, "Out-of-Body Image," *Ms. Magazine*, Spring 2008, http://www.msmagazine.com/spring2008/outOfBodyImage.asp.

11. Fairchild and Rudman, 353.

12. Margaret T. Gordon and Stephanie Riger, *The Female Fear: The Social Cost of Rape* (Urbana: University of Illinois Press, 1991),120.

13. Langelan, 45.

14. Lauren Taylor, "The Assertive Response to 'Hey, Baby,' Options Go Beyond the Silent Treatment," *Washington Post*, October 27, 2003, C10.

15. Ibid.

16. Lauren Taylor, Defend Yourself Street Harassment Workshop, April 18, 2009, Washington, D.C.

17. Ibid.

18. Langelan, 83–95; see also Don't Be Silent Blog, "Highlights from the Martha Langelan Workshop," February 10, 2008, http://dontbesilent3. blogspot.com/2008/02/highlights-from-martha-langelan.html; see also Don't Be Silent Blog, "Response to 'Drive-by Hollas Drive Me Crazy!!'" February 11, 2008, http://dontbesilent3.blogspot.com/2008/02/response-to-drive-by-hollas-drive-me.html.

19. Lauren Taylor, "Speak Up! Basic Verbal Self Defense Guidelines," Defend Yourself, n.d., http://stopstreetharassment.com/docs/DefendYour selfVerbalTactics.pdf.

20. Bernice Sandler, "Handling Sexual Harassment When It Happens to You," 1997, http://www.bernicesandler.com/id37.htm.

21. Stop Street Harassment Blog, "Getting an Apology," February 24, 2009, http://streetharassment.wordpress.com/2009/02/24/getting-an-apology.

22. Isabel, comment on Anti-Harassment UK Blog, comment posted on July 25, 2003, http://www.anti-harassment.ik.com (accessed in May 2007).

23. Comment on HollaBack Arkansas, comment posted on May 30, 2008, http://hollabackar.blogspot.com/ (accessed July 10, 2009).

24. Rachael, comment on Anti-Harassment UK Blog, comment posted on December 5, 2006, http://www.anti-harassment.ik.com (accessed in May 2007).

25. Stop Street Harassment Blog, "Report It," December 7, 2009, http://streetharassment.wordpress.com/2009/12/07/report-it.

26. Anonymous, comment on HollaBack Canada, comment posted on July 27, 2006, http://hollabackcanada.blogspot.com/2006/07/again-with-harrassing-kids.html.

27. Laura, "Success Story on the Blue Line," HollaBack Toronto, June 28, 2009, http://hollabackto.blogspot.com/2009/06/success-story-on-blue-line.html.

28. Lauri, comment on HollaBack NYC Blog, comment posted October 16, 2006, http://hollabacknyc.blogspot.com/2006/10/hollasummons.html (accessed July 10, 2009).

29. HollaBack DC!, "Uniform Harassment," April 22, 2009, http://hollabackdc.wordpress.com/2009/04/22/uniform-harassment.

30. Stop Street Harassment Blog, "Successfully Ending Harassment," April 16, 2009, http://streetharassment.wordpress.com/2009/04/16/successfully-ending-harassment.

Chapter 9

Raising Public Awareness

Another important way to help end street harassment is raising awareness that it is a problem and speaking out against it. At an individual level, doing so can be as simple as sharing your story in person or online, or it can be as involved as raising community awareness through running an anti-street harassment Web site, holding a local event, producing a documentary, or creating an art project. One's involvement also could be somewhere in between, such as helping with those projects or donating to them, attending, or participating in them. Activists' initiatives are highlighted throughout the chapter to illustrate what people already are doing. At the end of each section you can find ideas for action you can take.

SHARING STORIES

One day in college I was walking along El Camino Real, a busy street in Santa Clara, California, traveling from my campus to a domestic violence shelter where I volunteered. Men routinely honked and hollered at me whenever I traveled by foot on this street. As I was walking, I was talking to my father on the phone and he heard one of the men and asked in surprise if he was targeting me. I said yes, almost dismissively, and said it always happened. My father sounded shocked, however, and in that moment I realized he had no idea how often men harass me in public. A few years later when I began researching street harassment for my master's thesis, I talked more to my father and male partner about my experiences. Since I am rarely harassed in their presence, they did not know how often it occurs. Sharing my stories and letting them know how

annoying, angering, and sometimes scary it is, has raised their awareness. Today, they both are strong allies in ending the problem.

Sharing one's street harassment stories—as the target or
bystander—in person or online is something anyone who wants to
help stop street harassment can do. It also seems to be one of the
most effective ground-level methods for raising awareness. We listen to people we know.

For women, raising awareness by sharing your stories can be as
simple as telling the men you trust about your experiences. Tell
them each time a man harasses you or each time a really scary or
frustrating incident happens. Or simply tell them about how street
harassment makes you feel and the impact it has on your life.
Through an informal online questionnaire I conducted in late 2009,
eighty-five male allies shared their thoughts on how best to reach
other men on this issue. "Having women in their life talk to them
about street harassment and share their stories/how it makes them
feel" was selected by 95 percent of the men as being the most effective method. Similarly, 87 percent of the men thought that telling
other men "women they care about probably experience street harassment" would be the most successful message for involving them
in addressing street harassment issues. One woman in Champaign,
Illinois, who took my 2008 online survey wrote, "One thing that I
think has been more effective is to talk to the men that I know
about how it makes me feel. I think for some of the men who do
this they don't really realize how disruptive it can be."

Sharing one's stories and experiences with other women also
raises their awareness. Since men often street harass women who
are alone, women may not realize how often it happens to other
women and instead blame themselves for its occurrence, including
by internalizing that it is a compliment prompted by their appearance. If a woman realizes that most women are harassed at some
point, she is less likely to engage in self-blame or self-objectification
and more likely to respond assertively to the harasser and speak
out against that behavior. Plus, women who are upset by harassment
may find comfort in realizing there are other women who have similar feelings, and that they can support each other.

Men and women, if you have seen street harassment occurring,
you can tell people about it. If you intervened or did something to
stop it, tell them how. If someone you care about is street harassed,
talk about how that makes you feel. Men listen to other men, so it
is very useful for male allies to talk to other men about street harassment in general, and 73 percent of the eighty-five male allies
who took my survey said that was a realistic measure to help end

street harassment that they would be willing to do. They also can share tactics for how to intervene if they see it occurring, help other men realize that it is an inappropriate behavior, and explain the difference between nonthreatening, appropriate flirting and predatory or disrespectful behavior.

If you have a blog or contribute to one, consider sharing your street harassment stories, feelings about street harassment, and ideas for ending it there, too. The next section explores other ways to raise awareness online, starting with the HollaBack anti-street harassment Web sites.

ONLINE ACTIVISM

As the end of this section details, there are many ways to raise awareness about street harassment online. Several people run Web sites on which they post stories women submit to them about their experiences. The most well known are the HollaBack sites and, to start, I will highlight a few of them.

HollaBack NYC

Over dinner one evening in 2005, seven friends (women and men), including Emily May, discussed street harassment in New York City and brainstormed action they could take to combat it. Inspired by a woman who recently had taken a cell phone picture of a man masturbating on the subway and used it to report him to the police, they decided to launch a Web site where women could safely "holla back" at harassers by posting cell phone pictures of harassers and/or writing what happened. On the site, women would be able to e-mail stories or send pictures directly from their cell phones.

Within months, the Web site was a success. Since then, at least weekly—and often daily—women submit stories, making Holla-Back NYC a rich repository of stories. HollaBack NYC's success and in-your-face attitude has captured the attention of news outlets and magazines nationwide, ranging from the *New York Times* and other local New York papers to coverage in the *Boston Globe, LA Times*, BBC World Radio, National Public Radio, and ABC's *Good Morning America*. In informal studies and conversations, I've found people to be more familiar with their work than that of any other street harassment activist.

May, a native of Richmond, Virginia, who coordinates projects for a nonprofit addressing poverty issues, manages the day-to-day work of posting stories and talking to the press and working with local activists on community issues. She said she never intended or expected to work on street harassment, but, after four years of activism, she has become an expert. May offers this important insight on working to stop street harassment:

My perspective on effecting change is that if you can come up with a creative idea to fix something or do something that you can measure and get tangible outcomes, then that is infinitely more effective than if you take on "solving street harassment" or "ending racism." That's too vague and you'll never win. . . . It's good to have it in the back of your mind, but then focus on tangible actions. You win it in pieces.[1]

In 2009, May helped cofound a grassroots organization called New Yorkers for Safe Transit to address harassment on public transportation. She also is spearheading an initiative to develop a Smartphone application through which people can immediately report street harassment incidents. Those incidents will be mapped and later analyzed in an annual "State of Our Streets" report, which will be sent to the police, public officials, and the media. Automatic e-mail alerts noting real-time harassment also will be available. May and those with whom she is working hope to have enough funds raised to launch the project in New York City in 2010, with plans to later expand the initiative to other cities and countries.

Across the last few years, May has helped more than 20 people start HollaBack Web sites. Four of them are highlighted next.

HollaBack Boston and HollaBack TALK

A native of the Midwest and a self-identified feminist from a young age, Brittany Shoot moved to Boston, Massachusetts, to pursue a master's degree in 2005. Street harassment was a common experience for Brittany, and after she learned about HollaBack NYC that year, she decided to cofound HollaBack Boston. She said, "There are too many untold stories, and we need to stop feeling so alone and disempowered in the innumerable ways we're constantly preyed upon and verbally subjugated. . . . I feel that every major city, like every small community, has its own unique problems with safety in public space, and I felt that Boston's public space problems could easily be documented and dissected."[2]

Three months later, Shoot also cofounded HollaBack TALK, a Web site on which she and her two cofounders could share their own opinions and analysis about street harassment stories, public space laws, and the spectrum of sexual violence. Both blogs grew and received hundreds of page hits a day, a steady stream of story submissions, and mentions in numerous news articles. When I asked Shoot about the impact of HollaBack Boston and its benefits, she said, "I think the Holla Back sites—especially the ones that publish frequently and maintain activity in their community—help show this as a common problem. . . . I think changing the mentality about what we expect from others and ourselves is the first step."[3]

After nearly three years, both HollaBack Boston and HollaBack TALK are on hiatus given changes in Shoot's and cofounder founders Michelle Riblett and Hilary Allen's lives.

HollaBack DC!

Activists on gender issues, Chai Shenoy, a native of Northern California, and Shannon Lynberg, from Atlanta, Georgia, met as volunteers at the Washington D.C. Rape Crisis Center. After talking about their life-long frustrations with street harassment, or, as they call it, public sexual harassment, in early 2009 they decided to relaunch a HollaBack DC! Web site that had been stagnant for over two years. Their site includes a companion online map where they add electronic pushpins at the locations where the street harassment incidents occur to visually demonstrate how pervasive street harassment is throughout the city and to identify "hot spots" of activity. When I talked to them a few months after the launch, Lynberg said the following about the site,

There were times that I felt I lost my voice and that it [street harassment] was just something I had to deal with. By taking action on the issue and working on Holla Back DC, I feel I have reclaimed my voice. I hope that other survivors of public harassment can do the same by sharing their stories, learning how to engage their oppressors in nonviolent ways, and talking about it with other community members.[4]

Their revamped site had only been running for a few months, but already they had been featured in local Washington, D.C., online newspapers and blogs and had received over one hundred story submissions. They feel the site is accomplishing what they want: generating discussions about and awareness of street harassment. Going forward, they are working to generate those discussions offline as well as online, particularly in collaboration with the LGBQT community, and engage in local activism.

When I asked them what advice they have for someone who wants to create a similar Web site in their community, they both said to go for it and do it. "It is definitely worth the work, time, and stress. Helping others and creating a community to address issues that aren't discussed is really important," said Shenoy.[5] Lynberg added, "Yes, it is a lot of work but well worth it."[6]

HollaBack Toronto

In the summer of 2008, right before she created the Web site HollaBack Toronto, college student Lisa Rahman was harassed so much that she began wearing sweaters when she took the subway alone in Toronto and regularly walked out of her way to try to avoid areas where she had been previously harassed. She said, "It all finally got too ridiculous and I had to do something. My boyfriend showed me HollaBack NYC and it inspired me to create a Toronto version because I knew lots of women were experiencing the same thing. . . . Plus it gave me an outlet for my own stories."[7]

Each month, as more people learn about the site, Rahman receives more story submissions. The response from the public has been supportive and positive. Of particular note, Toronto Transit Commission employees have contacted her to help educate her site readers about what they can do if they are victims of harassment while riding public transportation. Rahman said of this, "It's amazing to see that people are finally stepping up and taking the subject of street harassment seriously."[8]

When I asked her about the utility of a Web site like hers and what she would tell someone who wanted to start one on their own, she said,

I think every community needs an outlet where women can come together and try to create a solution. I think without a forum like HollaBack Toronto it's a lot harder to get the support women need to deal with this and feel not as alone. It's pretty cliché, but I believe there is power in numbers and the more people you have banding together against a certain issue, the more attention will be paid to it. I think once more and more cities and communities start creating outlets to combat street harassment, the better the chance that we'll actually be able to start beating it.[9]

Do you want to help raise awareness about street harassment online and/or add your voice to online anti-street harassment movements? Here are some ideas.

- Write about your street harassment experiences on a personal blog or post it as a comment on a relevant news story or blog post. Submit your stories to be posted on anti-street harassment Web sites like Stop Street Harassment or a HollaBack Web site.

- Submit an article or op-ed on street harassment to a local or campus newspaper. For example, see Ashley Nguyen's article "Saying Hello Is Just for the Sake of Saying Hello" for *Temple News Online* (September 2009),[10] or Emily May's op-ed "Beware the Closing Doors" in the New York *Daily News* (June 2009).[11]

- Join an anti-street harassment group or become a fan of one on social networking sites.

- Tweet street harassment stories on Twitter. Add @catcalled, #hbnyc, or #streetharassment to your post and it will be added to @Catcalled, @HollaBackNYC, or @StopStHarassmnt's respective thread of harassment stories. Keep your own log of harassment experiences the way @streetharassmnt does.

- Start an anti-street harassment Web site for your community. If you want to start your own HollaBack Web site but don't know how, contact HollaBack NYC (holla@ihollaback.org).

STREET HARASSMENT EVENT

Another way to raise public awareness, as well as to educate people about street harassment, is to hold a local event on the topic. The following section highlights the events a few activists have done in their communities.

"Don't Grab My Ass" Discussion

Each year, the University of California at Santa Barbara's (UCSB) Rape Prevention Education Program (RPEP) holds campus street harassment discussions called "Don't Grab My Ass." Kari Mansager, the assistant director of RPEP, and a master's student at UCSB, said the discussion is one of RPEP's most popular programs, and they often hold it for residence halls of first-years and sororities and cultural organizations. Attendance ranges from five to fifty people.

At the opening of the discussion, Mansager and other organizers ask attendees to shout out stereotypes about how men and women are supposed to behave. Attendees discuss what verbal and physical repercussions people face for acting outside those norms. They talk about how those strict gender roles relate to street harassment.[12]

Next, Mansager facilitates a general discussion about street harassment and asks questions like:

- "What happens on the streets? How does that make people feel?"

- "Why do you think this happens?" (She says she has to do a lot of myth busting for this question)
- "What could we do to stop this?"

They also discuss possible responses for targets of harassment and bystanders.[13]

Last, attendees break into small groups to discuss a street harassment situation they have experienced or witnessed. They talk about how it made them feel, what they did, and what a bystander did or could have done. They act out one of the scenarios in front of the full group, including what they would have liked to have done in the situation. Mansager noted that for many women of color, the harassment is racialized as well as sexualized, which has led to interesting discussions about power and control.[14]

Usually most participants are women, but Mansager said men who attend seem to respond well. She noted that men especially react well to the opening discussion about gender stereotypes and the role playing. Mansager offered the following advice to any campus group who wants to hold a similar event:

I would encourage folks making a program to think about the issue not just as a harasser/target issue but as a community problem. That's why we emphasize bystander/witness involvement throughout the program. There are many things we as friends of the harassee/harasser or as total strangers can do to step in or speak up. I would also emphasize for other groups to let the audience share stories and their own ideas of responses. The students seem to learn best from their peers, and they share great ideas.[15]

"Hey Baby!: Resisting Sexual Harassment in Public Spaces, One Bloque at a Time"

For the last five years, Erin Johnson has worked as a community organizer in Asheville, North Carolina. One of her areas of interest is the ways in which art supports social change. Because of their street harassment experiences in Asheville, Johnson and a few friends decided to hold an anti-street harassment event.[16] She said, "We were frustrated by how we felt unsafe, even in groups of people. So we thought, 'What are some ways that we can take the frustration and anger and make something productive?'"[17]

For the April 2009 event, Johnson and the other organizers accepted art submissions relating to street harassment that could be put on the streets, on harassers' cars, and posted in their favorite bars and restaurants. For her part, Johnson created magnetic bumper stickers with phrases like "You sexually harassed me," to place on the vehicle of a harasser. As she said, that way the harasser can take it off but he will have to think about it as he does so. Other submissions included bike flags and business cards with instructions for appropriate interaction. Johnson says, "Art . . . is something that engages people but doesn't threaten."[18]

At the event, the more than one hundred attendees had the opportunity to look through the submitted artwork and select pieces they would like to use to raise awareness about street harassment. Attendees could also participate in anti-harassment cheers, blog their street harassment stories, listen to music, and participate in a community dialogue about how to address and work to end street harassment. Johnson felt the event was successful because it helped generate conversations about street harassment and helped attendees think about the ways it impacts them and how they could work to end it.[19]

When I asked her what advice she would give to someone who wants to hold a community event on street harassment, she had a few things to say. First, based on their event, she said that pairing art with conversation always goes well. Second, it is important to have representatives from all kinds of organizing efforts present in the planning process and at the event because "none of us are free until everyone is free."[20] She mentioned including individuals working on immigration rights, LGBQTI rights, anti-racism work, and so forth. She emphasized ensuring that the folks who are most affected by the problem be part of the planning process, including teenagers.[21]

INCITE! Community Education Speak Out

INCITE! Women of Color Against Violence is a national activist organization founded in 2000 with grassroots chapters nationwide that works with groups of women of color and their communities to develop political projects that address multiple forms of violence women of color experience.[22] To this end, they have focused on street harassment in some of their forms of activism. On May 6, 2006, they organized a day of action against street harassment in Washington, D.C., called the Community Education Speak Out. Nearly one hundred community members attended, holding anti-street harassment signs and demanding an end to the "degrading behavior through community education and the development of a respectful view of girls and women."[23]

Throughout the day, girls and women had the opportunity to share their stories, read their poetry, and participate in drumming and chanting about street harassment. Martial arts and self -defense trainers gave presentations and taught attendees basic self-defense moves to help them feel more confident in public. Last, attendees learned about ways they can respond to street harassment and practiced role playing various strategies.[24]

I briefly spoke with one INCITE! DC activist, Katie Seitz, about street harassment and her work with INCITE! DC. When I asked her why she addresses street harassment, she said simply, "because I experience it every day." She said their goals for the day of action and other initiatives were to "address the street harassment that is so prevalent here and give women and girls of color ways to speak out about it and address it within their communities without relying on law enforcement."[25]

Do you want to help raise awareness about street harassment through a community event? Here are some ideas.

- Hold an event on street harassment in your community, including at the local community center or YMCA/YWCA, at a high school or college campus, or hold a rally in a local park.
- Help organize, fund, advertise, or donate in-house contributions (like a space to host it or food for attendees) for an event.
- Attend an event and invite friends to attend, especially men.

STREET HARASSMENT FILMS AND DOCUMENTARIES

Viewing street harassment, seeing women talk about its impact on their lives, watching men who harass explain why, and hearing men who do not harass speak out against the behavior, can drastically raise awareness about this problem. Of note, 51 percent of eighty-five male allies I surveyed felt that viewing a documentary was the best way to raise awareness among men that this is a problem. Also, media outlets love having video clips with their stories, so having some available can make street harassment a more marketable story, and of course, being covered in the news helps raise awareness.

Here is information about three anti-street harassment documentaries, followed by specific ideas.

War Zone

For her 1998 documentary *War Zone*, filmmaker, producer, and social justice activist Maggie Hadleigh-West walked the streets of

New York City, San Francisco, Minneapolis, New Orleans, and Chicago, with a video camera and a camera woman. She bought the camera at a garage sale. Across five weeks they filmed over 1,000 men who harassed women, usually Hadleigh-West. They filmed Hadleigh-West talking to the men. The film includes interviews with five women of color about their street harassment experiences, and Hadleigh-West, who is white, also talks about her lifelong experiences with harassment.[26]

Many of the fifty-three men featured in the film were upset that Hadleigh-West challenged their perceived right to comment on women. Others told her she made them feel uncomfortable. Of course, it was her intention to make them feel scrutinized and upset just as they make many women feel. Although there is a growing body of research on men who rape women, there is very little research on men who harass women. For this reason, the men's responses in the film are extremely valuable.[27]

In 1998 *War Zone* aired at several film festivals and it has been recognized by many prominent media outlets, from *20/20* and *The Today Show* to the BBC and NPR, to *USA Today* and *Ms.* magazine. Since 2002, the Department of Defense has been using *War Zone* as an educational tool for all branches of the military.[28]

Today, Hadleigh-West continues to speak about street harassment, and educators nationwide use her film to spark discussions in their classrooms. About the documentary's importance and impact, Hadleigh-West said, "The validation that I constantly get from women [when] I travel around the academic circuit talking about it . . . always reinforces the idea that this is not my experience alone . . . [The film] is touching on something that hasn't been talked about, something that hasn't been illuminated."[29]

Her film is available for purchase on her Web site in lengths of 76 or 30 minutes, visit www.yomaggie.com/store.html.

Hey . . . Shorty

Inspired by *War Zone* and their daily experiences with street harassment, five interns at the volunteer-run youth development organization Girls for Gender Equity (GGE) in Brooklyn, New York, created a 20-minute street harassment documentary. GGE founder and executive director Joanne Smith says the main goal of the organization is to provide girls and young women with the skills and self-esteem needed to succeed. Smith encouraged their documentary idea, saying, "Combating the reality of street harassment has to begin with a consciousness-raising conversation. I'm Haitian and where GGE is based there is a large West Indian community. In our Caribbean/West Indian culture there are no words to explain what sexual harassment is and why it's wrong."[30]

The GGE interns, ranging in age from 15 to 18, worked with the Malcolm X Grassroots Movement to film and produce *Hey . . . Shorty* in 2007. They spent eight months interviewing young women of color in their neighborhood about the impact of street harassment on their life, as well as interviewing several men of color, both young and old, about why they harass women.[31] In particular, the GGE interns noted that it was very hard to confront older men about their behaviors.

Their well-produced film illustrates how pervasive street harassment is for women and how little men understand its impact. Several older men said, on film, that it was their right to treat a woman disrespectfully if she looked like she was sexually available based on her clothing and appearance. One teenage boy, without hesitation, admitted to chasing and throwing trash at a girl with his friends when she ignored his friend's comments. As with *War Zone*, this documentary provides needed insight into why men harass women.

GGE aired the film at a free 2007 Street Harassment Summit in New York City and received local press coverage. The film is available for purchase from the GGE Web site, http://www.ggenyc.org/publications.php.

Black Woman Walking

While attending graduate school at New York University, writer and media-maker Tracey Rose thought a lot about black women's bodies, respectability, and the politics of public space because of her classes. Combined with the street harassment she experienced, she questioned what her body signified. She said:

What does a female body of color mean in a public space? I had to ask this question because my bus stop had become an auction block, standing there became synonymous with solicitation. Cars would pull up and honk the horn and wait for me to get in. . . . This happened a lot in my twenties, a time when I lived in t-shirts and jeans and I couldn't figure out why it kept happening. But I knew I wasn't the only one it was happening to.[32]

As a result, she created an 8-minute documentary *Black Woman Walking* comprised of interviews with women of color to explore these issues. The film tries to examine whether women of color experience a particular type of harassment due to their particular histories and the social narratives that surround them. While Rose never intended for the film to be about same race harassment, those were the stories most women told. She said, "When I began interviewing, it became clear that the majority of times, women experience harassment from men within their own communities and that's one of the reasons the experience is so fraught and painful."

Her documentary is available in its entirety online. Numerous people have reposted it on blogs and Web sites. In discussions, most women have felt validated by it and found it brought up harassment memories that they had buried over the years, but that had formed an essential part of how they relate to the world. It can be viewed online by searching for *Black Woman Walking* or at http://streetharassment.wordpress.com/2008/10/14/black-woman-walking.

Clips from these documentaries and numerous examples of other anti-street harassment videos are available at www.stopstreetharass ment.com/resources/video.htm. Here are ideas for what you can do if you're interested in using film to raise public awareness:

- If you have access to a video recording device (including on a cell phone), consider creating an informal clip and adding your voice to the growing online collection of videos. Across various social networking sites there are dozens of home videos by young women talking about their street harassment experiences. Some women, such as Women's Studies students at Pennsylvania State, have produced mini-documentaries. For a class project in 2007, the students made a 7-minute documentary interviewing male college students about sexual harassment. Unexpectedly, during the filming, men admitted they harass women walking by and they even harassed women while being filmed. The filmmakers also interviewed women about how harassment makes them feel.[33]

- Try interviewing people you know and/or conducting "person on the street" interviews. See if you can capture street harassment live. Post your video online or screen it at a street harassment event or community film festival. Upload it to the Stop Street Harassment YouTube Channel, www.youtube.com/user/stopstreetharassment.

- If someone you know is making a documentary on street harassment, volunteer to participate! The more voices—women's and men's—captured on film speaking out against this issue, the more powerful the movement can become.

- If you are planning a street harassment event, consider including a screening of a documentary. There are documentaries that range in length from less than 10 minutes to 76 minutes, so there are options that can fit any event.

- Support documentaries by donating money or time to their production and attending screenings. Invite people to attend who do not know about street harassment.

VISUAL AND PERFORMANCE ART

Art of all forms has the power to move people and creative portrayals of street harassment issues can help raise community awareness that it is a problem. The art may be visual and on display in a museum exhibit or the foyer of a school or conference hall, or it may be performance-based and occur on the streets near your home. The following projects by three anti-street harassment activists offer ideas for raising awareness.

Cat Calls

In 2002, Jenga Mwendo, a New Orleans native who moved to New York City to study visual arts, turned her experiences with street harassment into a multi-media exhibit. She said of her brainstorming process, "As soon as I set foot onto the street, the ogling and catcalling began and it didn't stop until I closed my door behind me . . . I wanted men to somehow experience what it feels like to have your personal space consistently invaded by catcallers wanting something from you, whether it's simply attention or sex."[34]

Along with other artists at Red Clay Arts Studio in Brooklyn, New York, she spent countless hours creating that experience in exhibit form. One of the components was the Walk of Shame. The artists built a hall with cloth walls onto which videos of men catcalling were projected. This was to give men who walked through a glimpse into what it feels like to be objectified walking down the street. Mwendo said, "Empathy isn't something you can learn by reading. You have to experience it."[35]

Another component was the Talking Heads. Mwendo interviewed men, women, and girls about street harassment, asking them all the same questions. Then she edited and compiled the video clips. The finished piece was a row of computers featuring each interviewee, synced so that when they played, it seemed like they were on a panel talking with one another.

A few components were more static and less high-tech, but still effective. For example, for one week, Mwendo noted when and what street harassment she experienced. Then she wrote it all in a long list format and posted it on a wall. She said that during a group discussion, a man stood up and said he did not understand the volume of the harassment before seeing her list.

Since the goal of the exhibit was to give men an understanding of what it feels like to be subjected to street harassment on a regular basis, Mwendo believes the exhibit was a success. When I interviewed her in 2009, she encouraged anyone who wants to do a similar project to "just do it. Talk to as many people as possible. Get men's perspectives."[36]

As of this writing, she is back in New Orleans, helping with the rebuilding efforts. When I asked her if she had done any other work to address street harassment, she said, "No. 'Cat Calls' was sort of a cleansing process for me. . . . I no longer felt threatened or objectified by catcalls. . . . I was able to approach men, when I felt like it, and talk with them on a peer level (most times, they'd apologize and/or we'd end up having a civil conversation, or I'd express my perspective and be done with it). It felt/feels good to be free."[37]

Blank Noise

A group of women in Bangalore, India, stand along a city block for an hour, looking at people passing by, but not initiating any interaction with them. This unusual behavior for women in India causes a reaction among the (mostly male) crowds walking past. Their presence elicits questions about why they are standing there, even though groups of men always congregate on the street for no apparent reason without being questioned. Other times these, women will stand together in a line near a busy street, each holding a sign with a letter of the alphabet so that when they stand side-by-side, their collective message read "Y R U LOOKING AT ME?" They are silent, letting the question on the poster stand on its own.

Using performance art, as well as visual art and online activism, Jasmeen Patheja and members of her organization Blank Noise are challenging the notion that public spaces are for men and are opening a dialogue around the ways women and men occupy and interact in them. In particular, she and Blank Noise members address the problem of "eve teasing," as street harassment is called in India.[38]

During her last year studying visual arts in college, Patheja, a native of Kolkata who lives in Bangalore, created a personal reaction project because of her eve teasing experiences. Her multimedia exhibit included video, sound, and photography of young women and their experiences in public. The exhibit also looked at eve teasing generally, including the perspectives of the women being harassed, the men who harass, and the silent spectator (men and women). It was displayed throughout India and New York City.[39]

After graduation, Patheja's project quickly evolved into a large scale movement. Over six years later, there are Blank Noise chapters all over India, with members who engage in forms of public perform-ance and street action, with guidance from Patheja. Patheja also oversees many online and offline projects, including ones targeting men and silent spectators, and the "I Never Ask for It" campaign.

Women in India who wear jeans and other nontraditional cloth-ing are blamed for causing eve teasing. At one point in her life, Patheja had internalized this belief and changed the way she dressed to wear traditional Indian clothes. But she was still harassed. To combat such harmful and false victim-blaming, she is collecting clothing for a "I Never Ask for It" campaign to visually demon-strate the range of clothing women are wearing when men eve tease them. As of October 2009, she had collected over 200 articles of clothing and she hopes to have 1,000 articles before she exhibits them.[40]

When I met Patheja in October 2009, I asked her what advice she would give to someone who wanted to become an activist in their community. She suggested first collecting people's stories to show, as "an irrefutable truth that street harassment is an issue in your area." Then determine the best way to disburse the stories in the community so everyone is aware of the problem and can work together to fix it.[41]

Do you want to participate in Blank Noise or start your own chapter? Contact Patheja at blurtblanknoise@gmail.com.

Street Signs

A Brooklyn native educated in Philadelphia and Chicago, in the late 1980s artist Ilona Granet used her art skills to develop a unique approach for raising awareness about street harassment in New York City. Often bothered by street harassers, Granet decided to design several anti-harassment street signs. Her goal was to "get the word out that women usually find street harassment unpleasant, annoying to grotesque, and intolerable." One sign says, "Curb your animal instincts" in both English and Spanish and another says, "No Cat Calls, Whistling, Kissing Sounds." They are made of the same type of material as a stop sign and are about the same size.[42]

Granet exhibited her signs at the Museum of Modern Art in New York and various traveling shows. Most impressively, she worked with the New York City Department of Transportation (DOT) to get several of her signs posted in public for about a year. To achieve this feat, she spoke with the DOT about her idea and she was told to make a presentation to various community boards to plead her case and ask them to let her post her signs in their neighborhoods. She was able to do so successfully in locations near the World Trade Center, the Brooklyn Bridge, South Street Seaport, Borough of Manhattan Community College, and Battery Park. Through the Lower Manhattan Cultural Council she got insurance and worked with a government department to install her signs on lamp posts in well traveled and highly visible spots.[43]

Her signs generated a huge amount of press across the world, including radio, television, newspapers, and magazines. Granet told me that CNN filmed and aired footage worldwide of the signs and people's reactions—some men in the Wall Street area were not happy and vandalized the posted signs and stole some from her car. The footage also was used in CNN's Year in Review.[44]

Her signs and the press helped generate a lot of conversations about street harassment. Many women called Granet to tell her their street harassment stories and she said she watched as men began to think about the issues and recognize it as a problem. She told me she never imagined such a big response and that "it was a thrill that the subject was considered seriously."[45]

When I asked her what advice she would offer to someone who wants to do a similar project, she said, "I was lucky to have known someone who knew the man to go to in the city who worked with getting public art out and he liked the project. Do good work and find who can help you. . . . Funny [messaging] is good."[46]

Granet still has several signs and would love to see them used again. If you're interested, visit http://www.ilonagranet.com to contact her. Or create your own street signs and work with your local government officials to post them.

If you would like to use art to raise public awareness, here area a few ideas:

- Create an exhibit on street harassment for display at a local art gallery or a community event. For example, depict (photograph, drawing) women who have been harassed, accompanied by a quote about how it makes them feel. Create a 3-D map and cover it in blinking lights to signify every place a street harassment incident has occurred in a specific area during a certain timeframe. Collect clothing from women in which they were harassed and display them in a clothesline format. Include the harassment story for each article of clothing.

- Organize or participate in an anti-street harassment poster campaign on campus or in the community.
- Design anti-street harassment signs or posters to display in the community, including places where harassment tends to occur.
- Make your own "caution tape" that marks an area where you were harassed. Write your stories on the tape and name it a "street harassment zone."
- Organize or participate in street performance, such as role playing street harassment and encouraging audience participation in dialogue afterward. Create giant silhouette cutouts of men and play recordings of men's real vulgar comments in a busy pedestrian area while passing out information about street harassment (latter idea by Sarah VanDenbergh).
- Volunteer your artistic talents to help other efforts. For example, design a logo or banner for an anti-street harassment Web site or event, or design handouts and posters advertising an anti-street harassment documentary screening or event.
- Support local art by donating money or by attending the exhibits. Invite someone who does not know very much about street harassment to attend.

"JUST DO IT"

Echoing the advice of Jenga Mwendo, if you want to raise awareness about street harassment, then "just do it." From the simple act of sharing your stories in person or online to more involved forms of activism, there are a variety of ways to do something. All of the activists I highlighted are everyday people who one day decided to use their talents and resources to do something. Think about what your resources and talents are and be creative in how you want to address street harassment in your community. No action is too small to make a difference.

NOTES

1. Author interview with Emily May in New York City on September 13, 2008.
2. Brittany Shoot, e-mail message to author, April 23, 2007, and June 13, 2008.
3. Ibid.
4. Shannon Lynberg, e-mail message to author, June 9, 2009.
5. Chaitra Shenoy, e-mail message to author, May 12, 2009.
6. Lynberg, e-mail message to author, June 9, 2009.

7. Lisa Rahman, e-mail message to author, July 9, 2009.

8. Ibid.

9. Ibid.

10. Ashley Nguyen, "Saying Hello Is Just for the Sake of Saying Hello," *Temple News*, September 23, 2009, http://temple-news.com/2009/09/23/saying-hello-is-just-for-the-sake-of-saying-hello.

11. Emily May, "Beware the Closing Doors," *New York Daily News*, June 10, 2009, http://www.metro.us/us/article/2009/06/10/07/0408-82/index.xml.

12. Kari Mansager, e-mail message to author, October 26, 2009.

13. Ibid.

14. Ibid.

15. Ibid.

16. Erin Johnson, e-mail message to author, August 17, 2009.

17. Carol Motsinger, "In Pursuit of Respect: Art Hits the Street to Prevent Sexual Harassment," *Citizen Times*, April 5, 2009, cited on "Street Harassment Event in Asheville, NC," Stop Street Harassment Blog, April 5, 2009, http://streetharassment.wordpress.com/2009/04/05/street-harassment-event-in-asheville-nc.

18. Ibid.

19. Erin Johnson, e-mail message to author, August 17, 2009.

20. Ibid.

21. Ibid.

22. INCITE!, "About INCITE!" n.d., http://www.incite-national.org/index.php?s=35.

23. DC Indymedia, "Choose Respect! Pictures from the Community Education Speak Out against Street Harassment of Women and Girls," May 8, 2006, http://dc.indymedia.org/newswire/display/133765/index.php.

24. DC Indymedia, http://dc.indymedia.org/newswire/display/133765/index.php.

25. Katie Seitz, e-mail message to author, June 14, 2008.

26. Maggie, Hadleigh-West, "War Zone," Film Fatale, Inc., 1998 (71-minute version).

27. Ibid.

28. Media Education Foundation, "War Zone," n.d., http://www.mediaed.org/cgi-bin/commerce.cgi?preadd=action&key=213#film-festivals.

29. *Time* Yahoo Chat, "Watching All the Girls Go By: A Conversation with Maggie Hadleigh West, director of the film 'War Zone' about Sexual Harassment on the street," September 15, 1998, http://www.time.com/time/community/transcripts/chattr091598.html.

30. Chloe A. Hilliard, "'Ayo, Shorty!' Brooklyn Girls are Fighting Back against the Boys Who Harass Them," Village Voice, June 12, 2007, http://www.villagevoice.com/2007-06-12/news/ayo-shorty/, edited by Joanne Smith, e-mail message to author, December 30, 2009.

31. Girls for Gender Equity, Inc, "Publications," n.d., http://www.ggenyc.org/publications.php.

32. Tracey Rose, e-mail message to author, December 1, 2008.

33. MJS5083, "Sexual Harassment," YouTube, March 27, 2007, http://www.youtube.com/watch?v=WzVYRdyY5rI&feature=player_embedded.

34. Jenga Mwendo, e-mail message to author, December 9, 2009.

35. Lisa J. Curtis, "Street Fight: Arts Organization Creates an Exhibit in DUMBO Born out of One Harrowing Night," *Brooklyn Paper*, July 29, 2002, http://www.brooklynpaper.com/stories/25/29/25_29catcalls.html.

36. Jenga Mwendo, e-mail message to author, December 9, 2009.

37. Ibid.

38. Author interview with Jasmeen Patheja in New York City, October 13, 2009.

39. Ibid.

40. Ibid.

41. Ibid.

42. Ilona Granet, e-mail message to author, November 24, 2009, and December 24, 2009.

43. Ibid.

44. Ibid.

45. Ibid.

46. Ibid.

_____ *Chapter 10* _____

Making Street Harassment
an Issue

If so many women are negatively impacted by street harassment, where is the public outcry and widespread activism? This is a question I often have asked myself since I realized the extent of the problem of street harassment. This book was born because almost no one is writing about this problem.

While it is frustrating that so few people and groups are working to stop street harassment, it also is an exciting time for those who are. While a few academics have been writing about street harassment since at least 1981, it has not been an issue many activists have worked on in any significant way until the last five to ten years. I feel as though we are standing at the beginning of what will become a long-lasting, concerted, and ultimately successful movement to make all places safe and welcoming for women.

Movements to address rape, domestic violence, and sexual harassment at work and school each began this way too: a few dedicated academics writing on the issues and pockets of activists across the country doing what they can to address the issue locally. Stronger laws and policies followed as did widespread public awareness that this is unacceptable behavior. Each movement began in earnest only a few decades ago, and now, while rape, domestic violence, and sexual harassment at work and school still occur, they are no longer considered private problems or "the way things are," but are illegal, criminal actions. Street harassment is nowhere near as developed, but hopefully in a few more years, with more people working to end it, it can be.

Only in the last few years have large numbers of male allies begun working to address these largely male-perpetrated problems. We also need male allies to address the largely male-perpetrated problem of gender-based street harassment. Efforts to end it will have a better chance of succeeding with men involved. In addition to bringing different perspectives from many women, the benefit of men working on this issue is that when they speak, men who harass women will be more likely to listen. Policy-makers may only pay attention to the problem if men are involved in speaking out and working to end it, too.

In addition to educating men, empowering women, and raising awareness that street harassment is a problem, to help stop it we can turn it into an "issue" that organizations, groups, and individuals can work on in a cohesive, comprehensive way. To start, we need a common name and definition to use and rally around. Then, to better understand the complexities of the issue, we need more research and we need conferences where we can discuss a range of experiences and viewpoints and to share ideas. Last, we need local anti-street harassment campaigns to engage their communities in the issue and to lobby for local policies and ordinances that will make public spaces safer. This chapter explores each of these areas.

NAMING THE PROBLEM

Legal scholar Robin West wrote in her article "The Difference in Women's Hedonic Lives: A Phenomenological Critique of Feminist Legal Theory" that "an injury uniquely sustained by a disempowered group will lack a name, a history, and in general a linguistic reality."[1] This aptly describes what has happened to the experiences women have had in public spaces for centuries at the hands of unknown men.

Street harassment is the most commonly used term to describe the insulting, annoying, threatening, and unwelcome behavior of men toward girls and women they do not know in public places. But you will be hard pressed to find the term used in mainstream media or even used consistently among activists who want to end the problem. It is more difficult to rally around an issue and work to end it if it has no name, or if people call it different names. For that reason, I will continue to call it street harassment and, for consistency's sake, I encourage anyone working on this issue to use the term when describing the issue. It will be easier to educate the public and create change if everyone uses the same term to describe the same behaviors.

Agreeing about what behaviors constitute street harassment is part of naming it. While it is empowering for each person to define for themselves what constitutes street harassment, it also is important that there be a broad definition that is commonly used so that when we say "street harassment" we all know what that means. Also, if we want men to stop engaging in street harassment behaviors, we have to be clear about what these behaviors are and what men should stop doing. Giving them conflicting or contradictory messaging will not help to end the problem.

Fortunately, there is basic consistency among activists working on this issue as to what constitutes street harassment. Building off those definitions and my informal survey results, this is what I offer to clarify what constitutes street harassment:

- First and foremost, street harassment is any unwelcome behavior from men toward women in public spaces initiated because of their gender. Women are the ones who dictate if it is unwelcome. For "public places" I usually exclude bars and clubs because of the differences in expectation about interactions, but include any other place that is open to the general public.

- As to what specific behaviors constitute street harassment, I include: leering/staring, whistling, honking, kissy noises, "psst's," vulgar gestures, sexist or racist or homophobic comments, commands like "smile," sexually explicit comments, purposeful touching, flashing, masturbating, following, intentionally blocking the path, and assault. Persistently talking to a person when they clearly do not want to talk also is harassment. In some circumstances and at some times, there are women who like or do not mind behavior like positive comments on their appearance or being asked for their phone number. In general, such behavior is inappropriate for public spaces. If it is done, however, it should be done in a respectful and nonthreatening manner, and it should immediately cease if a woman does not respond positively (silence is not a positive response).

- Mutual flirting in public between strangers is acceptable, but it always must be done with respect (meaning no sexually explicit or sexist remarks), without threatening posture or words, and in such a way that either party has the opportunity to indicate if it is unwelcome. And if one party chooses to stop the advance, then the interaction immediately stops, without insults, threats, or violence on the part of the other person.

While street harassment is the name and these guidelines are how I propose to define street harassment, ultimately, we need more research and national and/or global conferences to share and discuss this topic in order to build consensus and cohesion.

RESEARCH AND CONFERENCES

While several scholars have written about street harassment, very few have actually studied it. In fact, among academics, I have found only five such studies. Several governments and communities also have studied the prevalence of street harassment, particularly on public transportation. I conducted two informal online surveys to gather more women's experiences, but my findings are not statistically significant and can only suggest problems. To be able to further address street harassment, we need to better understand it.

In 2009, I interviewed psychology professor Kimberly Fairchild about her research on street harassment. I asked her what advice she would offer to someone considering academic research, and she said,

I think the field is wide open for research on street harassment. The obvious starting point for a social psychological viewpoint is to become familiar with the research on sexual harassment because the best way to situate street harassment is under the greater umbrella of unwanted sexual attention and sexual harassment. There is so little understood academically about the experience of street harassment that research on any and all aspects is necessary: why do men do it, how does it make women feel, how do women react, how do men interpret women's reactions, how can we reduce incidents of street harassment.[2]

I wholeheartedly agree with all of her suggestions. Finding out why men do it is particularly important and an area where there is virtually no comprehensive study. I also propose a few more areas where more research is necessary:

- The role of race, class, sexual orientation, gender identity, disability, and age in harassment encounters.
- The impact street harassment has on women's lives.
- The most empowering and effective ways for women to deal with harassment.
- The ways street harassment can vary by region and by city, suburb, and rural areas.
- If there is a correlation between evidence of gender equity and the volume of street harassment in an area.

Only with more research can we better address the problem and know what strategies to use to end it.

Holding street harassment conferences is important so that people can come together to formulate and name the problem, and share their experiences and findings through panels with experts and activists, workshops, and discussion groups. Annual regional, national, and/or global conferences will help women and men strategize on this issue and put the problem on the agenda of regional, national, and/or global leaders.

In February 2009, in Cairo, there was a three-day conference about street harassment in Egypt with workshops covering the sociological, legal, and psychological perspectives of the problem. Conference attendees created a campaign proposal for dealing with the harassment and the best campaign was selected for implementation by a nongovernmental organization. Leaders in the country took notice and spoke at the conference, including the Minister of Education and an Egyptian ambassador.[3] In December 2009, a second conference was held in Cairo, this time it included activists from seventeen countries in the region. Attendees discussed the widespread problem of public harassment and brainstormed ideas for why it occurs and how they can address it.[4] The conference, which at the time of this writing, occurred a few days ago, has garnered global media attention and has inspired numerous blog posts on the topic.

Street harassment is not a problem that should be kept at an individual level and be regarded as one that women should have to deal with on their own. Gathering women and men together will make the movement strong and bring regional, national, and even global attention to the problem. It can also help lead to anti-street harassment campaigns, through which individuals can engage in more concrete and comprehensive approaches to ending the problem in their local communities.

ANTI-STREET HARASSMENT CAMPAIGNS

Anti-street harassment campaigns can serve many purposes. They can raise public awareness that street harassment is a problem and educate people about why it occurs. They also can lead to concrete changes, like anti-harassment public service announcements on the subway and street lamps on a busy but darkened road. This section highlights four grassroots anti-street harassment campaigns in Chicago, New York City, Mauritius, and Cairo, all of which are ongoing as of December 2009. Specific suggestions and ideas for carrying out one's own campaign conclude the section. Before highlighting the individual campaigns, I will discuss the use of the law to combat street harassment. This can help inform the structure for future debate for local, state, and national anti-harassment ordinances people can lobby for.

Anti-Harassment Ordinances

If confronted or called out on their behavior, men who harass women may claim they are doing nothing wrong or that their acts are not illegal. To make street harassment an issue akin to domestic violence or sexual harassment at the workplace and to help stop it, we need to make it illegal. Several legal scholars have examined criminal and civil law to see if either can be used by women who want to prosecute street harassers, including legal scholars Cynthia Grant Bowman in her 1993 *Harvard Law Journal* article "Street Harassment and the Informal Ghettoization of Women," and Tiffany Heben in her 1994 *South California's Review of Law and Women's Studies* article "A Radical Reshaping of the Law: Interpreting and Remedying Street Harassment." Their conclusion is that some forms of street harassment apply as crimes under current laws, including sexual touching, masturbating, and direct threats; however, men can engage in the most common types of street harassment like whistling and commenting on a woman's appearance without legal consequences. They suggested ways to redefine existing laws to encompass street harassment, guidelines for creating new ordinances, and they proposed their own.

From her research, Bowman determined that the goal of any new law should be the general deterrence of harassing behavior toward women through realistic and effective remedies. To that end, she came up with several factors that need to inform the creation of a law.

- The remedy should not define the offense in terms based on the intent of the harasser; it should incorporate a "reasonable woman" standard as to the offensiveness of the conduct and to the reasonableness of the woman's response to it.
- The law should apply to both verbal and nonverbal conduct.
- The ability to press charges should not require a course of conduct (meaning the person had to have committed the harassment more than once).
- The law's application needs to be limited to speech that is not general public discourse but street harassment.
- Pressing charges needs to be cheap enough that women can realistically do it.
- The consequences with being charged of harassment must be great enough that they deter most people from committing the crime.[5]

Taking these factors into consideration, the following is her proposed public ordinance for street harassment at the state or municipal level.

It shall be a misdemeanor, punishable by a fine of $250, to engage in street harassment. Street harassment occurs when one or more unfamiliar men accost one or more women in a public place, on one or more occasions, and intrude or attempt to intrude upon the woman's attention in a manner that is unwelcome to the woman, with language or action that is explicitly or implicitly sexual. Such language includes, but is not limited to, references to male or female genitalia or to female body parts or to sexual activities, solicitation of sex, or reference by word or action to the targets of the harassment as the object of sexual desire, or similar words that by their very utterance inflict injury or naturally tend to provoke violent resentment, even if the woman did not herself react with violence. The harasser's intent, except his intention to say the words or engage in the conduct, is not an element of this offense. This section does not apply to any peaceable activity intended to express political views or provide public information to others. A woman's dress and prior sexual history are irrelevant to the issue whether the harassment was welcome or unwelcome to her. . . . Any person aggrieved under this statute shall have a private cause of action for damages.[6]

Bowman concedes that the ordinance she proposed is subject to First Amendment challenge. Since the ordinance is both gender-based and content-based in its description of the prohibited behavior and "underbroad" in the conduct it prohibits, the statute could be argued to be invalid. Nonetheless, she says that these possible problems should not deter women from working to pass such an ordinance because the process alone of introducing legislation and campaigning for its passage would likely incite public discussion about street harassment and raise consciousness of it as a problem.[7]

Heben came to similar conclusions as Bowman and generally agrees with Bowman's proposed ordinance. The biggest hurdle she foresees in passing such a law is the inability to predict if women will actually use it and report harassment. Based on precedent, she found that many women feel that the police and the legal system will continue to fail to acknowledge the gravity of women's experiences, so women may decide not to waste their time and energy reporting an incident that will not be taken seriously.[8] Heben fears that discrimination against homosexual women and women of color might also deter women in those groups in particular from reporting their experiences of harassment. Also, she says, women of color may fear that a law against street harassment will be used to unfairly prosecute men of color and may "regard an ordinance against it as yet another way to punish black men, rather than empower black women."[9] Thus, Heben writes, and I agree, all women need to collaborate to develop an ordinance that is sensitive and useful to all populations.[10]

Overall, despite the current short comings of Bowman's and Heben's proposed statutes, both women support the modification of current laws to deter street harassment and the introduction of a law that criminalizes severe street harassment. I also support this and think that a harassment law will deter harassers, and, perhaps more importantly, it will cause a societal shift away from trivializing and dismissing street harassment and offer women more options for dealing with their harassers. Furthermore, in most cities there are public ordinances against nuisances like littering, not picking up dog waste, and panhandling. Male harassment is a bigger problem in many women's lives as it can negatively impact their quality of life and limit their access to public spaces. If these issues have ordinances, surely we can have one for harassers.

Some street harassers are men who are harassing women while they are technically on the job, for example, construction workers, gardeners, delivery persons, taxi drivers, or movers. Legal scholar Deborah Thompson had a very interesting idea about how to use the law to address these harassers (which, of course, primarily impacts working class men). She writes:

While Title VII [of the Civil Rights Act of 1964, which prohibits workplace discrimination] was never intended to apply outside the workplace, its hostile environment principles provide a useful framework from which to develop a liability regime to protect all women who are street harassed by "men at work." This regime would hold employers vicariously liable for public sexual harassment by their employees if the employer failed to warn workers that street harassment is intolerable, failed to implement a system by which members of the public could formally file a complaint, or failed to take remedial action when members of the public complained about harassment by their employees.

It would be relatively easy to develop a complaint procedure for street harassment. For example, instead of signs on the back of company trucks that read, "How's my driving, call 1-800-555-1212," trucks and taxis could display signs that read, "If the driver of this vehicle harasses you, call 1-800-555-1212." Similarly at construction sites, there should be a number for women to call to complain about harassment by workers. Such a "Harassment Hotline" would be a first step in ending the hostile environment of outdoor workplaces. It would send a valuable message that a particular company cares about its image and does not tolerate workers who invade and bombard communities with sexual harassment. . . . In sum, the societal interest of promoting the privacy, safety, mobility, and equality of women should outweigh the desire of employees to engage in recreational sexual harassment while on the job.[11]

I think Thompson's ideas are realistic measures to lobby for and have enforced. Employers tend to respect women's complaints because they do not want to lose business or gain a bad reputation as a place that hires harassers. Asking them to post a number on a delivery truck or on a sign next to a worksite that people can call if they experience or witness harassment (sexual, racial, or homophobic) is something many employers might consider and could make a big difference in deterring harassers and giving women the means by which to respond.

As part of their efforts, several of the anti-street harassment campaigns highlighted next are lobbying for various anti-street harassment laws, which add to the ideas for potential ways laws can be utilized to stop street harassment.

New York City

Within a short period of time in 2004, in separate incidents in North Brooklyn, New York, neighborhoods, men assaulted women who were walking home alone late at night. When Oraia Reid heard about these assaults occurring near where she lived and worked, she was outraged and, as a survivor of sexual violence, afraid. She described her overwhelming anger and fear to her then-partner Consuelo Ruybal, who in turn asked a simple question, "What do you want to do about it?" Reid's response was that she wished she could give every woman a safe ride home. Ruybal encouragingly said, let's do it![12]

They already owned a car and they bought a cell phone to use as a dispatch phone, and, after community needs assessment and grassroots advertising, they began giving free rides home to women and to members of the LGBQT community late at night on Saturdays, between 11:59 p.m. and 3 a.m. A community survey indicated that limited finances prevented many people from securing their own safe transportation home and yet, taking and walking home from mass transit late at night was dangerous. As word spread about the free safe ride service, other volunteers who owned cars offered to help. By 2005, they had given safe rides home to over 200 people on Saturday nights.

During 2005, their grassroots effort became an official organization, RightRides for Women's Safety (RightRides) and gained a 501(c)3 non-profit status. Their mission statement is, "To build safer communities by addressing gender-based violence, ranging from harassment to assault," while their motto is, *"Because Getting Home Safely Shouldn't Be a Luxury."*

In 2006, RightRides secured a fleet of donated Zipcars for volunteers to drive and they were able to expand the neighborhoods they served. At the end of 2006, they had driven nearly 600 riders safely home within nineteen neighborhoods throughout New York City on Saturday nights. RightRides continues to expand, and in 2009 they began offering rides home on Friday nights in addition to Saturday nights within forty-five neighborhoods. Also in 2009, they had about 150 driving team volunteers and drove their 2,000th rider safely home.[13]

When Reid and Ruybal began the services that became RightRides, they had no long-term vision. Reid said their thought was, "we have to do something about the increase in assaults, right now." She continued, "We took action quickly and soon after, we realized in addition to providing rides home, that it would be equally important to provide safety advocacy and education. I'm really excited that we've successfully mobilized many diverse communities to address sexual harassment and assault first hand, and in ways that resonate with them."[14] As of late 2009, Reid was working with activists in San Francisco and Washington, D.C. (including HollaBack DC! facilitators Chai Shenoy and Shannon Lynberg), to raise money and bring RightRides chapters to those cities[15]

Reid, who works as the executive director of RightRides, also focuses on community initiatives to make public spaces safer for women and the LGBQTI community. Since 2007, she has been working with groups like HollaBackNYC and Girls for Gender Equity to make public transportation safer and in 2009 they formed the group New Yorkers for Safe Transit (NYFST).

Although not yet organized with a name, the organizations comprising NYFST began their work in 2007 when they helped with a survey on sexual harassment and assault on the subway, conducted by the Office of the Manhattan Borough President Scott M. Stringer. Of the 1,790 people who responded to the online survey (the majority of whom were women), 63 percent said they had been harassed and one-tenth had been sexual assaulted on the subway system. Only four percent of people who were harassed reported it, as did only 14 percent of those who were assaulted. Forty-four percent said they had witnessed sexual harassment.[16]

One of the report recommendations was a Public Service Announcement (PSA) campaign about sexual harassment on the subway. The next year, the Metropolitan Transportation Authority (MTA) printed ads but shied away from posting them, claiming they were afraid they would encourage sexual harassment. Through a number of grassroots tactics, including an op-ed in *the New York Daily News* by HollaBack co-founders Emily May and Sam Carter,[17] combined with a joint collaboration between RightRides, the offices of Council Member Peter Vallone and Manhattan Borough President Scott Stringer, the nascent NYFST coalition issued letters calling for the release of the campaign with the ultimatum of holding a press conference on the topic. The MTA caved and posted the ads; a significant victory for the activists.[18]

In August 2008, MTA posted the PSA in 300 subway cars with 2,000 posters. It reads "Sexual Harassment is a Crime in the subway, too—A crowded train is no excuse for an improper touch. Don't stand for it or feel ashamed, or be afraid to speak up. Report it to an MTA employee or police officer."[19] In February 2009, the MTA launched an audio version of the PSA for the newest subway cars.[20]

After continuing to work together to put pressure on the MTA to better address the problem of sexual harassment and assault on the subway system, in March 2009, the coalition members who had worked on the subway report and pushed for the PSAs, met for a strategy planning session and formally created NYFST. They began a series of community dialogue projects with various nonprofit agencies serving women, youth, elders, LGBTQ and LGBTQ persons of color communities, and low-come individuals to better capture quantitative and qualitative data of harassment and violence in mass transit. They also began working to secure funding to conduct a scientific survey of 5,000 people to capture the mass transit harassment and assault numbers not being recorded.[21]

When I spoke with Reid and May in late 2009, they had made progress in their fundraising goals and were collecting mass transit stories online and through focus groups. They also had made progress on several other initiatives. For example, they worked with Take Back Our Union to advocate for increased transparency and safety for both transit riders and workers and to protest the closing of 100 token booths, which has serious safety repercussions. They met with various legislators about the need for policies that would require public transportation crime data transparency.[22] With their support, in November 2009, Councilwoman Jessica S. Lappin, a Manhattan Democrat, introduced a bill that would require the police to collect data on sexual harassment in the subways. "This is important because historically, harassment is overlooked by law enforcement authorities," said Reid during a joint City Council hearing on sexual harassment on the subway.[23]

In December 2009, their continued efforts and pressure led to more change in the public transit system. MTA reports they will increase the number of automated messages in the subway stations warning against assaults and they will begin distributing anti-groping posters and brochures. MTA will meet with NYFST in early 2010 to create a more comprehensive anti-harassment PSA that takes the onus off the survivor, provides a hotline number, bystander information, and details about how perpetrators will be held accountable for their actions.[24] Building off the method Holla Back NYC uses for "hollaback"ing at harassers with camera phone photos, NYPD is working on a pilot program that would enable victims to send photos of harassers to police officers, who can investigate the case even after the harasser has slipped away into a crowd.[25] The NYPD also released new tips for dealing with sexual harassment on the subway.

Look up NYFST to find out their latest initiatives and, if you live in New York City, how you can become involved (http://nyfst.org).

Chicago

Since 2003, members of the Rogers Park Young Women's Action Team (YWAT) have been leading an anti-street harassment campaign in Chicago, Illinois. YWAT is a youth-led, adult-supported group that empowers young women under age 21 to take action on issues that affect their lives.

To start, the eight founding YWAT members surveyed 168 neighborhood girls, ages 13 to 19, about street harassment and interviewed 34 more in focus groups. They published their findings in a report titled "Hey Cutie, Can I Get Your Digits?" The results were astounding: 86 percent had been catcalled on the street, 60 percent said they felt unsafe walking in their neighborhoods, and 53 percent said they felt there was nothing they could do about the harassment.[26]

With their report in hand, the young women began a successful and well-organized anti-street harassment campaign. For example, they worked with local business owners to let them know men standing outside their stores harassed them and made them feel unsafe. Over 120 business owners agreed to post signs in their windows that said, "R-E-S-P-E-C-T let me tell YOU what it means to ME! Respect my body. Respect my mind. Respect ME. STOP STREET HARASSMENT." The efforts of YWAT led to fewer men loitering outside businesses, harassing girls and women.[27]

YWAT also held public forums on street harassment and worked with local leaders, including police and elected officials, to address public safety. One of the YWAT's major victories was the installation of more street lights along Howard Street and Morse Avenue. City officials also installed a camera on Morse Avenue to better monitor street activities.[28]

In May 2006 and May 2007, YWAT organized a Citywide Day of Action against Street Harassment Campaign to convey the message "the streets belong to ALL OF US."[29] They encouraged people to participate in some form of activity that day. The following highlight some of the 140 forms of action of thousands of people in Chicago:

- Handing out anti-street harassment literature and flowers with a note saying "Flowers are beautiful, unwanted comments are not. Give a gift to mothers STOP STREET HARASSMENT" while wearing t-shirts with messages like "My name is not Baby" and "Stop Street Harassment."
- Wearing buttons saying "Because the Streets Belong to All of Us."
- Holding anti-street harassment workshops on campuses, in high schools, and at community centers.
- Distributing informational materials to teachers at 50 Chicago high schools about street harassment and asking them to discuss street harassment with their students.
- Hosting screenings of the documentary *War Zone* followed by a discussion.
- Participating in YWAT's community anti-street harassment march.[30]

The young women also hold anti-street harassment workshops at high schools, conferences, and community events.[31] Their latest initiative is working to make public transportation safer in Chicago.

During the spring of 2009, the group of teenage and college-age women surveyed 639 Chicago Transit Authority (CTA) riders, mostly young women. They found that sexual harassment is common on CTA buses and trains. Over half of the survey respondents said they had been sexually harassed and 13 percent said they had been sexually assaulted. Forty-four percent of those surveyed said they had witnessed harassment or assault. Only nine percent of those who had been harassed or assaulted had reported it.[32]

Armed with their survey results, YWAT met with the CTA Board and other key decision makers and asked that CTA employees receive training on how to deal with harassment and that CTA post more information about how people can report harassers. In a major victory for YWAT, only one month later in July 2009, the CTA announced it would expand its policies on how bus and rail operators deal with harassers. Operators are being instructed to ask harassers to stop, and, if the harasser does not, the operator will call the Control Center to receive instructions on what to do. The CTA said it would update its public safety tips brochures to include information about harassment and how to report it. The existing "If you see something, say something" posters and audio announcements will be updated to include sexual harassment. Lastly, sexual harassment complaints filed with the CTA customer service line will have a special code to enable better monitoring of the problem.[33] This was an amazingly fast and thorough response to the survey findings and town hall meetings YWAT organized.

A few weeks later, a new *Chicago Sun Times* article revealed that transit workers were worried about having this new responsibility and would prefer to call 911 for intervention from the offset rather than deal with harassers alone.[34] At the time of this writing, the CTA was still working out its new policies. In November 2009, however, the CTA made good on their word to create PSAs about harassment. Their new print PSA states, "If it's unwanted, it's harassment. Touching. Rude comments. Leering. Speak up. If you see something, say something." At the bottom of the poster there is information for whom to contact if a rider is the target of sexual harassment. CTA spokeswoman Sheila Gregory said, "An important part of improving safety and security on the system is knowing when, where and how often these types of violations occur so the campaign is intended to help reinforce the importance of reporting incidents."[35]

In their work, YWAT members stress that "teenagers can make a big difference in their community."[36] Their example and successes are inspiring and show that well-organized and dedicated teenagers can indeed make a huge difference. Visit their Web site to find out about their latest initiatives and how you can become involved, if you're in the area (www.youngwomensactionteam.org/).

Mauritius

Street harassment is common in Mauritius, an island off the coast of southern Africa. Alyssa Fine, a native of the American Midwest went to Mauritius as a Fulbright scholar to conduct research on sexual harassment in the workplace. During her data collection and analysis, it became clear that many women also wanted to talk about public harassment.

Because of the anecdotes she heard, Fine decided to research and write a report on street harassment in Mauritius; it was the first of its kind, sponsored by Soroptimist International Ipsae Mauritius.

A companion 2009 anti-street harassment campaign called Respekte Nu (Creole for Respect Us) became part of a six-year, worldwide Amnesty International campaign of Stop Violence Against Women (SVAW). With the help of colleagues, Fine designed the campaign and oversees its implementation. Notably, the director of AIMS is male and Fine said that when she first brought the idea for a report and campaign to him, he did not know street harassment was a serious problem. Only after talking to the women and girls in his life did he discover that it is and he agreed to the initiatives.[37]

The campaign launched with a press conference attended by representatives from non-governmental, private and governmental agencies. Alyssa and her colleagues shared the results of their study and details of the campaign and ended with a participatory activity in which attendees could write down their ideas about how best to address street harassment. Fine said, "As a result of this, we were able to develop partnerships with interested organizations and collect a number of ideas about how to move ahead."[38]

The anti-street harassment campaign is multi-dimensional and at the time of this writing several components are on-going. Some activities that have occurred include a Fam a Fam—or Woman to Woman—forum where 45 women and girls had a safe space to talk about street harassment. There also was a youth art contest for which 30 young people submitted essays/poems and drawings/photographs on street harassment. A postcard campaign is ongoing and people are asked to sign and send the card to the government urging them to take action on street harassment and violence against women. They are still developing brochures and conducting trainings and workshops for schools and women's associations to help facilitate discussions on street harassment. They also are working to develop a man to man platform with trainings, youth education, brochure distributions, and street theater.[39]

Fine said one of their most successful campaign initiatives has been speaking on radio shows. "We were able to convey important information and also engage with the audience [when people called in]. In addition, radio gave us much more control over the message than print media sources."[40]

When I asked Fine what advice she would give to someone who wants to raise awareness about street harassment in their area, she said,

It can be very difficult explaining to men and boys what it's like to be a woman or girl in public. Even the most well intentioned men can have trouble comprehending the fear, anger or humiliation that a comment or stare can provoke. Be ready to explain this and try to recruit male allies who may have better luck getting through to other men. Be positive in your message, especially when speaking to children. . . . Telling them what not to do is only effective if they are given an alternative. Put anti-street harassment messages within a bigger picture of respect, sex and relationships.[41]

Cairo

Because of the sharp increase in the number of women sharing their experiences with public harassment and a lack of societal awareness of the problem, in 2005 the Egyptian Centre for Women's Rights (ECWR) launched an anti-sexual harassment campaign called "Making Our Streets Safer for Everyone." Volunteers are the driving force of ECWR's campaign. They meet monthly to discuss ideas and plan initiatives.[42]

Initially, ECWR conducted informal, voluntary surveys of over 2,000 people. An overwhelming number of female respondents said sexual harassment was part of their daily life. Eighty-three percent of women said men had sexually harassed them and 62 percent of men admitted to perpetrating sexual harassment. Fewer than two percent of women reported going to the police for help. ECWR published their results in a 2008 report "Clouds in Egypt's Sky, Sexual Harassment: from Verbal Harassment to Rape." The report garnered lots of attention in Egypt and around the world.[43]

Next, ECWR organized several forms of public awareness, including:

- Distributing flyers with information like definitions of harassment, existing laws, how to file a police report, and how to campaign on the issue.
- Creating public service radio announcements about sexual harassment.
- Staging an anti-sexual harassment demonstration with 250 women and men on the steps of the Press Syndicate.
- Holding press conferences and public awareness days at cultural centers, institutions, and hotels. Events have featured presentations and discussions on Egypt's sexual harassment laws, women's image in the media, the sociological and psychological impacts of harassment, group discussions on how to address the problem, self defense workshops, and live music and relevant films.[44]

ECWR said they have received positive feedback on their initiatives, including hearing from many people that they had not realized verbal comments could constitute sexual harassment.

On the advocacy front, ECWR has worked with legal volunteers to draft a new sexual harassment law that increases jail time and fines for violation and puts more pressure on police to stop incidents and take the concerns of targets seriously. At the time of this writing, ECWR was working with allies in parliament to have this legislation introduced.[45] They also have been working on holding roundtable discussions with ministry of interior representatives.[46]

ECWR has been reaching out to youth, too, by training teachers and social workers to sensitize them to the issues of public sexual harassment and helping them know how to discuss the issues with their students. They recently released an animated five minute educational film and workbook for teachers to further help facilitate school discussions, including through painting and coloring. The resources teach children to trust others but to be careful and aware of inappropriate behavior and to learn the difference between appropriate and inappropriate language.[47]

Last, at the time of this writing, ECWR was looking for funding to launch a HarassMap Project to implement a system in Egypt for reporting incidences of sexual harassment via SMS messaging. The tool will give women a way to anonymously report incidences as soon as they happen, using text message. By mapping these reports online, the entire system will act as an advocacy, prevention, and response tool, highlighting the severity and pervasiveness of the problem.[48]

STRATEGIES

If you want to start or participate in an anti-street harassment campaign (large or small), here are some ideas and tips to help you. Also note that you do not need to be a professional to get started or to organize; campaigns often are run by regular people volunteering their time and expertise.

- Form a coalition of concerned persons and/or organizations to work on the issue. If possible, include individuals who can offer a variety of viewpoints and experiences, including teenagers and young women, women of color, members of the LGBQTI community, women with disabilities, sex workers, low-income women, and homeless women.
- Decide on preliminary goals for the campaign and create a plan for collecting data about women's experiences.
- Find out the experiences of women in your community by surveying them, interviewing them, and/or holding focus groups. Draft a report with the findings.
- With the report findings, decide, as a group, what changes need to be made and what initiatives to work on.

- Divide up the task work among groups, and plan to have regular meetings to share progress, ideas, and help each other with any challenges.
- Create goals for specific timeframes, such as, in one month we will do X, and in six months we will have done Y, and in one year, we will have achieved Z.
- Work on the goals, issue press releases to inform the public about your intentions and progress. Include ways for members of the public to become involved in the initiatives (from attending events to lobbying their local congress person to posting anti-street harassment signs in their neighborhoods).

The following are some ideas for action campaign members could do:

- Take the report to local council people who are sensitive to women's issues and discuss street harassment with them. Propose a law that fines men who verbally harass women in a sexual or sexist manner. Ask them to introduce it and support it.
- Meet with the local police departments about street harassment. If they do not already, ask that police officers receive sensitivity training regarding street harassment. Also, when surveying women about their harassment experiences you can ask them where they are harassed and create a map tracking this data. If there are problem areas, show the data to the police officers and ask them to have officers patrol the area.
- Talk to local businesses that have employees who work outside about the general problem of street harassment. Ask them to be proactive and to publish a phone number on their work vehicles and/or on a sign at a worksite that people can call if the employees harass women. Ask them to post signs saying "This is a harassment-free zone."

THE TIME IS NOW!

At some point in their life, most women and girls around the world will face harassment and even assault at the hands of unknown men while they are in public places, simply because they are female. For most women, the harassment begins when they reach puberty and for some, it never ends. Young women, women who live in cities, women who commute by foot or on public transportation, women who often are alone in public, and women who are members of communities that experience discrimination tend to face the most frequent harassment, but women everywhere are susceptible. Factors like race, sexual orientation and gender expression, socioeconomic status, disability, and one's global location can add layers to how women experience street harassment. Women's fear of stranger rape and assault and an inability to always respond when harassed mean that most women pretend to ignore harassers and try to avoid encountering them all together. Both strategies mean that women have a more limited access to public space and have to be on guard when they are there. Most men live in ignorance that street harassment negatively impacts women's lives. Many who engage in the behavior believe it is their right and they do not care how it makes women feel.

Street harassment is indicative of a lack of gender equality. It limits women's ability to participate in public life. If you want to live in a world where women and girls are safe and welcome in public, take action! Ending street harassment will require a concerted, multi-level, comprehensive strategy. Any size actions people take will make an impact. No act is too small to make a difference.

Men in particular must join this movement for it to succeed. Men are the perpetrators of gender-based street harassment and many men engage in it to impress each other or to prove their masculinity. For some men, only by seeing other men leading the way in speaking out on this issue and holding events and campaigns will they pay attention and listen. We all need to come together to make public places safe for our sisters, mothers, daughters, cousins, friends, and for all the women we do not know.

Only through the efforts of people of all ages, sexes, genders, sexual orientations, races, nationalities, and classes can we combat this problem. So, take action. Make a difference. Make public places safe and welcoming for women.

NOTES

1. Robin L. West, "The Difference in Women's Hedonic Lives: A Phenomenological Critique of Feminist Legal Theory," *Wisconsin Women's Law Journal* 3 (1987), 81; as cited in Olatokunbo Olukemi Laniya, "Street Smut: Gender, Media, and the Legal Power Dynamics of Street Harassment, or 'Hey Sexy' and Other Verbal Ejaculations." *Columbia Journal of Gender and Law* 14 (2005): 99; see also Deirdre Davis, "The Harm that Has No Name: Street Harassment, Embodiment, and African American Women," in *Gender Struggles: Practical Approaches to Contemporary Feminism*, ed. Constance L. Mui and Julien S. Murphy (Oxford: Rowman & Littlefield Publishers, Inc., 2002), 223; see also Tiffanie Heben, "Reshaping of the Law: Interpreting and Remedying Street Harassment," *South California's Review of Law and Women's Studies* 4, no. 1 (1994), 185–186.

2. Kimberly Fairchild, e-mail message to author, September 16, 2009.

3. Nourhan Elsebahy, "LEAD Program Organizes Conference on Sexual Harassment," *Caravan*, The American University in Cairo student paper, February 24, 2009, http://www.auccaravan.org/2009/02/24/sexual-harassment-conference-begins-this-week.

4. Sarah El Deeb, "Harassment across the Arab World Drives Women Inside," Associated Press, December 15, 2009, http://news.yahoo.com/s/ap/20091215/ap_on_re_mi_ea/ml_arabs_sexual_harassment.

5. Cynthia Grant Bowman, "Street Harassment and the Informal Ghettoization of Women," *Harvard Law Review* 106, no. 3 (January 1993), 574.

6. Bowman, 575–576.

7. Bowman, 577.

8. Heben, 216.

9. Heben, 217–218.

10. Heben, 218.

11. Deborah Thompson, "'The Woman in the Street:' Reclaiming the Public Space from Sexual Harassment," *Yale Journal of Law and Feminism* 6 (1994), 336, 338.

12. Oraia Reid, e-mail message to author, December 30, 2009.

13. Right Rides for Women's Safety, "Mission and History," n.d., http://rightrides.org/templates/about.php?page=mission.

14. Oraia Reid, e-mail message to author, September 25, 2008.

15. Oraia Reid, e-mail message to author, December 30, 2009.

16. Scott M. Stringer, "Hidden in Plain Sight: Sexual Harassment and Assault in the New York City Subway System," July 2007, http://www.nytimes.com/packages/pdf/nyregion/city_room/20070726_hiddeninplainsight.pdf.

17. Emily May and Sam Carter, "MTA Must Crack Down on Epidemic of Subway Groping," *New York Daily News*, July 19, 2008, http://www.nydailynews.com/opinions/2008/07/19/2008-07-19_mta_must_crack_down_on_epidemic_of_subwa.html?page=0.

18. Author interview with Emily May in New York City on September 13, 2008; see also New Yorkers for Safe Transit, "NYFST Actions to Date," n.d., http://nyfst.org/actions.

19. Sewell Chan, "Fighting Sexual Harassment on the Subways," *New York Times*, October 2, 2008, http://cityroom.blogs.nytimes.com/2008/10/02/fighting-sexual-harassment-on-the-subways.

20. "NYFST Actions to Date," http://nyfst.org/actions.

21. Author interview with Emily May and Oraia Reid in New York City on June 20, 2009.

22. Oraia Reid, e-mail message to author, December 30, 2009.

23. Jennifer Lee, "Sexual Harassment Is 'No. 1 Quality of Life Offense' on Subways, Police Say," *New York Times*, November 19, 2009, http://cityroom.blogs.nytimes.com/2009/11/19/sexual-harassment-is-no-1-quality-of-life-offense-on-subways-police-say.

24. Oraia Reid, e-mail message to author, December 30, 2009.

25. Jenny Tai, "Combating Subway Harassment," New York University News, December 1, 2009, http://nyunews.com/news/2009/dec/01/harassment.

26. Amaya N. Roberson, "Anti-Street Harassment," *Off Our Backs,* May–June 2005, 48.

27. Young Women's Action Team, "Accomplishments since July 2003," n.d., http://www.youngwomensactionteam.org/index.php?option=com_content&task=view&id=61&Itemid=112.

28. Ibid.

29. Young Women's Action Team, "Respect Is Due: Youth Take a Stand against Street Harassment," Area Chicago, n.d., http://www.areachicago.org/p/issues/issue-2/respect-is-due.

30. Kittenb comment, Bust Magazine online forum thread, comment posted on May 1, 2006, http://www.bust.com/lounge/lofiversion/index.php/t755.html.

31. Roberson, 48.

32. Mary Wisniewski, "Tired of Being Harassed on the CTA, Women Fight Back," *Chicago Sun-Times,* June 15, 2009, http://www.suntimes.com/news/transportation/1622746,CST-NWS-ride15.article.

33. *Chicago Sun-Times,* July 16, 2009, http://www.suntimes.com/news/transportation/1668966,CST-NWS-harass16.article.

34. *Chicago Sun-Times,* "CTA Bus Drivers: We're Not Harassment Cops," July 27, 2009, http://www.suntimes.com/news/transportation/1686362,CST-NWS-heybaby27.article.

35. CBS Chicago Area Local News, "New Ads Target Sexual Harassment on CTA," November 9, 2009, http://cbs2chicago.com/local/cta.sexual.harassment.2.1300843.html.

36. "MO'Talks" Channel 25, March 2005, http://www.youtube.com/watch?v=Vw9n4x8VeqM&feature=player_embedded#.

37. Alyssa Fine, *Roadblocks: The Street Harassment of Women and Girls in Mauritius* (Rose Hill, Mauritius: Soroptimist International Ipsae, 2009).

38. Alyssa Fine, e-mail message to author, October 11, 2009.

39. Ibid.

40. Ibid.

41. Ibid.

42. Modern Discussions, "Campaign against Sexual Harassment," March 19, 2007, http://www.ahewar.org/eng/show.art.asp?aid=292.

43. The Egyptian Center for Women's Rights, "'Clouds in Egypt's Sky': Sexual Harassment: from Verbal Harassment to Rape," July 2008, http://ecwronline.org/images/pub/ssh/sexualHarassmentResearchResults2008English.pdf.

44. Child Rights Information Network, "The Egyptian Center for Women's Rights Campaign against Sexual Harassment," n.d., http://www.crin.org/docs/ECWR_Harassment_Campaign_Fact_Sheet.pdf.

45. Bikya Masr, "Egypt: Sexual Harassment Law Coming?" Bikya Masr, November 2, 2009, http://bikyamasr.com/?p=5417; see also Joseph

Mayton, "Egypt Puts Tougher Sex-Harassment Law on Agenda," *Women's E News*, February 4, 2009, http://www.womensenews.org/story/the-world/090204/egypt-puts-tougher-sex-harassment-law-agenda.

46. Child Rights Information Network, http://www.crin.org/docs/ECWR_Harassment_Campaign_Fact_Sheet.pdf.

47. Association for Women's Rights in Development, "A New Resource: The ECWR Very Important Games Booklet," April 8, 2009, http://www.awid.org/eng/Women-in-Action/New-Resources/A-New-Resource-The-Egyptian-Center-for-Women-s-Rights-ECWR-Very-Important-Games-Booklet. Access the booklet online here: http://www.awid.org/eng/content/download/54971/612638/file/Games%20Booklet-%20Combats%20Sexual%20Harrasment%20of%20Childern.pdf.

48. Netsquared, "HarassMap: Reporting and Mapping Sexual Harassment on the Streets Via SMS," February 23, 2009, http://www.netsquared.org/projects/harassmap-reporting-mapping-sexual-harassment-sms.

Bibliography

PUBLICATIONS

AAUW. "Pay Equity Statistics." n.d. http://aauw.org/advocacy/laf/lafnet work/library/payequity_stats.cfm (accessed July 14, 2009).

AAUW. "Sexual Harassment in the Workplace: Facts and Statistics." n.d. http://aauw.org/advocacy/laf/lafnetwork/library/workplaceharssment facts.cfm (accessed November 22, 2008).

ABC News. "Japan Tries Women-Only Train Cars to Stop Groping." June 10, 2005. http://abcnews.go.com/GMA/International/story?id=803965 &CMP=OTC-RSSFeeds0312 (accessed March 15, 2009).

Abdelhadi, Magdi. "Egypt's Sexual Harassment 'Cancer.'" *BBC*, July 18, 2008. http://news.bbc.co.uk/2/hi/middle_east/7514567.stm (accessed July 20, 2008).

African Press International. "Few Available Jobs Pay as Well as Sex Work." November 18, 2009. http://africanpress.wordpress.com/2009/ 11/18/few-available-jobs-pay-as-well-as-sex-work (accessed November 22, 2009).

Alas, A Blog. "The Male Privilege Checklist." n.d. http://www.amptoons. com/blog/the-male-privilege-checklist (accessed December 18, 2009).

Alexander, Leigh. "And You Thought Grand Theft Auto Was Bad." Slate. com, March 9, 2009. http://www.slate.com/id/2213073 (accessed March 10, 2009).

Allen, Charlotte. "Cleaving over Hillary's Cleavage." *Los Angeles Times*, August 5, 2007. http://www.latimes.com/news/opinion/sunday/commentary/ la-op-allen5 aug05,0,4948945.story (accessed August 23, 2009).

All Headline News. "Survey Finds Majority of Delhi Women Fear Sexual Harassment in Public Places." November 17, 2009. http://www.allhead linenews.com/articles/7017019900 (accessed November 22, 2009).

Amer, Mildred, Jennifer E. Manning, and Colleen Shogan. "Women in the United States Congress: 1917–2009." Congressional Research Service, July 27, 2009. http://www.senate.gov/CRSReports/crs-publish.cfm? pid='0E%2C*PLS%3D% 22%40%20%20%0A (accessed August 23, 2009).

American Psychology Association. "Report of the APA Task Force on the Sexualization of Girls." 2007. http://www.apa.org/pi/women/programs/ girls/report.aspx? item=2 (accessed December 20, 2009).

Ammar, Manar, and Joseph Mayton. "A Majority of Cairo Women Face Street Harassment." Alternet.org, October 21, 2008. http://www.alternet. org/reproductivejustice/103130/a_majority_of_cairo_women_face_street_ harassment (accessed November 14, 2009).

Amnesty International. "Colombia: Scarred Bodies, Hidden Crimes: Sexual Violence against Women in the Armed Conflict." 2004. http:// www.amnesty.org/en/library/asset/AMR23/040/2004/en/eeb9c46a-d598- 11dd-bb24-1fb85fe8fa05/ amr230402004en.html (accessed November 9, 2009).

Amnesty International. "Take Action for the Women of Juarez." n.d. http://www.amnestyusa.org/artists-for-amnesty/bordertown/take-action- for-the-women-of-juarez/page.do?id=1101544 (accessed November 8, 2009).

Anti-Harassment UK Blog, http://www.anti-harassment.ik.com.

Arnst, Cathy. "Will the Recession Change Gender Roles?" *Business Week*, February 6, 2009. http://www.businessweek.com/careers/workingparents/ blog/archives/2009/02/will_the_recess.html (accessed September 3, 2009).

Associated Press. "Saudi Arabia's Religious Police Undergo Change Slowly." July 7, 2009. http://www.miamiherald.com/news/world/AP/ story/1138310.html (accessed November 9, 2009).

Association for Women's Rights in Development. "A New Resource: The ECWR Very Important Games Booklet." April 8, 2009. http://www. awid.org/eng/Women-in-Action/New-Resources/A-New-Resource-The- Egyptian-Center-for- Women-s-Rights-ECWR-Very-Important-Games- Booklet (accessed October 27, 2009).

Authentic Ireland Travel. "A Woman's Guide to Safe Travel." n.d. http:// www. authen ticireland.com/womens+guide+to+safe+travel (accessed November 8, 2009).

BBC. "Egyptian Sexual Harasser Jailed." October 21, 2009. http://news. bbc.co.uk/2/hi/africa/7682951.stm (accessed November 14, 2009).

BBC. "Saudi Cleric Favours One-Eye Veil." October 3, 2008. http://news. bbc.co.uk/2/hi/middle_east/7651231.stm (accessed November 9, 2009).

BBC. "Tokyo Trains Tackle Groping Problem." December 5, 2000. http:// news. bbc.co.uk/2/hi/asia-pacific/1055599.stm (accessed March 15, 2009).

BBC. "Viewpoints: Europe and the Headscarf." February 10, 2004. http:// news. bbc.co.uk/2/hi/3459963.stm (accessed November 9, 2009).

Benard, Cheryl, and Edith Schlaffer. "The Man in the Street: Why He Harasses." In *Feminist Frameworks*, edited by Allison M. Jaggar and Paula S. Rothenberg. New York: McGraw Hill, 1984.

Benard, Cheryl, and Edith Schlaffer, "The Man in the Street: Why He Harasses." *Ms. Magazine*, May 1981, 18–19.

Bielski, Zosia. "Female Managers Face More Harassment, Study Says." *Globe and Mail*, August 13, 2009. http://www.theglobeandmail.com/life/work/female-managers-face-more-harassment-study-says/article1247187 (accessed August 14, 2009).

Bird of Paradox Blog. http://birdofparadox.wordpress.com/2009/08/17/street-harassment.

Blackwell, Gloria. "Back to School for the Media: Tweens, Thongs, and 'Coffee Sluts,'" AAUW Blog, September 1, 2009. http://blog-aauw.org/2009/09/01/back-to-school-for-the-media-tweens-thongs-and-coffee-sluts (accessed November 22, 2009).

Blenford, Adam. "Guatemala's Epidemic of Killing." *BBC*, June 9, 2005. http://news.bbc.co.uk/2/hi/americas/4074880.stm (accessed December 18, 2009).

Blow, Charles M. "Two Little Boys." *New York Times*, April 24, 2009. http://blow.blogs.nytimes.com/2009/04/24/two-little-boys (accessed December 11, 2009).

Bohner, Gerd and Norbert Schwarz. "The Threat of Rape: Its Psychological Impact on Nonvictimized Women." In *Sex, Power, Conflict: Evolutionary and Feminist Perspectives*, edited by David M. Buss and Neil M. Malamuth. Oxford: Oxford University Press, 1996.

Boswell, Laura. "Olympians Posing Nude, Poses Questions." ESPN, n.d. http://sports.espn.go.com/espn/page3/story?page=boswell/040823 (accessed November 20, 2009).

Bowman, Cynthia Grant. "Street Harassment and the Informal Ghettoization of Women." *Harvard Law Review* 106, no. 3 (January 1993): 518–580.

The Brian Lehrer Show. "Taking Back the Streets." WNYC, July 16, 2007. http://www.wnyc.org/shows/bl/episodes/2007/07/16/segments/82164 (accessed October 1, 2009).

Brown, Campbell. "Commentary: Sexist Treatment of Palin Must End." CNN, September 24, 2008. http://www.cnn.com/2008/POLITICS/09/24/campbell. brown.palin (accessed November 20, 2009).

Brownmiller, Susan. "Against Our Will: Men, Women, and Rape." In *Feminism in Our Time: The Essential Writings, World War II to the Present*, edited by Mariam Schneir. New York: Vintage Books, 1994.

Buchwald, Emilie. "Raising Girls for the 21st Century." In *Transforming a Rape Culture*, edited by Emilie Buchwald, Pamela R. Fletcher, and Martha Roth. Minneapolis, MN: Milkwood Editions, 1993.

Buss, David M. "Sexual Conflict: Evolutionary Insights into Feminism and the 'Battle of the Sexes.'" In *Sex, Power, Conflict: Evolutionary and*

Feminist Perspectives, edited by David M Buss and Neil M. Malamuth. Oxford: Oxford University Press, 1996.

Bust Magazine. http://www.bust.com/lounge/lofiversion/index.php/t755. html.

Canada.com. "Priest Blames Girls for Abuse He Caused." January 18, 2007. http://www.canada.com/nationalpost/news/story.html?id=a9b28 207-58bd-4e0d- b8fe-57be11a56f73 (accessed November 22, 2009).

Cawthorne, Alexandra. "The Straight Facts on Women in Poverty." Center for American Progress, October 8, 2008. http://www.americanprogress. org/issues/2008/10/women_poverty.html (accessed September 3, 2009).

CBC News. "Mounties Scour Vancouver Park for Clues in Jogger's Killing." April 6, 2009. http://www.cbc.ca/canada/british-columbia/story/ 2009/04/06/bc-jogger-slaying.html (accessed April 16, 2009).

CBS Chicago Area Local News. "New Ads Target Sexual Harassment on CTA." November 9, 2009. http://cbs2chicago.com/local/cta.sexual. harassment.2.130 0843.html (accessed December 14, 2009).

CBS News. "Female Jogger Reportedly Raped in Fairmount Park." August 13, 2009. http://cbs3.com/topstories/fairmount.park.philadelphia.2.11 25141.html (accessed September 4, 2009).

CCH Aspen Publishers. "Employment Law: EEOC Examines 'Caregiver Discrimination.'" May 4, 2007. http://hr.cch.com/news/employment/ 050407a.asp (accessed August 23, 2009).

Chambers, Veronica. *Kickboxing Geishas: How Modern Japanese Are Changing Their Nation.* New York: Free Press, 2007.

Chan, Sewell. "Fighting Sexual Harassment on the Subways." *New York Times*, October 2, 2008. http://cityroom.blogs.nytimes.com/2008/10/02/fighting-sexual- harassment-on-the-subways (accessed October 10, 2009).

Chan, Sewell. "Subway Harassment Questionnaire Garners a Big Response." *New York Times*, July 26, 2008. http://cityroom.blogs. nytimes.com/2007/07/26/big-response-to-subway-harassment-question (accessed February 8, 2009).

Chan, Stacey. "Off the Map—Power on the Street." Kirwan Institute Blog. August 13, 2009. http://kirwaninstitute.blogspot.com/2009/08/off-map-power-on-street_13.html (accessed August 16, 2009).

Chen, Edith Wen-Chu. "Sexual Harassment from the Perspective of Asian-American Women." In *Everyday Sexism in the Third Millennium*, edited by Carol Rambo Ronai, Barbara A. Zsembik, and Joe. R. Feagin. New York: Routledge, 1997.

Chicago Sun-Times. "CTA Bus Drivers: We're Not Harassment Cops," July 27, 2009. http://www.suntimes.com/news/transportation/16863 62,CST-NWS-hey baby27.article (accessed July 28, 2009).

Child Rights Information Network. "The Egyptian Center for Women's Rights Campaign against Sexual Harassment." n.d. http://www.crin. org/docs/ECWR_Harassment_Campaign_Fact_Sheet.pdf (accessed October 27, 2009).

Chynoweth, Sarah K., and Erin M. Patrick, "Sexual Violence during Firewood Collection: Income-Generation as Protection in Displaced Settings." In *Gender-Based Violence*, edited by Geraldine Terry and Joanna Hoare. Oxford: Oxfam Great Britain, 2007.

CNN Money. "Abercrombie's Sexy Undies 'Slip.'" May 28, 2002. http://money.cnn.com/2002/05/22/news/companies/abercrombie (accessed November 22, 2009).

Cohen, Patricia Cline. "Safety and Danger: Women on American Public Transport, 1750–1850." In *Gendered Domains: Rethinking Public and Private in Women's History*, edited by Dorothy O. Helly and Susan M. Reverby. Ithaca, NY: Cornell University Press, 1992.

Collins, Patricia Hill. *Black Feminist Thought: Knowledge, Consciousness, and the Politics of Empowerment*. New York: Routledge, 1990.

Colvin, Jill. "Hillary's Cleavage Problem." *New York Press*, August 15, 2007. http://www.nypress.com/article-16988-hillarys-cleavage-problem.html (accessed August 23, 2009).

Comstock, Gary. *Violence against Lesbians and Gay Men*. New York: Columbia University Press, 1991.

Crenshaw, Kimberle. "Race, Gender, and Sexual Harassment." *Southern California Law Review* 65 (1991–1992): 1467–76.

Curtis, Lisa J. "Street Fight: Arts Organization Creates an Exhibit in DUMBO Born Out of One Harrowing Night." *Brooklyn Paper*, July 29, 2002, http://www.brooklynpaper.com/stories/25/29/25_29catcalls.html (accessed October 20, 2006).

Daily Mail. "That's One Hell of a Shot, Serena! Tennis Champ Courts Attention with Nude Magazine Cover." October 6, 2009, http://www.dailymail.co.uk/tvshowbiz/article-1218530/Serena-Williams-courts-attention-nude-magazine-cover.html (accessed November 20, 2009).

Dana, C. "Talking Back to Harassers." *Washington Post*, August 19, 1986, C5.

Davies, Lizzy. "Why Not Ban Full Veil, Says French Government Spokesman." *Guardian*, June 19, 2009. http://www.guardian.co.uk/world/2009/jun/19/veil-burka-france-muslim-women (accessed November 9, 2009).

Davis, Deirdre. "The Harm that Has No Name: Street Harassment, Embodiment, and African American Women." In *Gender Struggles: Practical Approaches to Contemporary Feminism*, edited by Constance L. Mui and Julien S. Murphy. Oxford: Rowman & Littlefield Publishers, Inc., 2002: 214–225.

DC Indymedia. "Choose Respect! Pictures from the Community Education Speak Out Against Street Harassment of Women and Girls." May 8, 2006. http://dc.indymedia.org/newswire/display/133765/index.php (accessed August 9, 2009).

Dejohn, Irving, and Brendan Brosh. "Two Arrested in Queens Bias Attack on Transgender Female." *New York Daily News*. July 10, 2009. http://www.nydailynews.com/news/ny_crime/2009/07/10/2009-07-10_

2_arrested_in_queens_transgender_attack.html (accessed November 5, 2009).

de Sanches, Annie Slezickey. "Rogers Park YWAT Also a Peace-Builder." *Rogers Park 2000*, Fall 2009. http://www.rogerspark.org/images/ September_2009.pdf (accessed October 27, 2009).

Dhakal, Prem. "The Sorry Side of Public Transport." My Republica, February 16, 2009. http://www.myrepublica.com/portal/index.php?action=news_ details&news_id=173 (accessed November 14, 2009).

di Leonardo, Micaela. "Political Economy of Street Harassment." *Aegis* (Summer 1981): 51–57.

Don't Be Silent Blog. "Highlights from the Martha Langelan Workshop." February 10, 2008, http://dontbesilent3.blogspot.com/2008/02/high lights-from-martha-langelan.html (accessed September 5, 2009).

Don't Be Silent Blog. "Response to 'Drive-by Hollas Drive Me Crazy!!'" February 11, 2008. http://dontbesilent3.blogspot.com/2008/02/response-to-drive-by-hollas-drive-me.html (accessed September 5, 2009).

Doumato, E. A. *Women's Rights in the Middle East and North Africa: Citizenship and Justice—Saudi Arabia Country Report.* Washington, DC: Freedom House Inc., 2005.

Drucker, Susan J., and Gary Grumpert. "Shopping Women, and Public Space." In *Voices in the Street: Explorations in Gender, Media, and Public Space*, edited by Susan J. Drucker and Gary Gumpert. Cresskill, NJ: Hampton Press, Inc., 1996.

Duneier, Mitchell. *Sidewalk.* New York: Farrar, Straus, and Giroux, 2000.

Echidne of the Snakes Blog. "The Right to Go Out." October 16, 2008. http://echidneofthesnakes.blogspot.com/2008_10_01_archive.html#40 19843672375903459 (accessed October 20, 2008).

Egyptian Center for Women's Rights. "'Clouds in Egypt's Sky' Sexual Harassment: From Verbal Harassment to Rape." July 2008. http://ecwr online.org/images/pub/ssh/sexualHarassmentResearchResults2008English. pdf (accessed October 27, 2009).

eHow. "How to Avoid Being Raped at College." n.d. http://www.ehow. com/how_2126457_avoid-being-raped-college.html (accessed November 20, 2009).

El Deeb, Sarah. "Harassment across the Arab World Drives Women Inside." Associated Press, December 15, 2009. http://news.yahoo.com/s/ap/ 20091215/ap_on_re_mi_ea/ml_arabs_sexual_harassment (accessed December 20, 2009).

Elliot, Cath. "So Angry I Could Strip!" *Guardian*, May 28, 2008, http:// www.guardian.co.uk/commentisfree/2008/may/28/soangryicouldstrip (accessed July 30, 2008).

Elsebahy, Nourhan. "LEAD Program Organizes Conference on Sexual Harassment." *Caravan*, The American University in Cairo student paper, February 24, 2009. http://www.auccaravan.org/2009/02/24/ sexual-harassment-conference-begins-this-week (accessed December 10, 2009).

ERA: Women and Poverty. "Women and Poverty." n.d. http://www.equal rights.org/professional/welfare/welfback.asp (accessed September 3, 2009).

Fairchild, Kimberly, and Laurie A. Rudman. "Everyday Stranger Harassment and Women's Self-Objectification." *Social Justice Research* 21, no. 3 (2008): 338–357.

Farrar, Kate. "Baby Spice to Burkas." AAUW Dialog, September 24, 2009. http://blog-aauw.org/2009/09/24/baby-spice-to-burkas (accessed November 14, 2009).

Fayer, Joan. "Changes in Gender Use of Public Space in Puerto Rico." In *Voices in the Street: Explorations in Gender, Media, and Public Space*, edited by Susan J. Drucker and Gary Gumpert. Cresskill, NJ: Hampton Press, Inc., 1996.

Feminist.com. "The Sex Industry." n.d. http://www.feminist.com/resources/ourbodies/ viol_sexind.html (accessed November 22, 2009).

Fernandez, Colin. "Tesco Condemned for Selling Pole Dancing Toy." *Daily Mail*, October 24, 2006. http://www.dailymail.co.uk/news/article-412195/Tesco-condemned-selling-pole-dancing-toy.html (accessed November 22, 2009).

Fieser, Ezra. "Guatemalan Gangs: Swagger, Tattoos, But No Rules." *Global Post*, November 23, 2009. http://www.globalpost.com/dispatch/the-americas/091109/guatemala-gang-culture-rape?page=0,1 (accessed December 18, 2009).

Fieser, Ezra. "Guatemala Slowly Confronts Widespread Rape of Women." *Christian Science Monitor*, November 20, 2009. http://www.csmonitor.com/World/Americas/2009/1120/p90s01-woam.html (accessed November 25, 2009).

Fine, Alyssa. *Roadblocks: The Street Harassment of Women and Girls in Mauritius*. Rose Hill, Mauritius: Soroptimist International Ipsae, 2009.

Flowers, R. Barri. *The Prostitution of Women and Girls*. London: McFarland & Company, Inc., Publishers, 1998.

Fogg-Davis, Hawley. "Theorizing Black Lesbians within Black Feminism: A Critique of Same-Race Street Harassment." *Politics and Gender* 2 (2006): 57–76.

Fraser, Christian. "Egyptian Women Learn to Fight Back." *BBC*, March 18, 2009. http://news.bbc.co.uk/2/hi/middle_east/7936071.stm (accessed November 14, 2009).

French, Marilyn. *From Eve to Dawn: A History of Women in the World, Volume 1*. New York: The Feminist Press at CUNY, 2008.

French, Marilyn. *The War against Women*. New York: Ballantine Books, 1992.

Friedman, Ann. "Girls Just Wanna Have Fun . . . Without Getting Raped." Feministing Blog, March 28, 2006. http://feministing.com/archives/002955.html (accessed November 22, 2009).

Fukada, Takahiro. "In Anonymous Packed Train Lurk Gropers." *Japan Times*, August 18, 2009. http://search.japantimes.co.jp/cgi-bin/nn2009 0818i1.html (accessed September 10, 2009).

Gardner, Carol Brooks. *Passing By: Gender and Public Harassment*. Berkeley, CA: University of California Press, 1995.

Girls for Gender Equity. *Hey . . . Shorty*. Documentary directed by Ashley Lewis and Sala Cyril. 2007.

Girls for Gender Equity. "Publications." n.d. http://www.ggenyc.org/public ations.php (accessed October 25, 2009).

Givhan, Robin. "Hillary Clinton's Tentative Dip into the New Neckline Territory." *Washington Post*, July 20, 2007. http://www.washington post.com/wp-dyn/content/article/2007/07/19/AR2007071902668.html (accessed September 3, 2009).

Gizmodo. "Pole Dancer Doll Doesn't Really Set the Perfect Role Model." August 30, 2009. http://gizmodo.com/5348675/pole-dancer-doll-doesnt-really-set-the-perfect-role-model (accessed November 22, 2009).

Global Action Project. "Crossed Lines." July 9, 2007. http://www.youtube. com/watch?v=oW0dViXyS1o (accessed July 10, 2009).

Golden, Stephanie. "Lady versus Low Creature: Old Roots of Current Attitudes Toward Homeless Women." In *Women: A Feminist Perspective, Fifth Edition*, edited by Jo Freeman. Mountain View, CA: Mayfield Publishing Company, 1995.

Gordon, Margaret T., and Stephanie Riger. *The Female Fear: The Social Cost of Rape*. Urbana, IL: University of Illinois Press, 1991.

Grauerholz, Elizabeth. "Gender Socialization and Communication: The Inscription of Sexual Harassment in Social Life." In *Conceptualizing Sexual Harassment as Discursive Practice*, edited by Shereen G. Bingham. Westport, CT: Praeger, 1994.

Grier, Beverly. "Making Sense of Our Differences: African American Women on Anita Hill." In *Sexual Harassment Issues and Answers*, edited by Linda LeMoncheck and James P. Sterba. Oxford: Oxford University Press: 2001.

Grimes, Andrea. "Street Objectification: A Call against Cat-calling." Heartless Doll, June 17, 2009. http://www.heartlessdoll.com/2009/06/italian_ women_tired_of_italian_objectification.php (accessed September 25, 2009).

Grossman, Anna Jane. "Catcalling: Creepy or a Compliment?" CNN, May 14, 2008. http://www.cnn.com/2008/LIVING/personal/05/14/lw.catcalls/ index.html (accessed May 14, 2008).

Guano, Emanuela. "Respectable Ladies and Uncouth Men: The Performative Politics of Class and Gender in the Public Realm of an Italian City." *Journal of American Folklore* 120 (475): 48–72.

Hadleigh-West, Maggie. *War Zone*. Film Fatale, Inc., 1998 (71-minute version).

Hannah, Daryl C. "First Black-Woman Fortune 500 CEO." *DiversityInc*, May 22, 2009, http://www.diversityinc.com/public/5879.cfm (accessed August 23, 2009).

"Harassment Rampant on Public Transportation." *Shanghai Star,* April 11, 2002. http://app1.chinadaily.com.cn/star/2002/0411/cn8-4.html (accessed March 15, 2009).

Harik, Ramsay M., and Elsa Marston. *Women in the Middle East: Tradition and Changes.* New York: Franklin Watts, a Division of Grolier Publishing, 1996.

Harris, Ian M. *Messages Men Hear: Constructing Masculinities.* London: Taylor & Francis, 1995.

Hausmann, Ricardo, Laura D. Tyson, and Saadia Zahidi. "The Global Gender Gap Report." World Economic Forum. 2009. http://www. weforum.org/pdf/gendergap/report2009.pdf (accessed October 30, 2009).

Hazeur, Monique, and Nijla Mumin, *BACK UP! Concrete Diaries.* A documentary that is still in production. The author attended a screening of the documentary in-progress in Washington, D.C., in July 2009.

Heben, Tiffanie. "Reshaping of the Law: Interpreting and Remedying Street Harassment." *South California's Review of Law and Women's Studies* 4, no. 1 (1994): 183– 219.

Heldman, Caroline. "Out-of-Body Image." *Ms. Magazine,* Spring 2008. http://www.msmagazine.com/spring2008/outOfBodyImage.asp (accessed December 19, 2009).

Hilliard, Chloe A. "'Ayo, Shorty!' Brooklyn Girls Are Fighting Back against the Boys who Harass Them." *Village Voice,* June 12, 2007. http:// www.villagevoice. com/2007-06-12/news/ayo-shorty (accessed October 25, 2009).

Hira, Nadira. "Fortune 500 Women CEOs." *CNN,* April 21, 2009. http:// money.cnn.com/galleries/2009/fortune/0904/gallery.fortune500_women_ ceos.fortune/index.html (accessed August 23, 2009).

HollaBack Arkansas, http://hollabackar.blogspot.com.

HollaBack Canada, http://hollabackcanada.blogspot.com.

HollaBack DC! "Uniform Harassment." April 22, 2009. http://hollabackdc. wordpress.com/2009/04/22/uniform-harassment (accessed April 25, 2009).

HollaBack NYC. "Antiracism." October 2, 2005. http://hollabacknyc. blogspot. com/2005/10/antiracism.html (accessed November 5, 2009).

HollaBack Toronto. "Success Story on the Blue Line," June 28, 2009. http://hollabackto.blogspot.com/2009/06/success-story-on-blue-line.html (accessed July 10, 2009).

hooks, bell. *Ain't I a Woman? Black Women and Feminism.* Boston, MA: South End Press, 1981.

hooks, bell. *Black Looks: Race and Representation.* Boston, MA: South End Press, 1992.

hooks, bell. "Seduced by Violence No More." In *Transforming a Rape Culture,* edited by Emilie Buchwald, Pamela R. Fletcher, and Martha Roth. Minneapolis, MN: Milkwood Editions, 1993.

Horowitz, Jason. "World Briefing, Europe: Italy: Court Rules 'Bottom Pinching' Is Assault." *New York Times*, January 20, 2005. http://query.nytimes.com/gst/fullpage.html?res=9507E3DB1038F933A15752C0A96 39C8B63 (accessed November 8, 2009).

HOTGIRLS. "Anti-Street Harassment Campaign." n.d. http://www.helping our-teengirls.org/programs/street_harassment_campaign.htm (accessed October 26, 2009).

Hussain, Rummana. "Suspect Held without Bail in Jackson Park." *Chicago Sun Times*, August 21, 2009. http://www.suntimes.com/news/24-7/1728510, jackson-park-rapes-suspect-bail-082109.article (accessed September 4, 2009).

INCITE! "About INCITE!" n.d. http://www.incite-national.org/index.php?s=35 (accessed October 19, 2009).

Indian Express. "82% Delhi Women Find Buses Most Unsafe: Study." November 14, 2009. http://www.indianexpress.com/news/82-delhi-women-find-buses-most-unsafe-study/541230 (accessed November 14, 2009).

Institute for Women's Policy Research. "The Gender Wage Gap by Occupation." April 2009. http://www.iwpr.org/pdf/C350a.pdf (accessed September 3, 2009).

Jack. "Race, Class, and Street Harassment." Feministe, July 20, 2007. http://www.feministe.us/blog/archives/2007/07/20/race-class-and-street-harassment (accessed November 5, 2009).

James. "Train Molesting Remains a Major Problem!" Japan Probe, August 22, 2006. http://www.japanprobe.com/?p=413 (accessed March 15, 2009).

Japundit Blog. "Chikan Choo Choo." September 28, 2006. http://blog.japundit.com/archives/2006/09/28/3627 (accessed March 15, 2009).

Johnson, Alex. "Damsels in Distress: If You're Missing, It Helps to be Young, White and Female." MSNBC, July 23, 2004. http://www.msnbc.msn.com/id/5325808 (accessed August 23, 2009).

Johnston, Erin. "Women Feel Tokyo Train Gropers." *Guardian*, November 24, 2004. http://www.guardian.co.uk/world/2004/nov/24/japan (accessed August 10, 2009).

Johnston, Cynthia. "Two-thirds of Egyptian Men Harass Women?" *Reuters*. July 17, 2008. http://www.reuters.com/article/email/idUSL17325 81120080717 (accessed July 20, 2008).

Johnston, Joey. "ESPN's Vitale to Help with Bradenton Teen's Funeral Expenses." Tampa Bay Online, September 8, 2009. http://www2.tbo.com/content/2009/sep/08/081251/counselors-attend-students-after-bradenton-cheerle/news-metro (accessed September 9, 2009).

Jones, Charisse, and Kumea Shorter-Gooden. *Shifting: The Double Lives of Black Women in America*. New York: HarperCollins, 2003.

Katz, David S. "Personal Safety for Women Traveling Abroad on Business." WITI, 2004. http://www.witi.com/careers/2004/travelsafety.php (accessed November 8, 2009).

Katz, Jackson. *The Macho Paradox: Why Some Men Hurt Women and How All Men Can Help.* Naperville, IL: Sourcebooks, Inc., 2006.

Kaufman, Michael. "The Construction of Masculinity and the Triad of Men's Violence." In *Men's Lives* (second edition), edited by Michael S. Kimmel and Michael A. Messner. New York: Macmillan Publishing Company, 1992.

Kearl, Holly. "Women Still Face Pregnancy Discrimination." AAUW Legal Advocacy Fund Update Newsletter, Winter 2009. http://aauw.org/publications/updates/upload/LAF-Update-Winter-2009.pdf.

Kearl, Holly. "Want a Female Taxi Driver?" AAUW Dialog, January 8, 2009. http://blog-aauw.org/2009/01/08/want-a-female-taxi-driver.

Kenney, Florence. "Men and Women Lived with the Seasons." In *Messengers of the Wind: Native American Women Tell Their Life Stories*, edited by Jane Katz. New York: Ballantine Books, 1995.

Kenney, Sally J. "Gap on Federal Bench? 8th Circuit Here We Come." *Women's E News*, April 17, 2009. http://www.womensenews.org/article.cfm?aid=3983 (accessed September 3, 2009).

Kissling, Elizabeth Arveda. "Street Harassment: The Language of Sexual Terrorism." *Discourse and Society* 2, no. 4 (1991): 451–460.

Klein, Ezra. "Catcalling." *American Prospect,* May 15, 2008.http://www.prospect.org/csnc/blogs/ezraklein_archive?month=05&year=2008&base_name=catcalling (accessed September 25, 2009).

Knickmeyer, Ellen. "In Egypt, Some Women Say that Veils Increase Harassment." *Washington Post*, August 17, 2008. http://www.washingtonpost.com/wpdyn/content/article/2008/08/16/AR2008081602063_pf.html (accessed November 23, 2009).

Koenig, Ronnie. "Why Do Men Catcall?" AlterNet, October 21, 2009. http://www.alternet.org/sex/143383/why_do_men_catcall/?page=1 (accessed November 2, 2009).

Koskela, Hille. "'Bold Walk and Breakings': Women's Spatial Confidence versus Fear of Violence." *Gender, Place and Culture* 4, no. 3 (1997): 301–320.

Krantz, Matt. "Women CEOs Slowly Gain on Corporate America." *USA Today*, January 2, 2009. http://www.usatoday.com/money/companies/management/2009-01-01-women-ceos-increase_N.htm (accessed September 3, 2009).

Landau, Elizabeth. "Men See Bikini-clad Women as Objects, Psychologists Say." *CNN*, April 2, 2009. http://www.cnn.com/2009/HEALTH/02/19/women.bikinis. objects/index.html (accessed December 13, 2009).

Langelan, Martha. Back Off! How to Confront and Stop Sexual Harassment and Harassers. New York: Fireside Press, 1993.

Laniya, Olatokunbo Olukemi. "Street Smut: Gender, Media, and the Legal Power Dynamics of Street Harassment, or 'Hey Sexy' and Other Verbal Ejaculations." *Columbia Journal of Gender and Law* 14 (2005): 91–130.

Lauzen, Martha M. "Behind-the-Scenes Women in the 2008–09 Prime-time Television Season: Executive Summary." Center for the Study of Women in Television and Film, 2009. http://womenintvfilm.sdsu.edu/files/2008-09_Boxed_in_Summary.pdf (accessed November 22, 2009).

Lauzen, Martha M. "The Celluloid Ceiling: Behind-the-Scenes Employment of Women on the Top 250 Films of 2008." Center for the Study of Women in Television and Film, 2009. http://womenintvfilm.sdsu.edu/files/2008_celluloid_ceiling.pdf (accessed November 22, 2009).

LaVallee, Andrew. "Only 13% of Wikipedia Contributors are Women, Study Says." *Wall Street Journal*, August 31, 2009. http://blogs.wsj.com/digits/2009/08/31/only-13-of-wikipedia-contributors-are-women-study-says (accessed September 3, 2009).

Lee, Jennifer. "Sexual Harassment Is 'No. 1 Quality of Life Offense' on Subways, Police Say." *New York Times*, November 19, 2009. http://cityroom.blogs.nytimes.com/2009/11/19/sexual-harassment-is-no-1-quality-of-life-offense-on-subways-police-say (accessed December 13, 2009).

Lee, Sunhwa, and Louis Shaw. "From Work to Retirement: Tracking Changes in Women's Poverty Status." AARP, February 2008. http://www.aarp.org/research/ppi/econ-sec/low-income/articles/from_work_to_retirement__tracking_changes_ in_women_rsquo_s_poverty_status.html (accessed September 3, 2009).

Levy, Ariel. *Female Chauvinist Pigs: Women and the Rise of Raunch Culture*. New York: Free Press, 2005.

Lisaius, Som. "Sexual Assault Suspect Caught on Surveillance Tape at Circle K." CBS KOLD News 13, April 28, 2008. http://www.kold.com/Global/story. asp?S=10267317&nav=menu86_3 (accessed November 20, 2009).

Los Angelista. "No, You Can't Touch My Hair." September 13, 2009. http://www.losangelista.com/2009/09/no-you-cant-touch-my-hair.html (accessed September 20, 2009).

MacCallum, Martha. "Have Fun Girls." Fox News, March 8, 2006. http://www.fox news.com/story/0,2933,187244,00.html (accessed November 22, 2009).

MacKinnon, Catherine. "Sexual Harassment as Sex Discrimination." In *Sexual Harassment: Confrontation and Decisions*, edited by Edmund Wall. Buffalo, NY: Prometheus Books, 1992.

MacKinnon, Catherine. "The Social Causes of Sexual Harassment." In *Sexual Harassment: Confrontation and Decisionw,* edited by Edmund Wall. Buffalo, NY: Prometheus Books, 1992.

MacMillan, Ross, Annette Nierobisz, and Sandy Welsh. "Experiencing the Streets: Harassment and Perceptions of Safety among Women." *Journal of Research in Crime and Delinquency* 37, no. 3 (August 2000): 306–322.

Madriz, Esther. *Nothing Bad Happens to Good Girls: Fear of Crime in Women's Lives*. Berkeley, CA: University of California Press, 1997.

Marcotte, Amanda. "Catcalling Is NOT a Compliment." Alternet.org, May 16, 2008. http://www.alternet.org/blogs/peek/85566 (accessed September 25, 2009).

Marquet, Julie. "Fighting Sexual Harassment in Egypt." *The Observers*, April 14, 2009. http://observers.france24.com/en/content/20090414-fighting-sexual- harrassment-egypt-women-rights (accessed November 14, 2009).

Martin, Brian. "Men: Help Stop Public Harassment." In *Perspectives on Social Problems, Volume 9: Public Harassment*, edited by Carol Brooks Gardner. Greenwich, CT: JAI Press, 1997.

Masr, Bikya. "Egypt: Sexual harassment law coming?" November 2, 2009. http://bikyamasr.com/?p=5417 (accessed November 14, 2009).

May, Emily. "Beware the Closing Doors." *New York Daily News*, June 10, 2009. http://www.metro.us/us/article/2009/06/10/07/0408-82/index.xml (accessed June 15, 2009).

May, Emily, and Sam Carter. "MTA Must Crack Down on Epidemic of Subway Groping." *New York Daily News*, July 19, 2008, http://www.nydaily news.com/opinions/2008/07/19/2008-07-19_mta_must_crack_down_on_epidemic_of_subwa.html?page=0 (accessed October 27, 2009).

Mayton, Joseph. "Egypt Puts Tougher Sex-Harassment Law on Agenda." *Women's E News*, February 4, 2009. http://www.womensenews.org/story/the-world/090204/egypt-puts-tougher-sex-harassment-law-agenda (accessed November 14, 2009).

McEwan, Melissa. "CNN Still Doesn't Know How to Cover Sexual Assault." Shakesville, October 6, 2009. http://shakespearessister.blog spot.com/2009/10/cnn-still-doesnt-know-how-to-cover.html (accessed November 22, 2009).

McEwan, Melissa. "Feminism 101." Shakesville, October 18, 2008. http://shakespearessister.blogspot.com/2008/10/feminism-101.html#disqus_thread (accessed October 1, 2009).

McEwan, Melissa. "Judge Blames 10-Year-Old Victim for Her Own Rape." Shakesville, June 28, 2007. http://shakespearessister.blogspot.com/2007/06/judge-blames-10-year-old-victim-for-her.html (accessed November 22, 2009).

McEwan, Melissa. "How Odd!" Shakesville, November 2, 2007. http://shakespeares sister.blogspot.com/2007/11/how-odd.html (accessed November 22, 2009).

McEwan, Melissa. "Rape Culture 101." Shakesville, October 9, 2009. http://shakespearessister.blogspot.com/2009/10/rape-culture-101.html (accessed November 20, 2009).

McEwan, Melissa. "Take My Cunt, Please." Shakesville, January 4, 2007. http://shakespearessister.blogspot.com/2007/01/take-my-cunt-please.html (accessed November 22, 2009).

McEwan, Melissa. "Three Boys under 10 Charged with Rape." Shakesville, November 19, 2007. http://shakespearessister.blogspot.com/2007/11/

three-boys-under-10-charged-with-rape.html (accessed November 22, 2009).

McKeganey, Neil, and Marina Barnard. *Sex Work on the Streets: Prostitutes and Their Clients.* Buckingham, UK: Open University Press: 1996.

McNamara, Mei-Ling. "Travel Tips for Women Travelers: Safely Experience the Freedom of the Unaccompanied Female." TravelChannel.com, n.d. http://www.travelchannel.com/Travel_Ideas/Girlfriend_Getaways/ci.Travel_Tips_for_Women_Travelers.artTravelIdeasFmt?vgnextfmt=artTravelIdeasFmt (accessed November 9, 2009).

Media Education Foundation. "*War Zone.*" n.d. http://www.mediaed.org/cgi-bin/commerce.cgi?preadd=action&key=213#film-festivals (accessed October 25, 2009).

Media Report to Women. "Industry Statistics." February 2009. http://www.media reporttowomen.com/statistics.htm (accessed September 3, 2009).

Men Can Stop Rape. "Strength Mediaworks." n.d. http://www.mencansto prape.org/info-url2698/info-url.htm (accessed December 13, 2009).

Men Can Stop Rape. "Strength Training," n.d. http://www.mencanstoprape.org/info-url2696/info-url.htm (accessed December 13, 2009).

Men Can Stop Rape. "Youth Development: The Men of Strength (MOST) Club." n.d.http://www.mencanstoprape.org/info-url2696/info-url_show.htm?doc_id=697523 (accessed December 13, 2009).

Mike. "Hemlines Don't Rape People, Rapists Do." Science Blogs, January 3, 2007. http://scienceblogs.com/mikethemadbiologist/2007/01/hemlines_dont_rape_people_rapi.php (accessed November 22, 2009).

Miller, Emily. "Cankles Make Hillary Clinton One of the Girls." *Free Republic*, July 23, 2009. http://www.freerepublic.com/focus/chat/2301 301/posts (accessed August 23, 2009).

Miller, Jody. *Getting Played: African American Girls, Urban Inequality, and Gendered Violence.* New York: New York University Press, 2008.

Mills, Melinda. "'You Talking to Me?' Considering Black Women's Racialized and Gendered Experiences with and Responses or Reactions to Street Harassment from Men." Masters of Arts thesis, Georgia State University, 2007.

MJS5083. "Sexual Harassment." YouTube, March 27, 2007. http://www.youtube.com/watch?v=WzVYRdyY5rI&feature=player_embedded (accessed December 10, 2009).

Modern Discussions. "Campaign against Sexual Harassment." March 19, 2007. http://www.ahewar.org/eng/show.art.asp?aid=292 (accessed October 27, 2009).

"MO'Talks." Channel 25. March 2005. http://www.youtube.com/watch?v=Vw9n4x8VeqM&feature=player_embedded# (accessed October 27, 2009).

Motsinger, Carol. "In Pursuit of Respect: Art Hits the Street to Prevent Sexual Harassment." *Citizen Times*, April 5, 2009. Cited on Stop Street Harassment Blog. "Street Harassment Event in Asheville, NC." April 5, 2009. http://streetharassment.wordpress.com/2009/04/05/street-harassment-event-in-asheville-nc.

Mroz, Jacqueline. "Female Police Chiefs, A Novelty No More." *New York Times*, April 6, 2008. http://www.nytimes.com/2008/04/06/nyregion/nyregionspecial 2/06Rpolice.html (accessed September 3, 2009).

MSNBC. "Mexico's Pink Taxis Cater to Fed-up Females." October 19, 2009. http://www.msnbc.msn.com/id/33385984 (accessed November 22, 2009).

Mukhopadhyay, Samhita. "Catcalling Is Creepy." Feministing.com, May 20, 2008. http://www.feministing.com/archives/009231.html (accessed July 24, 2009).

Mwanagombe, Lewis. "Education-Zambia: Bicycles Help Girls Go Further." IPS, September 7, 2009. http://ipsnews.net/news.asp?idnews=48349 (accessed November 14, 2009).

My Fox Orlando. "Teen Dies Weeks after Being Shot." June 4, 2008.http://www.myfoxorlando.com/myfox/pages/News/Detail?contentId=6690282&version=3&locale=EN-US&layoutCode=TSTY&pageId=3.2.1 (accessed June 10, 2008).

Najibullah, Farangis. "Acid Attack on Afghan Schoolgirls Causes Fear, Anxiety among Parents." Afghanistan Online. November 15, 2008, http://www.afghan-web.com/woman/acidattacks.html (accessed November 15, 2009).

National Center for Transgender Equality. "It's Official: First Federal Law to Protect TransgenderPeople." October 22, 2009. http://transequality.org/news. html#first_law (accessed November5, 2009).

National Coalition against Domestic Violence. "Domestic Violence Facts." n.d. http://www.ncadv.org/files/DomesticViolenceFactSheet%28National%29.pdf (accessed September 3, 2009).

National Governors Association. "Current Governors." 2009. http://www.nga.org/portal/site/nga/menuitem.42b929b1a5b9e4eac3363d10501010a0/?vgnextoid=d54c8aaa2ebbff00VgnVCM1000001a01010aRCRD&vgnextfmt=curgov (accessed November, 22 2009).

National Poverty Center. "Poverty in the United States, FAQ." n.d. http://www.npc.umich.edu/poverty/#4 (accessed September 3, 2009).

National Public Radio. "Young Women in Brooklyn Fight for Respect." July 2, 2007. http://www.npr.org/templates/story/story.php?storyId=11654299 (accessed October 25, 2009).

New Yorkers for Safe Transit. "NYFST Actions to Date." n.d. http://nyfst.org/actions (accessed October 27, 2009).

Netsquared. "HarassMap: Reporting and Mapping Sexual Harassment on the Streets Via SMS." February 23, 2009.http://www.netsquared.org/projects/harassmap-reporting-mapping-sexual-harassment-sms (accessed October 27, 2009).

Ng, Terry. "Japan's Simulated Train Café: Groping Allowed." Kineda, January 25, 2006. http://www.kineda.com/japans-train-cafe-groping-allowed (accessed March 15, 2009).

Nguyen, Ashley. "Saying Hello Is Just for the Sake of Saying Hello." *Temple News*, September 23, 2009. http://temple-news.com/2009/09/23/saying-hello-is-just-for-the-sake-of-saying-hello (accessed September 25, 2009).

Nielsen, Laura Beth. *License to Harass: Law, Hierarchy, and Offensive Public Speech*. Princeton, NJ: Princeton University Press, 2004.

Oldenburg, Ray. "The Sexes and the Third Place." In *Voices in the Street: Explorations in Gender, Media, and Public Space*, edited by Susan J. Drucker and Gary Gumpert. Cresskill, NJ: Hampton Press, Inc, 1996.

The OpEd Project. "More about the OpEd Project." n.d. http://www.theoped project.org/cms/index.php?option=com_content&view=article&id=57 &Itemid=63 (accessed September 3, 2009).

Organisation for Economic Co-operation and Development. "Gender Equality and Social Institutions in Afghanistan." Social Institutions and Gender Index. n.d. http://genderindex.org/country/afghanistan (accessed November 9, 2009).

Organisation for Economic Co-operation and Development. "Gender Equality and Social Institutions in Egypt." Social Institutions and Gender Index. n.d. http://genderindex.org/country/egypt-arab-rep (accessed November 9, 2009).

Organisation for Economic Co-operation and Development. "Gender Equality and Social Institutions in Iraq." Social Institutions and Gender Index. n.d. http://genderindex.org/country/iraq (accessed November 8, 2009).

Organisation for Economic Co-operation and Development. "Gender Equality and Social Institutions in Kuwait." Social Institutions and Gender Index. n.d. http://genderindex.org/country/Kuwait (accessed November 9, 2009).

Organisation for Economic Co-operation and Development. "Gender Equality and Social Institutions in Saudi Arabia." Social Institutions and Gender Index. n.d. http://genderindex.org/country/saudi-arabia (accessed November 9, 2009).

Organisation for Economic Co-operation and Development. "Gender Equality and Social Institutions in Sudan." Social Institutions and Gender Index. n.d. http://genderindex.org/country/sudan (accessed November 8, 2009).

Organisation for Economic Co-operation and Development. "Gender Equality and Social Institutions in Tunisia." Social Institutions and Gender Index. n.d. http://genderindex.org/country/tunisia (accessed November 9, 2009).

Organisation for Economic Co-operation and Development. "Gender Equality and Social Institutions in United Arab Emirates." Social

Institutions and Gender Index. n.d. http://genderindex.org/country/united-arab-emirates (accessed November 9, 2009).

Organisation for Economic Co-operation and Development. "Gender Equality and Social Institutions in Yemen." Social Institutions and Gender Index. n.d. http://genderindex.org/country/yemen (accessed November 9, 2009).

Oshynko, Norma Anne. "No Safe Place: The Legal Regulation of Street Harassment." Thesis for Masters of Law in Faculty of Law, University of British Columbia, 2002.

Osunsami, Steve, Chris Strathmann, and Joshua Gaynor. "Finding Kristi Cornwell: Missing Georgia Mother Snatched Off the Street." ABC News, August 17, 2009. http://abcnews.go.com/GMA/story?id=8341741&page=1 (accessed September 4, 2009).

Pacific Lutheran University. "World Expert Addresses Masculinity, Violence." April 11, 2008.http://news.plu.edu/node/2507 (accessed December 11, 2009).

Paddock, Barry, Henry Karoliszyn, Jotham Sederstrom, Alison Gendar, and Wil Cruz. "Van Crashes in Midtown; Kills Pregnant Woman Driver Allegedly Attempted to Flirt With." *New York Daily News*. March 27, 2009. http://www.nydailynews.com/ny_local/2009/03/27/2009-03-27_van_crashes_in_midtown_kills_pregnant_wo.html (accessed March 27, 2009).

Parker, Sheila. "Metro Police Investigate Sexual Assault." WSAV, May 25, 2009. http://www2.wsav.com/sav/news/local/article/metro_police_investigate_sexual_assault/12822 (accessed May 30, 2009).

Parkinson, Dan. "Should Women Be More Responsible?" *BBC*, November 16, 2006. http://news.bbc.co.uk/2/hi/uk_news/6153822.stm (accessed November 22, 2009).

Peters, Jenny. "Female Directors on the Hunt for Work." *Variety*, June 11, 2009. http://www.variety.com/article/VR1118004830.html?categoryid=3284&cs=1&query=Few+Females (accessed November 22, 2009).

Peterson, Latoya. "Catcalling Is a Cross Cultural Annoyance." Racialicious. June 29, 2007. http://www.racialicious.com/2007/06/29/catcalling-is-a-cross-cultural- annoyance (accessed August 16, 2009).

Pilgrim, David. "Jezebel Stereotypes." Jim Crow Museum of Racists Memorabilia. Ferris State University. n.d. http://www.ferris.edu/jimcrow/jezebel (accessed November 1, 2009).

Pitcher, Jane Rosie Campbell, Phil Hubbard, Maggie O'Neill, and Jane Scoular. *Living and Working in Areas of Street Sex Work: From Conflict to Coexistence*. York, UK: Joseph Rowntree Foundation, 2006.

Pleck, Joseph H. "Men's Power with Women, Other Men, and Society: A Men's Movement Analysis." In *Men's Lives* (second edition), edited by Michael S. Kimmel and Michael A. Messner. New York: Macmillan Publishing Company, 1992.

Pratto, Felicia. "Sexual Politics." In *Sex, Power, Conflict: Evolutionary and Feminist Perspectives*, edited by David M. Buss and Neil M. Malamuth. Oxford: Oxford University Press, 1996.

Prime, Jeanine, and Corinne A. Moss-Racusin. "Engaging Men in Gender Initiatives: What Change Agents Need To Know." Catalyst, May 2009. http://www.catalyst.org/publication/323/engaging-men-in-gender-initiatives-what-change-agents-need-to-know (accessed August 28, 2009).

Prime Minister's Office. "Violence Against Women—Just Because They're Women!" November 26, 2002. http://www.pmo.gov.il/PMOEng/Archive/Press+Releases/2002/11/Speeches6916.htm (accessed March 15, 2009).

Radio Free Europe. "Russia to Introduce Women-Only Train Compartments." November 15, 2006. http://www.rferl.org/content/Article/1072739.html (accessed March 15, 2009).

Rape, Abuse, and Incest National Network. "The Offenders." n.d. http://rainn.org/get-information/statistics/sexual-assault-offenders (accessed December 21, 2009).

Rape, Abuse, and Incest National Network. "RAINN's 2009 Back-To-School Tips for Students." August 10, 2009. http://www.rainn.org/news-room/sexual-assault-news/2009-back-to-school-tips (accessed November 20, 2009).

Rape, Abuse, and Incest National Network. "Who Are the Victims?" n.d. http://www.rainn.org/get-information/statistics/sexual-assault-victims (accessed November 1, 2009).

Remember Our Dead. "Transgender Death Statistics 2009." http://www.transgenderdor.org/?page_id=192 (accessed November 15, 2009).

Revolutionary Association of the Women of Afghanistan. "On the Situation of Afghan Women." n.d. http://www.rawa.org/wom-view.htm (accessed November 9, 2009).

Right Rides for Women's Safety. "Mission and History." n.d. http://rightrides.org/templates/about.php?page=mission (accessed October 18, 2009).

Roberson, Amaya N. "Anti-Street Harassment." *Off Our Backs*. May–June 2005.

Rodriguez, Teresa, Diana Montane, and Lisa Pulitzer. *Daughters of Juarez: A True Story of Serial Murder South of the Border*. New York: Atria Books, 2007.

Saeed, Ali, and Nadia Al-Sakkaf. "Sexual Harassment Deters Women from Outdoor Activities." *Yemen Times*, January 21, 2009. http://www.yementimes.com/article.shtml?i=1226&p=report&a=2 (accessed March 15, 2009).

Saltzberg, Elayne A., and Joan C. Chrisler. "Beauty Is the Beast: Psychological Effects of the Pursuit of the Perfect Female Body." In *Women: A Feminist Perspective, Fifth Edition*, edited by Jo Freeman. Palo Alto, CA: Mayfield Publishing Company, 1995.

Sanchanta, Mariko. "Train Operators Fight Groping by Creating Women-Only Cars." *Los Angeles Times*. January 2, 2006. http://articles.latimes.com/2006/jan/02/business/ft-subways2 (accessed March 15, 2009).

Sanday, Peggy Reeves. "Rape-Prone versus Rape-Free Campus Cultures." *Violence against Women* 2, no. 2 (June 1996): 191–208.

Sanday, Peggy Reeves. "The Socio-Cultural Context of Rape: A Cross-Cultural Study." In *Confronting Rape and Sexual Assault*, edited by Mary E. Odem and Jody Clay-Warner. Lanham, MD: The Rowman & Littlefield Publishing Group, Inc., 1998.

Sandler, Bernice. "Handling Sexual Harassment When It Happens to You." 1997. http://www.bernicesandler.com/id37.htm (accessed September 14, 2009).

Sandler, Bernice. "How Men Can Tell If Their Behavior Is Sexual Harassment." n.d. http://www.bernicesandler.com/id18.htm (accessed December 18, 2009).

The Sarah Palin SexismWatch Blog. http://palinsexismwatch.blogspot.com.

Savage, Sara. "Study Abroad Safety Tips for Female Students." IIEPassport, n.d. http://info.iiepassport.org/tipsforfemalestudents.html (accessed November 8, 2009).

Schwyzer, Hugo. "Staring at Janae's Legs." In *Men Speak Out: Views on Gender, Sex and Power*, edited by Shira Tarrant. New York: Routledge, 2008.

Sheffield, Carole J. "Sexual Terrorism." In *Women: A Feminist Perspective, Fifth Edition*, edited by Jo Freeman. Palo Alto, CA: Mayfield Publishing Company, 1995.

Slack, Donovan. "Fearless in the City: Some Women Still Party as if Invulnerable." *Boston Globe*, March 9, 2006. http://www.boston.com/news/nation/articles/2006/03/09/fearless_in_the_city (accessed November 22, 2009).

Smith, Catherine, and Cynthia Greig. *Manly Maidens, Cowgirls, and Other Renegades, Women in Pants*. New York: Harry N. Abrams, Inc, 2003.

Smith, Julia Llewellyn. "'If We Put Every Man Who Touched a Woman's Bum in Jail, There'd Be No Room for the Drug Dealers.'" *Telegraph*, July 13, 2003. http://www.telegraph.co.uk/news/worldnews/europe/italy/1435997/If-we-put-every-man-who-touched-a-womans-bum-in-jail-thered-be-no-room-for-the-drug-dealers.html (accessed November 8, 2009).

Smuts, Barbara. "Male Aggression against Women: An Evolutionary Perspective." In *Sex, Power, Conflict: Evolutionary and Feminist Perspectives*, edited by David M. Buss and Neil M. Malamuth. Oxford: Oxford University Press, 1996.

Spain, Daphne. *Gendered Spaces*. Chapel Hill, NC: The University of North Carolina Press, 1992.

Street Harassment Project. "History." http://www.streetharassmentproject.org/history.html (accessed November 22, 2009).

Stevens, Allison. "Moore: Women's Poverty Should Top Our Agenda." *Women's eNews*, January 14, 2009. http://www.womensenews.org/article.cfm/dyn/aid/3887 (accessed September 3, 2009).

Stringer, Scott M. "Hidden in Plain Sight: Sexual Harassment and Assault in the New York City Subway System." July 2007. http://mbpo.org/uploads/HIDDEN %20IN%20PLAIN%20SIGHT.pdf (accessed February 8, 2009).

Stop Street Harassment Blog. "Anti-Black Woman Harasser in Arlington." August 7, 2009. http://streetharassment.wordpress.com/2009/08/07/anti-black-woman-harasser- in-arlington.

Stop Street Harassment Blog. "Blogging Against Disablism Day: Street Harassment Edition." May 1, 2009. http://streetharassment.word press.com/2009/05/01/blogging-against-disablism-day-street-harassment-edition.

Stop Street Harassment Blog. "Getting an Apology." February 24, 2009. http://streetharassment.wordpress.com/2009/02/24/getting-an-apology.

Stop Street Harassment Blog. "Going to the Movies Is Soooooo Fun." September 10, 2009. http://streetharassment.wordpress.com/2009/09/10/going-to-the-movies-is-soooooo-fun.

Stop Street Harassment Blog. "NYC Steps Up Efforts to Make Subways Safer." December 2, 2009. http://streetharassment.wordpress.com/2009/12/02/nyc-steps-up-efforts-to-make-subways-safer.

Stop Street Harassment Blog. "Report It." December 7, 2009.http://street harassment.wordpress.com/2009/12/07/report-it.

Stop Street Harassment Blog. "Successfully Ending Harassment." April 16, 2009. http://streetharassment.wordpress.com/2009/04/16/successfully-ending-harassment.

Stop Street Harassment Blog. "An Ugly Girl's Story." August 31, 2009. http://street harassment.wordpress.com/2009/08/31/an-ugly-girls-story.

Stop Street Harassment Blog. "Unpleasant Reminder." May 28, 2009. http://streetharassment.wordpress.com/2009/05/28/unpleasant-reminder.

Stop Street Harassment Blog, "You Think You're Better than Me?" June 12, 2009. http://streetharassment.wordpress.com/2009/06/12/you-think-youre-better-than-me/#comments.

T., Josh. "TransFeminism/CisFeminism: Why Can't We Be Friends?" Community Feministing. April 17, 2009. http://community.feministing.com/2009/04/trans feminismcisfeminism-why-c.html (accessed August 8, 2009).

Tai, Jenny. "Combating Subway Harassment." New York University News, December 1, 2009. http://nyunews.com/news/2009/dec/01/harassment (accessed December 2, 2009).

Taneja, Amit. "From Oppressor to Activist: Reflections of a Feminist Journey." In *Men Speak Out: Views on Gender, Sex and Power*, edited by Shira Tarrant. New York: Routledge, 2008.

Taylor, Lauren. "The Assertive Response to 'Hey, Baby,' Options Go Beyond the Silent Treatment." *Washington Post*, October 27, 2003, C10.

Thompson, Deborah. "'The Woman in the Street:' Reclaiming the Public Space from Sexual Harassment." *Yale Journal of Law and Feminism* 6 (1994): 313–348.

Time Yahoo Chat. "Watching All the Girls Go By: A Conversation with Maggie Hadleigh West, Director of the Film 'War Zone' about Sexual Harassment on the Street." September 15, 1998. http://www.time.com/time/community/transcripts/chattr091598.html (accessed October 25, 2009).

United Nations Security Council. "Security Council Demands Immediate and Complete Halt to Acts of Sexual Violence." June 19, 2008. http://www.un.org/News/Press/docs//2008/sc9364.doc.htm (accessed December 17, 2009).

University of Chicago. "Safety Tips for Students Studying Abroad." n.d. http://study-abroad.uchicago.edu/safety.html (accessed November 8, 2009).

USA Today. "Mexico City Debuts Women-only Buses." January 24, 2008. http://www.usatoday.com/news/world/2008-01-24-mexicpcity-buses_N.htm (accessed March 15, 2009).

Valenti, Jessica. "High Heels for Babies. Really." Feministing.com, June 13, 2008. http://www.feministing.com/archives/009385.html (accessed November 22, 2009).

Valenti, Jessica. "Is Segregation the Only Answer to Sexual Harassment?" *Guardian*, August 3, 2007. http://www.guardian.co.uk/lifeandstyle/2007/aug/03/healthandwellbeing.gender (accessed March 15, 2009).

Valenti, Jessica. "Padded Bras for Six Year-Olds." Feministing.com, September 11, 2006. http://feministing.com/archives/005685.html (accessed November 22, 2009).

Valenti, Jessica. *The Purity Myth.* Berkeley, CA: Seal Press, 2009.

Venkatesh, Sudhir. "Skinflint: Did Eliot Spitzer Get Caught Because He Didn't Spend Enough on Prostitutes?" *Slate*, March 12, 2008. http://www.slate.com/id/2186491 (accessed November 22, 2009);

Wardani, Lina. "Egypt Voices: Sexual Harassment." *BBC*, September 3, 2008. http://news.bbc.co.uk/2/hi/middle_east/7593765.stm#nancy (accessed November 14, 2009).

Warnock, John W. "The Status of Women in Karzai's Afghanistan." Global Research, April 14, 2009. http://www.globalresearch.ca/index.php?context=va&aid=13184 (accessed November 9, 2009).

Warr, Mark. "Fear of Rape among Urban Women." *Social Problems* 32, no. 3 (February 1985): 238–250.

Weber, Mark C. *Disability Harassment.* New York: New York University Press, 2007.

West, Robin L. "The Difference in Women's Hedonic Lives: A Phenomenological Critique of Feminist Legal Theory." *Wisconsin Women's Law Journal* 3 (1987): 81–145.

White, Deborah Gray. *'Ar'n't I a Woman? Female Slaves in the Plantation South.* New York: Norton, 1999.

Wilson, Michael. "Woman Slashed While Jogging in Park Behind Gracie Mansion." *New York Times*, January 4, 2009. http://www.nytimes.

com/2009/01/05/nyregion/05jogger.html?_r=2&ref=nyregion (accessed January 6, 2009).

Wise, Sue, and Liz Stanley. *Georgie Porgie: Sexual Harassment in Everyday Life*. London: Pandora, 1987.

Wisniewski, Mary. "Tired of Being Harassed on the CTA, Women Fight Back." *Chicago Sun-Times*, June 15, 2009. http://www.suntimes.com/news/transportation/1622746,CST-NWS-ride15.article (accessed June 15, 2009).

Wolf, Naomi. *The Beauty Myth*. New York: Anchor Books, 1992.

Wood, Julia. "Saying it Makes it So: The Discursive Construction of Sexual Harassment." In *Conceptualizing Sexual Harassment as Discursive Practice*, edited by Shereen G. Bingham. Westport, CT: Praeger, 1994.

Woodhouse, Laura. "Hands Up If You've Experienced Street Harassment." The F Word Contemporary UK Feminism Blog. May 28, 2008. http://www.thefword.org.uk/blog/2008/05/hands_up_if_you (accessed July 15, 2008).

Writers Guild of America, West. "Rewriting an All-Too-Familiar Story? The 2009 Hollywood Writers Report." November 2009. http://www.wga.org/uploadedFiles/who_we_are/hwr09execsum.pdf (accessed November 22, 2009).

Yamaguchi, Mari. "Japanese Women Must Run Gantlet—Gropers are Common in Crowded Train Cars." *Seattle Times*, October 23, 1994. http://community.seattletimes.nwsource.com/archive/?date=19941023&slug=1937419 (accessed March 15, 2009).

Young Women's Action Team. "Accomplishments Since July 2003." n.d. http://www.youngwomensactionteam.org/index.php?option=com_content&task=view &id=61&Itemid=112 (accessed October 27, 2009).

Young Women's Action Team. "Respect Is Due: Youth Take a Stand against Street Harassment." Area Chicago, 2006. http://www.areachicago.org/p/issues/issue-2 /respect-is-due (accessed October 27, 2009).

E-MAIL MESSAGES TO AUTHOR AND INTERVIEWS WITH AUTHOR

C., M. E-mail message to author. August 20, 2009.

Fairchild, Kimberly. E-mail message to author. September 16, 2009.

Fine, Alyssa. E-mail message to author. October 11, 2009.

Granet, Ilona. E-mail message to author. November 24, 2009, and December 24, 2009.

G., L. E-mail message to author. August 18, 2009.

H., M. E-mail message to author. August 19, 2009.

Johnson, Erin. E-mail message to author. August 17, 2009.

Lynberg, Shannon. E-mail message to author. June 9, 2009.

M., A. E-mail message to author. September 3, 2009.

M., K. E-mail message to author. August 15, 2009.

Mansager, Kari. E-mail message to author. October 26, 2009.

May, Emily and Oraia Reid. Interview in New York City. June 20, 2009.

May, Emily. Interview in New York City. September 13, 2008.

Mwendo, Jenga. E-mail message to author. December 9, 2009.

Patheja, Jasmeen. Interview in New York City. October 13, 2009.

Rahman, Lisa. E-mail message to author. July 9, 2009.

Reid, Oraia. E-mail message to author. September 25, 2008, and December 29, 2009.

Rose, Tracey. E-mail message to author. December 1, 2008.

S., J. E-mail message to author. August 18, 2009.

S., M. E-mail message to author. August 18, 2009.

Seitz, Katie. E-mail message to author. June 14, 2008.

Shenoy, Chaitra. E-mail message to author. May 12, 2009.

Shoot, Brittany. E-mail message to author. April 23, 2007, and June 13, 2008.

Smith, Joanne. E-mail message to author. December 30, 2009.

ANTI–STREET HARASSMENT EVENTS ATTENDED BY AUTHOR FOR RESEARCH

Defend Yourself Street Harassment Workshop. Washington, D.C., April 18, 2009.

Docs in Progress, screening of *Back Up! Concrete Diaries*. Washington, D.C., July 10, 2009.

Girls for Gender Equity. Street Harassment Summit. New York City, May 5, 2007.

Index

About the Author

HOLLY KEARL is the creator of the website www.StopStreet Harassment.org , which educates the public about this problem, helps women deal with it, and gives victims a place to tell their stories. A graduate of Santa Clara University, Kearl has an M.A. in Women's Studies from George Washington University. She has been a women's rights activist since high school, and volunteers with the Rape, Abuse, and Incest National Network Online Hotline. She is a manager of the Legal Advocacy Fund of the American Association of University Women (AAUW).